Dear Sterling,

Be the Blue Door:
a writer's journey

Kay McCracken

Thank you for all your support. I'm looking forward to reading your next book!
hugs,
Kay

Beyond the Blue Door: a writer's journey
Copyright © Kay McCracken 2018

Author: Kay McCracken

Publisher: Rutherford Press

For information, contact:
Rutherford Press,
PO Box 648
Qualicum Beach, BC, Canada V9K 1A0
info@rutherfordpress.ca
https://rutherfordpress.ca

Printed in the United States of America and Canada

All rights reserved. No part of this book may be reproduced in whole or in part, materially or digitally, including photocopying, without the express written permission of the author or publisher.

ISBN (book)   # 978-1-988739-12-0
ISBN (ebook)   # 978-1-988739-13-7

Book design by George Opacic

Poems copyright of the author or as noted

Photo of Kay McCracken © Jim McCracken 2017

Cover pen & ink and water colour by Frieda Martin, "The Journey"

Acknowledgements

I wish to thank the Gracesprings Collective editorial board for their guidance, suggestions, and for giving me a round of thumbs up to keep going: Alex Forbes, Craig Brunanski and Deanna Barnhardt Kawatski. You are awesome writers, poets, and friends.

My heartfelt gratitude to Cathy Sosnowsky, author, poet, workshop leader and editor, who read and edited an earlier draft of "Blue" and for her honesty and bravery in publishing *Snapshots: A Story of Love, Loss and Life*. Thank you for showing me that love and life exists beyond loss and grief, and that for some of us who are driven to do so, writing is the key to healing.

Thank you to my brother, Michael McCracken and to my friend, Carol Stuike, for their careful reading of "Blue" and for their comments and encouragement. And to two more dear friends, Dorothy Rolin, for steering the title in the right direction, and Dave Harper for everything computer related, and more.

Most importantly, I thank my daughter Teri-Ann, aka Nahanni, for allowing me to write about her struggles with mental health, and for her bravery in confronting her demons, as we all must at some point.

Thank you, too, to the grandkids. It's for you that I put pen to paper: Shasta, Faith, Melissa, Ty, Robert, Savanna, Riley, Logan and Destiny Kathleen.

My gratitude extends to three more people: to Dr. H's help during a transition from bookseller to caregiver to an ailing mother. And some time later, for another Dr. H for his understanding and compassion. These days, the mindfulness meditation classes I attend once a week, courtesy of Madeleine Eames, are a life line to sanity, also known as inner peace.

Contents

Part 1: Time to Heal

1. Hanging On
2. Unplugged
3. The Miracle of Easter Sunday
4. Wild Thing
5. The Blue Stone
6. Writers' Retreat
7. Pigs in the Snow
8. The Lone Pine Ranch Odyssey
9. River Song
10. Mindful Kitten

Part 2: Moving On

11. Six Lessons
12. Too Sharp the Day
13. Dorothy and the Writers' Group
14. Upward Spiral
15. Little Blue Monkey
16. The Blue Room
17. Did Father Know Best?
18. Writers' Soirée
19. Two Spirals Clash
20. Deliverance
21. Raven Magic
22. Gentle Souls
23. Getting to Know Mom
24. April 19, 2001
25. Writers' Gathering, Summer, 2001
26. September 11, 2001
27. Angie

Part 3: Getting to Yes

28. Creative Writing with Chris, Winter 2002
29. The Devil and Miss Lolita
30. Like Father, Like Daughter
31. Red-haired Boy
32. Unloved
33. The Strange & the Baffling
34. The Ryga Centre, June 2002
35. Whyte and his Passion to Write
36. Surrey Writers' Conference, October 2002
37. Busy
38. Reluctant Chrysalis
39. Butterfly Blues
40. A Festival to Be Proud of
41. Xcellent Birds

Part 4: It's Never Too Late to Reinvent Your Life

42 Timing is Everything
43 The Wheel of Fortune Keeps Turning
44 Robbie and Stormy Arrive
45 More Poetry
46 Artistic Personality
47 Writers' Festival, 2005
48 Divided Loyalties
49 The Ups and Downs of Life on 3rd Street
50 Poetry Launch for bill bissett
51 The Wind Changes Everything
52 Secwepemc Cowboy
53 Gracesprings Collective
54 Richard Wagamese
55 Lakeland
56 Too Good to be True
57 Enchanted Forest
58 My Book Launch: June 13, 2009
59 Full Circle
60 Writers' Festival 2010

Part 5: The Final Years

A series of short vignettes, some humorous, some sad, about the last year of Marion's life:

Extreme Laughter
Coyote
After the High, the Low
Family & Food
Saying Goodbye
Blue Flower
Revealing Photos
The Incredible Shrinking Mother
John's Fall
Marilyn
Another Diagnosis
Little Brown Bird
Nightly Intrusions
Admitting Defeat
Love You Forever
God, the great Trickster
Raven on the Fence
The Honouring
What's Next?
Not Bridgey, too

Part 6: Starting Over

A River to Skate Away On
Unexpected Love
Afterword

Beyond the Blue Door:

a writer's journey

for my mother, Marion Kathleen McCracken,

whose favourite colour was green

Title page photo by Richard Morton:

Kay and Marion on Marion's 80th birthday

Introduction

Most people don't make changes until they've hit bottom. After losing my bookstore, Reflections, along with my health, I was alone, frightened and grief stricken. I was getting on in years and didn't think I'd be able to pull my life together after the failure. That's the place where people are faced with two choices: either you live, or you die. And if you decide to live you dig deep to find out what's important to you. Hiding isn't an option any more. I found my reason to go on when I began writing about the experience.

Beyond the Blue Door is the sequel to my memoir, *A Raven in My Heart: Reflections of a Bookseller*, that was inspired by all those readers who asked "What happened next?"

I never intended to write a sequel memoir, but let's face it, a lot happened next.

When I began writing many things conspired to get in the way. I was still healing after burning out when I found myself duty bound to care for my ill and ageing mother. She needed help after the first of many mini strokes.

The road was rocky at first as two independent, strong-willed women shared a space, but I discovered something: the more I accepted my mother for who she was, the more I was able to accept parts of myself that I'd denied.

What I couldn't have anticipated was that I would spend the next twelve years caring for the woman who had always been an enigma. Who was my mother really, and why had I aligned myself with my father over her?

As I struggled with the mystery of who my mother was, I experienced the healing power of writing, and of becoming part of the writing community in Salmon Arm, an area known as the Shuswap in south central British Columbia, and in the wider writing community of British Columbia. Writing revealed things to me about my mother, our family, and how we are connected in ways I hadn't understood before.

Unearthing memories reminded me of the archaeological digs I took part in at university. At first, I might not have understood what I'd uncovered, but eventually a picture emerged from a fragment of bone, or stone. The writing process was like that. As I dug up buried memories I was able to see a clearer picture. My mother was the biggest surprise, for the woman was so much more than I had imagined.

The colour blue weaves its way through the narrative, illuminating different phases of my life. My blue phase began with the blue stone, an unexpected gift from a Shuswap (Secwepemc) First Nations friend, during my book selling days. Or it may have even begun even earlier, with the little blue monkey—I was eleven or so then—or with the Blue Room when I was sixteen.

When I began writing this memoir I found myself walking through the metaphorical blue door to explore how the colour had, or hadn't, influenced me. What meaning, if any, did I attach to blue with its many shades and hues, its many associations to music, mood, nature, and art? Stepping beyond the blue door I experienced an astonishing richness in all things blue.

This is also a story about starting over, with a few twists and turns, because starting over never travels in a straight line. Indeed, my life had never moved in a straight line. Join me on my journey through the labyrinth.

This story is also for anyone who has ever lost anything or anybody, and for any poor soul who is, or who has ever been, lost. It's also for anyone who has ever cracked up.

All these years later the story of "what happened next" has been given life.

Part One

Time to Heal

Shades of Blue

out of the blue   a blue stone   a blue star
the blue canoe

I grew up loving the blues
 music of my soul

and early one morning
a Lazuli Bunting
seen only once in a blue moon
alone at the bird feeder
wearing bright turquoise feathers
he lingered for a moment
leaving me
astonished for the day

and I read about the 5th chakra
an energy centre relating to the throat
spirals of bright blue
helping me
 to speak my truth
late in life
truth or dare

baby blue   powder blue
midnight blue
the hierarchy of blue
from innocent   to seductive
from spiritual highs to blue-black depths

1: Hanging On

The phone rang. "Hi, Mom." I tried to sound upbeat.

"I want my bonds back," she said. The tone of her voice alarmed me, but I tried to stay calm.

"I know Mom, a businessman is coaching me about how to approach the manager at the loan company. He seems to think there won't be a problem." I paused.

"Well, I want them back," she demanded in a way that didn't sound like my mother, but then she had every right to be upset—not that she was destitute. My father had left her well looked after and the bonds were but a small part of her overall finances.

"So do I, believe me. I'm doing everything I can. I'll let you know when I find out. Try not to worry. I'm sure you'll get them back."

If only I hadn't listened to my friend, William, and taken out another loan to expand my bookstore when the other bookstore in town closed. The original loan would be paid off with nothing to worry about. But I couldn't blame him. He was only trying to help.

When I hung up the phone tears sprang to my eyes. Did she understand how unwell I was and what closing the bookstore, losing everything, after hanging on for so long and so tight, what that had cost me in terms of my health? Didn't she know that I had nothing left, not money, not health, not my bookstore, or even a way to make a living? Did she realize that I was barely hanging on now, and that for a time I didn't see much reason to?

Will I survive this?

I picked up the phone to talk to another one of the publishers I still owed money to. I hung up shaking. Every day was a struggle that I didn't see an end to, although eventually with some help, and selling off more equipment from my bookstore, the phone calls started to fall off.

The cabin at Gardom Lake was my life raft. Thank God I found this place about a twenty minute drive from Salmon Arm—where my bookstore lived on Shuswap Street—before Reflections closed. The peace and quiet of the small lake suited me in my current state. I was thankful I lived in a cozy, out-of-the-way place where people weren't going to put any demands on me.

Long ago, an asylum was meant to act as a place of respite, offering protection and security, where men and women would be cared for until they were well enough to rejoin society. I recalled hearing that when Riverview Hospital in Coquitlam closed in early 2000 the homeless population in Vancouver grew to three or four thousand on the Downtown Eastside. Not wanting to ask for help, people with severe mental health issues only had one recourse for the hell that afflicted their minds: Hospital Emergency. Hundreds of people a day go there, sometimes two or three times a day. Lucky for me I had a perfect place to retreat to where nature and beauty would help heal me.

The rhythm of Gardom Lake was unhurried, mostly unpopulated in the winter, except for a couple of permanent residents further along on the same property, but I rarely saw anyone.

I watched the ravens play above the old growth forest on the island just off shore. The ravens, whose presence had kept me company on my long walks when the world was soft and deep with blessed snow, hushed and slumbering except for a solitary raven's call that so belonged to the winter forest, the towering fir, spruce, and cedar, dark winter green. Swish of powerful wings, ink black against the pale winter sky. And raven talk, unique among birds, the sound resonant and clear in the stillness.

The beauty of the place was one thing, but anxiety about how I would live plagued me. And what about the bonds? And my mother, what about her? We were very different people. I don't know if I ever really understood her—so good natured and simple next to my moody, complicated father—but she had stuck by me during my crazy teenage years, I'll give her that. I probably gave her more grief than all the other kids combined, although not on purpose. I guess she didn't hold it against me because she offered me a few bonds to secure the small loan I needed to open my bookstore. She loved visiting Reflections for lunch, or coffee, and to buy books for the grandkids, which I let her have at cost. She supported me and my bookstore venture wholeheartedly. That's why the last phone call from her had been so odd, so out of character.

January's rent was paid at least, but the new year didn't look promising. Some days all I could do was sit at the window and watch the snow, big lazy flakes drifting endlessly toward the earth from a white sky. The drifts grew larger daily, piling up on the porch railing, weighing down the curtain of fir and cedar branches that hung between me and the frozen lake. The falling snow mesmerized and insulated, so that I could almost forget the rest of the world existed.

Of course, now more than ever I had to believe there was something beyond, for part of me knew that I couldn't hide away in that cocoon forever.

2: *Unplugged*

I recalled the last night sitting in Reflections with a few friends who had dropped by with pizza and beer—our version of a wake for my bookstore. All that was left were a few chairs and the holes in the walls where once artwork had hung. The Shuswap is home to an abundance of incredible artists.

The irony of the date escaped me at the time, New Year's Eve, 1998, on the cusp of a new year with no idea how I would survive, or what my new reality would look like.

As January drew to a close, I thought it's now or never. At the beginning of February, I began writing. I'd dabbled—short stories and some poetry—and had always kept a journal to record thoughts, events, descriptions, and emotions, although facing the blank computer screen to begin my story was different. *Where do I start?* I knew I had a story, for the adventure had everything: mystery, fascinating characters, love gained and love lost, a First Nations mentor, white supremacists, a bookstore ghost, and Raven—and all this against the backdrop of the beautiful bookstore I'd created.

The daily ritual of sitting down in the same chair at the same time to spend four or five hours writing was an inexplicable joy, as if a door opened up before me and beyond that door lay freedom and a magical realm where creativity swept me up in her arms, leaving the cares of daily life far away. I was free. I looked forward to getting up again. Hallelujah.

I found it curious that I could write but my brain wasn't good for much else, something I discovered when I attended a morning job search session. I was the only person in the class who couldn't follow the instructions or keep up on the computer. I panicked. Everything moved too fast for me to grasp. My head spun. I wanted to disappear. The experience shook me. Apparently, my brain had crashed just like the computer had during the dying days of my bookstore.

The damage was on the inside where people couldn't see it. The mysterious malfunction was something I didn't know how to explain should anyone ask.

I kept glancing at the clock, but with every minute that passed my self-worth plummeted. Eventually, I was called, and followed a woman who led me down a rabbit warren of hallways and offices. Nervous, sick, but mostly humiliated, I sat across a desk from a social worker, who looked stressed. No smile. *If she's in charge of my fate, I'm screwed.*

When I told her my story she said I would have to move into a rooming house. I pictured myself in a small, shabby room down the hall from a bathroom that I'd be sharing with lonely, unemployed men. *Don't cry. Not yet.* There were forms to sign. Here, here, and here, she said. That's when I felt like I'd given up my rights as a human being. By accepting social assistance, I'd committed myself to a kind of mental prison.

My rent was already low but I got up the courage to phone the owner of the cabin, who I'd never met, to explain my situation and to ask if he would consider lowering the rent for a time. He said yes. What a blessing. Now if I was really careful, and continued to eat rice and beans, maybe I wouldn't find myself in a rooming house.

Afraid that social assistance would define who I was, I jumped into the next business venture. A kind, enthusiastic woman helped me get started in an herbal business. I could work from home, aside from going to people's homes to do presentations, and attend the product meetings. The herbs would heal me. All would be well.

Or did I forget who I was, how I throw everything I've got into whatever I'm trying to achieve?

I started to miss my daily walks in nature, my daily ritual of prayer and meditation before sitting down to write. I had a lot to learn about the product, and before long I noticed myself working as hard as I ever did at Reflections. I began to lose my balance. Too many meetings. Pushing myself too hard. And then one night everything came crashing down when I had a misunderstanding with a woman at a meeting. I thought I'd done something wrong. It's difficult to say what happened to me for there seemed to be no words, only confusion and devastation inside me.

The dark, winding road took me home, where I collapsed into the worn, brown rocking chair beside the cold fireplace. Tears that were beyond my control streamed down my face. I heard the sobs of a desperate woman, a woman who had lost her way. *Will I ever stop crying? Is this what a nervous breakdown is?*

I told myself to hang on, that surely this would pass, but I knew this was different from anything I'd ever experienced. I couldn't move out of the chair, as if the life force had drained out of me. There was no way out. *You've really done it this time. This is the big one you've been postponing for most of your life.*

Eventually, I reached over and unplugged the phone and crawled off to bed. After a night of tossing and turning, I sat up and wrote down my dream. There was a fox, two men, and me. One of the men shot and wounded the fox. The beauty of that animal was beyond anything in the physical realm alone. I felt the thick soft fur, saw the wound, and asked the man not to kill her. He seemed to realize how wrong it would be to take the fox's life, too. We arranged an operation to remove the bullet.

Reflecting on the dream, I thought the men represented the masculine side of me, that busy, focused, linear thinking creature, which in Jungian terms is the animus. I figured that's what happened with my business. I could never stop doing things to make the business successful. I didn't go for walks in nature or take time to smell the wild roses that I loved so much. Work, work, work. No balance. Was I the wounded fox? Wounded by my own striving to make the business a success?

Did the fox represent my soul, the spiritual part of me that was in danger of dying? I thought the dream revealed that the feminine, instinctual energy, or anima, had triumphed in the end, the part of me that wanted to live. I needed time to just be. I needed time to reflect, to sink into the place of healing that wise women throughout the ages were in touch with.

Then I remembered what I'd read in *Women Who Run With the Wolves*, by Clarissa Pinkola Estés, and flipped through the book until I found it. Injured animal dreams, I read, coincide with devastation of the wilderness, both within and without. Okay, it really is time to disconnect from the world of business and busyness for a time. I left the phone unplugged.

3: The Miracle of Easter Sunday

So if I'd cracked up I hoped it was only temporary, but just in case, I called to make an appointment with a mental health professional. I was put on a waiting list. After resting for a week, I plugged back in and began winding down the herbal business, which hadn't made me any money anyway, even though I was signing up a lot of people. The woman at the top of my sales pyramid may have been making money but no matter how well I did, it didn't look like it was paying off. Unless I was willing to make the business my religion, in the sense that if I didn't proselytize or try to convert people to this product, attend what amounted to revival meetings with people giving testimonials about the miracle product, I didn't have a hope of supporting myself. The sad reality hit home.

Into this gloomy picture something positive arrived: my mother's bonds were released. Mom appeared to be her easy-going self again. I didn't quite know what I was: perhaps lost somewhere in between losing everything again, and starting over.

Some days I walked around the lake and at other times I did the Gardom Lake loop, a road that brought me back to my cabin in about an hour. I never encountered anyone on my walk and only rarely did I see a car. What houses there were, were few and far between and most were set well off the road among densely treed acreages.

In an effort to lift my spirits, when Easter Sunday arrived, I decided to walk the Gardom Lake loop. I felt buried beneath the burden of anxiety about the future, but the overcast sky and mild temperature called for a thin summer jacket that day, so off I went. Every so often a tiny spit of rain anointed my face.

My heart thumped as if trying to jump out of my chest and perspiration broke out as I approached what I called Scary Dog Drive. Recently two unchained, hostile dogs had dashed out to confront me, snarling, teeth bared, as I neared their property. The first time it happened I froze, but I forced myself to act as if I wasn't afraid. *Dogs sense fear.* In the sternest voice I could muster, I demanded, "*Go! Go home!*" I tried to look menacing. *Now turn slowly ... breathe ... keep walking!* Snap of teeth at my heel. I thought for sure I was a hair's breath away from being ripped apart. No one around. No one to call the dogs off. *Where are the owners?*

    I reached into my pocket for the dog biscuit I'd brought as a distraction for the scary dogs. By some miracle they didn't appear that day. My heart rate returned to normal and I turned the corner onto Magpie Junction, so called because that's where I always met a magpie. I adored the cheeky bird who always chattered at me, looking me over before flying off to Crow Flats, where a party of noisy crows—a murder of crows sounds too sinister—congregated in an aspen grove in the valley. Often, too, bald eagles, hawks and ravens flew overhead. Some days a downy woodpecker's hammering echoed through the pine forest.

    On that Easter Sunday, just before Magpie Junction, a bird with an enormous wingspan flew directly above me toward Crow Flats. Blue heron, I gasped, and ran after him until his long spindly legs disappeared over a ridge of trees. *Kinda looks like a flying cross.*

    Turning the corner at Magpie Junction, a movement on my right caught my attention. In the dense, dark green evergreen forest—and framed against the only birch tree—a brilliant blue Steller's Jay hopped about on a branch, flaunting his perky black crest. Stunning! After a while I became aware of a patch of pale blue in a tree to the left. Edging closer, I saw a little puffball of baby blue feathers. I marveled at how the day exposed unexpected pleasures.

    Further along I spotted three magnificent bald eagles circling above the flats. Red winged black birds pierced the day with clear, bright notes, while several silent crows flew overhead, their beaks stuffed with building material. A flash of black and white, a long graceful tail, and a magpie swooped into a thicket of trees in the open woodlands.

    My hiking boots crunched over a patch of pebbles on the dirt road until I came upon a pair of mallard ducks floating together in one of the pools left by the melting snow on the side of the road. Mr. Mallard's emerald green head and neck shone above his narrow white collar, and chestnut breast. At his side, his modestly feathered female partner in brown tones, except for a discreet indigo patch, which matched her mate's. Perfect symmetry. I admired them, their quiet composure, for several minutes before walking on.

Around the next bend, I passed a farm where two men talked in loud voices over a noisy engine. I stopped in my tracks, for right before me in a young birch tree, chips flying every which way, clung a Pileated Woodpecker. Wow! A vivid red pointed cap of feathers above a face of black and white face stripes with a vertical white band on his black body, and his size—at least half a meter. Surreal. Considering how close I stood to the huge, sharp-beaked bird, almost at eye level, I barely took a breath for fear of scaring him off. The amazing creature appeared unconcerned with my presence and kept on with his busy work, excavating for insects. The God who created the feathered creatures must have had a wild imagination and a box full of vivid colours to paint with.

I finally tore myself away and continued down the road, where the flats gave rise to forest on my left. I peered down a steep bank into serene green woods and felt drawn into that place despite a fence at the bottom. Stumbling over crumbling dirt and rocks on the way down I managed to step over the sagging barbed wire fence with ease. On the other side I found myself standing on a soft brown carpet of needles.

As I stood there, the silence seeped into me. Nothing stirred; not a leaf, branch, or bird.

A kind of awe came over me, as if I'd entered a holy place. That's when I noticed the levelled log set across two large stones. I sat down and breathed in the scent of cedar, like fine incense. I bowed my head in reverence as a choir of small birds began singing in the canopy. Feeling at peace, I gave thanks for the joy being awakened in me.

Saying goodbye to the Church of Nature, I crawled back up the bank and ambled down the dirt road again.

I came across a dark brown horse grazing on the other side of a log fence. When he noticed me, I hopped across a ditch to be close to him. He wore a midnight blue blanket with the name Rambo on it. *Rambo? With those gentle brown eyes?*

Further down Gardom Lake Road, a movement on my right woke me from my reverie. On the roadside, blending in with the brown earth and grey gravel, a ruffed grouse foraged for bugs. She glanced up at me before continuing with her business, unconcerned by my presence.

The miracle of that Easter Sunday was that I had resurrected my connection to nature, to the wonder and awe of the spiritual world. As I reflected on that day, I felt honoured that nature's creatures had accepted me without hesitation. I was just another one of God's creatures at one with all I met. Snuggling into bed, I lay quietly in the soft darkness, feeling grateful and at peace.

4: Wild Thing

The first time I saw wild thing, she was riding high in the palm of my nephew's hand. She looked straight at me with bright black eyes and in that moment, she had me. She had the air of confidence that befitted a queen, a tiny Cleopatra riding in on a barge, surveying her kingdom and her subjects.

She wore a black and white coat of fur, that royal impish kitten. I could see that she was fearless and it didn't take long to discover how mischievous she was. Mom's new kitten attacked anything that moved, including fingers and toes.

My sister Karen had brought the little one all the way from Sechelt on the Sunshine Coast as a gift for our mother, to replace her beloved cat Simon. Both my parents adored Simon, which made it even sadder when he disappeared on one of their camping trips in the van.

Dad had passed away several years earlier so Mom was alone and Karen thought that our mother should have another cat for company. The kitten was headed for the SPCA if no one would take her. My sister did her best to find a home for her—she couldn't take another cat herself—but nothing worked out in the kitten's favour. So here they were, my sister and her three children, delivering the surprise gift to Mom.

After a week of wild kitten antics, for she truly was a wild thing, Mom had had enough.

"She attacks me with her sharp claws if I move my feet under the covers at night," my mother cried.

"Do you want me to take her?"

My mother's resounding "yes" changed my life.

I did have a problem, however. When I'd first looked at the cabin where I lived, the young woman living there had a cat. I thought that was perfect as I pictured myself writing with a cat curled up in front of the fireplace during the long winter nights. Don't even think about it, I was told. The man who owned the cabin was coming with his family in the spring and he was deathly allergic to cats.

Another curious thing was that the tidy row of tourist cabins, plus mine, was called Cat Tale Cottages. An oval sign hung at the top of the driveways, leading down to the lake and cottages. The sign was painted with a black cat sitting among the cattails, looking at the lake. Very misleading, but I agreed not to get a cat.

The allergic man and his family had come and gone after a couple of months. The woman who owned the other cabins bought mine, and the attached one named Maple, named for the young maple planted nearby. After my mother's distressing call, I talked to Joan, the new owner, to ask if I could have a cat if I kept her indoors. Dogs and cats were not allowed to roam free, as the property was a sanctuary for wildlife. Joan said yes as long as I kept the cat inside.

I named the kitten Brigit after the Celtic/Irish goddess who connects the mystical to the practical. I called her Bridgey for short; and she did act as a bridge for me, to a world beyond myself, to a world of unconditional love that perhaps only a pet friend can provide.

At times, I'd catch Bridgey swinging from the six-foot fern that leaned into the colourful, framed photograph of two Tibetan nuns, their heads thrown back in ecstatic laughter. The poster had been a gift from Vancouver photographer Brian Harris, a co-worker at Banyen Books.

Bridgey made me laugh. I adored her too-big-for-her-head ears, her white whiskers, springing from her tiny black and white face. During the day, she napped on the apple-green windowsill in the warm sunshine among pink and purple petunias. Other than the windowsill, her favourite snoozing spot was on top of the two-set, hardcover Unabridged Webster's New Twentieth Century Dictionary that a friend had given me years earlier. A dictionary cat. *How appropriate.* I enjoyed pouring over that dictionary for hours at a time, while my little friend snoozed on it for hours at a time.

Bridgey, my writing, and my daily walk brought balance to my life. I was still shaky and unwell, but playing with my cat brought me happiness, and writing lifted my spirits.

One morning on CBC radio, I heard a woman interviewed about a day-long workshop she was offering on dream interpretation. I'd been having profoundly vivid dreams every night that I wrote down in the morning: broken milk bottles and spilled milk; mushrooms growing on my breasts.

I called a friend to join me, as the workshop was being held in Kamloops, several hours away, and I needed support to step out of the safe little world I'd created for myself.

When the day arrived, I was up very early, met Estelle, and we began the long drive to Kamloops. I had tucked the turquoise stone I'd been given at a sacred First Nations ceremony into the pocket of my jeans as an amulet against my fear of the unknown—or a possible panic attack—as I was still very much in the grip of crippling anxiety when it came to talking in groups, and I was still unwell. My mysterious malady. I hoped that the blue stone would give me courage, as it was known to be a healing stone. Some people carry Ativan as an antidote against panic, but I had my blue stone.

5: The Blue Stone

"to see the universe in a grain of sand"
William Blake. Auguries of Innocence

The year: 1996. Place: Reflections Books, Shuswap Street, Salmon Arm, BC

Mary Lou pushed open the door and walked over to the counter where I greeted her. She was about my age, a middle-aged white woman with sandy-coloured, short hair. I met her when I opened Reflections, as she worked next door to my bookstore at the Family Resource Centre. She worked with Native women on local reserves in her capacity as a social worker.

"I've got a message from George," she said. George was an Indigenous friend I respected. He sometimes shared knowledge of the old ways with me, the teachings that he lived by.

"What is it?"

"There's a Yuwipi tonight. He said to bring you along if you could make it."

"A what?"

"Yuwipi. It's a healing ceremony. A medicine man named Big Bear has come from down south to perform the ritual. I have to get back to work, but I can tell you more about it later on the drive out to the band office. Is 6:30 okay?"

"I should be able to get the clean-up done by then. I'll be ready." I had no idea what to expect, but if George invited me, I was going.

On the drive out to Squilax, Mary Lou explained the Yuwipi ceremony to me.

"It's an ancient Sioux healing ceremony. The medicine man calls on and opens a space for healing spirits to work with people. It takes place in the dark and the spirits often show themselves in the form of lights, birds or other allies, or as sounds."

"Wow," was all I could say. I'd never heard of such a thing.

Mary Lou said she'd heard that the spirits often picked up rattles on the altar and that the focus of the ceremony is on personal prayer to help heal ourselves and others.

"What do you mean it takes place in the dark?"

"You know the auditorium at the band office, well they tape up all the windows so no light can get in and the doors are locked. No one leaves till it's over. It can go on for hours or all night from what I've heard."

I felt the tug of anxiety in my stomach. What had I got myself into? I remember thinking that I should have brought my own car so I could leave before it began. I told myself to relax, which didn't help. My past anxieties, my fear of being trapped, or of going crazy even, was sneaking up on me like a ghost from my past.

I couldn't let the specter catch up with me or I'd be into a full-blown panic attack, something I hadn't had for many years, yet there was always the possibility that one day the work I'd done with a therapist would unravel, that I'd unravel, and that my life would be over. In some ways it was like a ticking time bomb.

I'd read that depression, anxiety and panic attacks were not a sign of weakness, but instead a sign of having tried to remain strong for far too long, and that one in three people will experience one or all of those life-altering, indeed life-threatening, conditions at some point in their lives. I thought how astonishing that nobody talked about it, which only served to make those of us afflicted feel more isolated and vulnerable. Maybe if I'd been able to confide in Mary Lou, but of course I didn't. When had I decided that it wasn't okay to talk about my fears, or my feelings?

We drove over the bridge toward the North Shore, over the river of deep blue that separated Shuswap Lake from Little Shuswap Lake, and turned left just before the bannock stand on the right. Off highway, we meandered along a quiet road flanked by Ponderosa pine, trees that inspired me with their ability to survive fire and drought, and their beauty—deeply etched cinnamon-coloured bark with tufts of elegant dark green needles. Past the silent pow wow grounds, and ... no turning back now ... we turned in at the Band office.

I took a deep breath to calm myself before entering the building. Men, women, elders, and teenagers milled about the empty auditorium, while more people kept arriving. The majority were First Nations, maybe about fifty or so by now. I noticed a couple of men on ladders taping black plastic over the windows, and then I saw George talking to several men across the room. He looked busy, so Mary Lou and I joined two women we knew on the far side of the room. Someone asked when it would begin. Someone else said we're on Indian time now and that means it will begin when the time is right.

I noticed that I was sweaty and a little shaky. I'm going to the washroom, I told Mary Lou. When I pushed open the washroom door, two young Native women stood talking at the sinks. I hung back, waiting, because all I wanted to do was to splash some cold water on my face.

One of the women turned to look at me, her expression clouded with dark emotion. My heart did a flip-flop. *Now what?*

"Hey, white girl, what're you doing here? This is a sacred ceremony. Only people who have prepared themselves with prayer should be here, and only people who haven't used alcohol lately." Her eyes narrowed as she stared at me. "This isn't something to play at."

Her words were like the stings of a wasp. I opened my mouth to speak. "I, I, ..." *oh my God, I'm stuttering.* "I was invited by Mary Lou and George." I didn't sound convincing. I wanted to run before more wasps overtook me, but I couldn't move.

The woman who hadn't spoken said, "She's with Mary Lou. She's okay." The woman nailing me with her stare mumbled something, then reluctantly, it seemed to me, turned her back on me and left with her friend.

I placed my hands on the counter to steady myself. *God, I'm pale. My appearance gives new meaning to the term "white girl".* I splashed cold water on my face; it felt good ... and I dabbed cool water on the back of my neck. I smoothed back my hair, took a hair tie from my purse, and pulled my hair into a ponytail. The dim light highlighted the dark shadows under my eyes.

I couldn't blame that woman, after all, who was I to sit in like a voyeur on this ceremony that I knew nothing about. We had denied the aboriginal people their dignity, their culture, and then forced our religion on them. How interesting that many, it appeared, embraced the old ways, a revival of great spiritual significance.

As I left the washroom, I speculated how it was that I found myself there at all. Not just in that auditorium, but also in the Shuswap. My metamorphosis had already begun and there was no holding it back: from girl, to mother, to grandmother … an elder, a woman who retreats from society's busyness to learn the secrets of the soul. Although I hadn't retreated—I'd opened a busy bookstore—and I was tired, so very tired.

I sat by myself on the floor, back against the wall, recalling the time when I left Vancouver. It was about three years after my father passed away unexpectedly.

Possessed by the idea of leaving life-as-I-knew-it for a more meaningful existence, I left my job as a bookstore clerk, my husband, friends, and family and drove to the Shuswap where my father's ashes lay resting in a churchyard in Sorrento. Dad's country, for that's how I thought of it, and possibly Dad himself, began to speak to me through the vessel of nature, for nature was his holy temple. He found interest in everything there and had a keen eye for the smallest detail. My gentle, soft-spoken father ambled through woods and valleys soaking up the glory of the Creator. His transformation from atheist to AA took place after he retired and moved to the Shuswap with my mother, a woman who still lovingly tended the gardens and his roses.

Dad read widely, enjoyed nature photography, and went on solitary sojourns into out-of-the-way places. During my drive up country to see Mom, I sensed that something more than a visit or a business opportunity was calling me, and as time went on, I was more convinced that Dad's spirit, the intangible essence of him, lingered here.

I sat watching people on the far wall. One or two people looked fierce, like nothing I'd ever seen before. A Native man I knew sat down beside me. He told me that the opening song had to do with the four directions, and the earth and sky.

"It's the most powerful of all songs," he said, "because it's directed at the entire universe and requests the spirits of all the directions to enter the meeting place. Three more prayer songs follow that song, and on the fourth the spirits arrive. Yuwipi is a spirit calling ceremony." I listened attentively, trying to take in the importance of the profound ritual. I couldn't believe I was there.

Everyone, old and young, had taken places along the walls of the room now that the windows were sealed and the door was locked. The floor felt hard and unyielding.

George sat on the floor holding his drum, along with other men, including Big Bear, a big man wearing jeans and a dark shirt. I noticed a blanket set out before them with items on it, and hundreds of colourful prayer ties hanging on lines. I didn't know the significance of all the things I was seeing, but I knew that many days of preparation would have been required, and that it probably involved many sessions of purification and prayer in the sweat lodge.

Next, much to my surprise, Big Bear, the medicine man, was tied up and wrapped in a blanket. The lights went out and it was blacker than night, blacker than anything. Everything disappeared, including my own body, an odd sensation.

Then the drumming, the drumming ... galloping into the hollows of my heart. Many drums and many male voices raised the hair on my arms. Nothing and everything.

Sparks of blue ... the sound of rattles... thrashing and thumping, coming from everywhere at once. I tried to hold on, but there was nothing to hold on to. I saw, or thought I saw, movement up high in a far corner of the ceiling ... no end ... no exit ... prayers, and more prayers ... me ... part of the energy in the room, free falling through the night, yet alert and connected to my beating heart ... swoosh .... something brushed past me ... my eyes strained to see ... nothing ... no control ... yet oddly, I was okay.

I don't know what time it was when the fluorescent lights burst upon us like an unwelcome guest, exposing tired human beings squinting against the intruder. As my eyes adjusted, I noticed Big Bear had freed himself from his bonds. Soon, men were setting up long tables and chairs while women carried in huge pots of steaming food. Delicious aromas filled the auditorium and my stomach rumbled in anticipation of the feast that would follow.

People chatted and laughed as they set up large urns of coffee and tea. The energy in the room felt electric. Standing in the middle of the commotion, I wasn't sure what to do. Just when I decided to look for Mary Lou, George appeared before me, his intense expression startled me. No words. Everything seemed to stop. In his right hand he held something, which he offered to me. I reached out to accept it, and stared at the blue stone in my palm, like nothing I'd ever seen before. My eyes met his, but before I could say anything he turned and disappeared into the crowd. I instinctively closed my fingers around the blue stone in a protective gesture. The cool, smooth stone warmed my hand and seemed to connect me to something beyond myself.

Blue is the colour of the throat chakra, which represents communication and is all about speaking one's truth. Uncanny, because it was as if my throat centre had been clamped shut for far too long.

I joined Mary Lou and others at a table and opened my palm to stare at the stone. A nugget of turquoise about the size of an acorn. I'd seen lots of turquoise, but nothing like that stone. It glowed. The orb held the essence of every blue: mountain lakes, Mediterranean seas, my father's eyes.

A memory emerged. As a child, I was surrounded by my father's lapidary interests. He collected stones and Indian arrowheads. The stones appeared ordinary, even drab, but when he sliced them open a rich, intricate, and colourful world lay hidden inside. I grew up believing stones were just stones, or did I? I remembered a dreamy child who saw enchantment and meaning in everything. What did Dad believe? He was the one with the imagination in the family, the storyteller. Maybe he saw more than beauty in the stones he so carefully polished. Maybe I am my father's daughter.

The next day at Reflections, when I wasn't making cappuccino or finding a book for a customer, I pulled the blue stone out of my pocket from time to time, marveling at how good it felt in my hand. The stone held a story. Mary Lou told me that the turquoise stone, along with other items, had been placed on the altar of blankets, where they had been blessed by the medicine man. "Turquoise is the most powerful of all healing stones," she said.

That stone comforted and connected me to the Secwepemc people; it belonged to a realm that was beyond me, yet part of me. It was my amulet against loneliness, a stepping-stone to the other side of grief, for my old life was slipping away and I had no idea what lay ahead.

First Nations, my Celtic ancestors, and every mystical tradition, including the Christian one, maintain that everything is connected and oddly, here in the Shuswap, that truth became self-evident for me. Or maybe I'd begun to see the world in a fresh way, for at the heart of it lay wonder … to see the universe in a blue stone.

6: Writers' Retreat

One day an invitation arrived in the mail for Deanna Kawatski's annual one-day writers' retreat in June. Excitement gripped me as I read a personal note from Deanna. I sensed the experience would take me out of my comfort zone, but, gazing out the window at the lake ruffled by a passing breeze, I knew the time had come.

Deanna and I had become acquainted when I carried her book *Wilderness Mother* about her experiences living in the wilderness in northern British Columbia for thirteen years. We arranged for her to do a reading at my bookstore. This was Deanna's first reading, but not her first publishing experience. Fiddlehead Press had published *Bird, Bubble and Stream*, a book of poetry, in 1980. Throughout the 80's and early 90's her feature articles appeared in six national magazines in both the U.S and Canada. For a time, *Mother Earth News* made her a contributing editor. I felt excited to have such an accomplished author appearing in Reflections.

When she and her husband separated, Deanna moved back to the Shuswap with her two children. She was born in Salmon Arm and had spent idyllic childhood summers with her grandmother at Magna Bay on Shuswap Lake. The rest of the year she went to school in Kamloops.

I remembered the evening of Deanna's appearance in Reflections well. Shelley, a friend of Deanna's from school, lived in Salmon Arm and when she heard about the reading she decided to surprise Deanna and say a few words on her behalf. She invited their Kamloops teacher. Even in grade seven, Mr. Turner had seen Deanna's writing talent and had encouraged her.

The bookstore was packed that evening. We had done a lot of promotion and as usual word-of-mouth created a buzz. My friend Carol was visiting from Vancouver, which made the event even more special. I always loved the energy that lingered in the bookstore after any kind of gathering.

When the day for the writers' retreat finally arrived, I was up early. It was a long drive, maybe an hour and a half from where I lived to the highlands beyond Celista, a town on the north shore of Shuswap Lake. The map was easy to follow and eventually I turned into Deanna and Eric's driveway, a country lane bordered by towering birch and cedar trees. *Enchanting.* I had the feeling that I was entering a realm set apart from the rest of the world.

A black lab and a sheltie ambled across the lawn toward me, tails wagging.

Beyond the lane and towering trees, a tidy yard opened up. Beyond that, fields and several cows. In a garden bordering the house, red tulips nodded in the morning breeze. Among the bold tulips, a plant hung with pink and white heart-shaped flowers. The air smelled of grass and fields and sweet blossoms—the scent of spring in the Shuswap.

As lovely as this welcome was, and as peaceful as the farm was, I experienced an all too familiar stab of anxiety in my stomach, but no matter how scared I was the time had come to get feedback, the necessary next step to moving forward with my writing.

This nervousness had plagued me ever since I could remember, which was far too long. It was a ridiculous setback in just about everything I tried to do. How could I ever forget the day that nerves turned into a full-blown panic attack? That was during a lengthy stressful time in my life. I thought I'd cracked up. That little break in the dam contaminated the rest of my life. Fear took a back seat to terror, for panic attacks are terrifying. A full-blown panic attack meant my heart raced uncontrollably as fear oozed from every pore. The urgent need to escape a nameless, formless terror, would shake me to my core. In ancient Greece, flute playing Pan, god of flocks, half man and half goat, sometimes caused unreasoning fear, known as panic, in people and in animals. I prayed that the spirit of the goat god wasn't lurking nearby. The last thing I needed right then was a panic attack as I faced one of my biggest fears: speaking in front of people, and a new one—reading my writing to people. With no blue stone to give me courage I wanted to turn and run before anyone saw me. The turquoise stone had mysteriously disappeared at the dream workshop I'd attended in

Kamloops.

Using all my will power to keep moving forward, I found the steps that would take me inside. I stopped to pet a tabby cat, sitting in quiet contemplation on the porch. Deep breath. Through the window on the timeworn wooden door, I saw people sitting around a table in the yellow kitchen. I knocked and turned the door knob.

Deanna embraced me and introduced me to the women around a long wooden table. Chairs shuffled on the linoleum as nearly a dozen people made room for me. I was surprised that I knew one woman. Estelle, a tall, slender, fair-haired photographer and author who had come to the dream workshop with me. I'd carried her books *Shuswap Pathways: A Trail Guide and Shuswap Secrets: a pictorial guide* in my bookstore.

I was aware of the smell of baking, crackle of fire in the wood cook stove, chatter of friendly voices ... and me, a little shaky.

Deanna sat at the head of the table, a petite woman, several years younger than me, probably in her late 40's. She stood out among the other women, even though most were taller than her. She was striking looking with waist-length dark hair that shone with auburn highlights. But it was more than that, or her expressive dark eyes. She possessed strength and gentleness. She respected people and didn't invade their space. It's what made me trust her.

When we settled, Deanna asked us to say a few words about ourselves. Without warning, an age-old panic threatened me like a demon unleashed from the basement. Please, God. Not now!

By the time they came to me, my heart pounded uncontrollably. My palms felt clammy. I looked at the sheets of paper I'd placed on the table in front of me. *Don't run. Hands flat on the table so they won't shake.*

"I'm Kay McCracken." I looked down at the paper in front of me.

Say something else.

"I guess I've always had a dream of writing, ever since I was young. I remember the first story I ever wrote in grade four or five. Writing that story was the most fun I ever had in school. And that teacher was my favourite. She was kind and grandmotherly."

I paused and smoothed the papers in front of me.

"And there were other scribblings and stories, and a lifelong dedication to playing with words and images in my journals but then life got in the way. Kids, jobs, marriages—the women laughed at that—and my fears, but after I closed my bookstore there came a time when I knew I had to try. I'm writing a book about the experience."

I'd been staring at my hands most of the time.

They're applauding! I looked around the table at the smiling faces. *I did it.*

I managed to relax a little with a few warm up writing exercises but when it was time to share the first page from the book I was working on, I got all knotted up again. *Pain in my stomach ... fear ... fear of appearing foolish or stupid ... squeezing the life out of me.*

"It flows well," Deanna said, when I finished reading. Thank God, I could breathe again. A couple of women offered suggestions. I'd survived.

When we took a break mid-morning, Deanna's daughter, Natalia, set out warm blueberry muffins and poured mugs of great smelling coffee. The sense of shared enthusiasm among us exhilarated me. I began to sense that Deanna and I might be kindred spirits. She was kind, a nature lover, and she possessed a vital creative energy that I responded to.

Deanna pulled out a book and read a passage from *Bird by Bird: Some Instructions on Writing and Life,* by Anne Lamott.

Lamott writes that writing can be a pretty desperate endeavor because it is about some of our deepest needs, including our need to be visible, to be heard, our need to make sense of our lives, to wake up and grow and belong.

I wanted to jump up and yell YES! I couldn't wipe the smile off my face.

In the afternoon we gathered outside to the sound of a raven croaking above us in a tall fir tree. I felt the connection in my heart, as the beautiful bird had become an important symbol for me—it was the great Trickster after all who brought the world out of darkness. I had struggled with depression, the darkness, when I worked so hard and long to make my bookstore a success, and again when I lost everything.

A cow bellowed a mournful lament for her bull in the next field and I thought about how it would be a long time, if ever, before I called a man to me again.

Deanna said we were free to wander into the woods to work on the next writing exercise. I found a log near the woodpile where Eric had been chopping wood. My senses were awakened by the scent of fresh wood chips as they mingled with the pungent scent of the fertile earth, of a forest throbbing with new life, sap rising, cedar bows swaying in the breeze.

Inspiration was everywhere, even far above me in a treetop, where raven had begun to coo like a dove.

7: Pigs in the Snow

I'd become friends with the permanent residents of the strata property where I lived. Long before my time, Sarah Weaver and Clive Callaway bought Twin Island Resort. At some point they shared the property with several other families and it became a strata. Joan Reid owned some of the cabins, which she rented to tourists on a weekly basis, mainly families from Alberta. Mine was the only cabin that rented year-round, so it was quiet in the fall, winter, and spring, and alive with the holiday spirit of families during the summer, with me in their midst, a quiet woman living alone with her cat, her porch a dazzling splash of colourful flowers.

Joan was an interesting woman. Despite being confined to a wheelchair as a paraplegic after a car accident, she didn't let that stop her from running Cat Tale Cottages efficiently, or riding horses, or driving her van. She loved life, people, and adventure and I never heard her complain, never a hint of "poor me," never a regret that I heard about. She carried on living her life as if the wheelchair was her chariot and her arms were the wings that bore her to freedom.

Residents living around the lake formed a group called the Friends of Gardom Lake. I attended a meeting or two and it was during the second meeting that I was asked to write a piece for their newsletter. I was taken by surprise and left the group somewhat stunned that I'd agreed to interview one of the pioneering families in the area. A neighbour would go with me, as I didn't know the woman we were to visit.

It was snowing heavily the day Denise and I walked over to Mrs. Sturt's place. As we walked we laughed, recalling the time in early spring when I stopped to chat to Denise on the road and a sudden snow storm blew up. To our astonishment a mother pig emerged, running straight at us through the blur of snowflakes. Right behind her, running as fast as their little legs could carry them, a dozen or so piglets. We stood aside, mouths agape, as they ran to freedom along Gardom Lake Road. Where had they escaped from and where they were going, we wondered aloud. Denise and

I laugh to this day every time we think about that surreal sight—pigs in the snow.

We had phoned to arrange a time for an interview with Mrs. Sturt. Her house was on the right as we turned onto the Bible Camp road. The weathered barn was hung with elk and moose hides, a sight that always caught my attention as I drove or walked by.

Mrs. Sturt asked us to call her Pearl and introduced us to her mini-poodle, Sandy. I noticed a couple of Manx cats scatter as we entered the porch. When we were sitting around Pearl's kitchen table, enjoying the warmth of the wood stove and the cup of coffee we were offered, I pulled out my pen and paper and asked about the hides. She said they were a reminder of her husband Art's hunting days and that the barn was on the property along with the house when Pearl and Art moved there fifty-four years ago in May, which meant they'd been there since 1946.

Pearl was a petite, soft-spoken woman. At eighty-three she said she had seen many changes and agreed to share some of her memories with us. I scribbled notes on a lined, yellow pad of paper, reveling in the novelty of my first experience as a journalist.

When the Sturts first moved to Gardom Lake Pearl said there was only one other woman in the area. She lived with her teenagers where the Bible Camp was now. Pearl remembers seeing a light moving in the dark hills at night as her neighbour rounded up her cows.

In those days they shared the wilderness with many animals. "You just had to look out any window. There were moose, bear, deer, and coyote roaming freely. There were also grebes nesting down here." Anger rises as Pearl remembers the Sunday that three men rowed over in a boat and poked at the nests with their oars.

Pearl's love of the local wild life ran deep. One night while Art, a fire warden, was away fighting a fire in Deep Creek, Pearl saw headlights in the field and ran out in her nightgown to yell at the men who she suspected of poaching deer. In fact, they were stealing her firewood!

As I glanced out Mrs. Sturt's kitchen window, I was mesmerized for a moment by the dance of snowflakes over the lake. Pearl told us about the winter that the snow was up to the top of her fence, and about the winter of '50, '51, when the temperature plunged to -40 degrees Fahrenheit. Another winter was so windy that it left the lake "looking like a mirror," she said. "It was a little unnerving walking on the polished ice because you could see stumps, and weeds moving below." She paused. "This year is unusual. It's the first time I've seen ice form and then disappear from the lake."

The Sturts raised five children at Gardom Lake and Pearl recalled how the children walked to school, which was on Schoolhouse Road. As their youngest daughter Cheryl grew she could be seen riding her buckskin horse, a black lab at her side. "She rode over the mountain by herself and we never had to worry back then."

Pearl survived her husband Art by five years—he passed away in 1995—and reminds us that he played an important part in the building of Gardom Lake Park. Pearl remembers people bringing horses and dogs to the park and turning them loose, and that she received flack for attempting to enforce the "No Dogs" rule.

I could hear a TV in the next room and someone laughing. "That's Sharon," Pearl said. Apparently, her daughter was disabled, causing Pearl great concern about what would happen to Sharon when she was gone. Another daughter lived nearby on the property. Pearl said she loved the lake and wouldn't be happy anywhere else.

"You can take a girl out of the country, but you can't take the country out of the girl," Pearl said, with a shy smile.

Back in my cabin, I read over my notes and began writing. I rewrote the article several times until I was finally happy with it. My confidence in writing was not great. I worried about every comma and used my dictionary to check the spelling of words. Spelling had never been my strong point. I finally handed it to Sarah and hoped for the best. When the Gardom Lake News, Fall 2000—6th Issue came out, I was thrilled.

Gardom's Past: Pioneering at Gardom Lake by Kay McCracken.

My first by-line. I stared at the title with my name below it. Something like a mixture of pride and elation welled up in me. *Oh ya, this is what happy feels like.*

8: The Lone Pine Ranch Odyssey

Joan and I turned off the highway and wound our way up a dusty road until we came upon the Lone Pine Ranch, a private working ranch in the Okanagan high country that overlooked both Kalamalka and Okanagan Lakes. The ranch had registered Quarter horses and Texas Longhorn cattle, a real ranch, and my yearning to go horseback riding was about to be fulfilled.

We waited, and waited. There had been an accident out on the trail. An ambulance was called for a woman, and a veterinarian for the horse. As one hour turned into two, anxiety wore me down. I'd been up early to drive Joan to Salmon Arm before we could head for the ranch on the other side of Vernon, an hour's drive from Salmon Arm. In the past, lack of sleep had been a trigger for anxiety to take hold.

Did I really want to go horseback riding? After all, I hadn't been on a horse since I was about ten years old. I felt uneasy and a bit queasy, but there was nothing to do but wait. I couldn't let Joan down. I'd been excited about this adventure when Joan set it up for us.

Ravens cavorted in the trees near us, the only diversion from my discomfort.

Finally, the time came for Joan and I, but when I stood next to the horse I felt sick. It was gigantic. Overwhelming. A mountain of horse to climb. I never had this feeling when I was younger, living in the Toronto suburbs and washing the neighbours' cars to make money for my riding lesson every weekend. I loved riding horses and spent time after the lesson grooming them in the stable. I learnt to ride bareback and the next thing I signed up for was jumping, but we moved again, Medicine Hat that time, before I could tackle the new challenge. The constant moving was hard on a shy kid like me and maybe that contributed to the feeling I had of never really fitting in anywhere, of being an outsider.

I watched Joan laugh and joke with the rugged-looking cowboy helping her into her saddle. My turn. With pounding heart, I let our trail guide boost me up and into the saddle. The ground appeared far below me. Vertigo, or nerves, threatened me. *What was I doing!* Let me off, I screamed—but that was only inside my head. I was exhausted and we were just starting out.

The saddle felt uncomfortable and awkward between my legs. No turning back now. A ripple of fear gripped me, but I hung on tight, trying to believe that the adventure wouldn't hurt me too badly. Within minutes I was in pain.

The guide joked that rattlesnakes lay in wait along the trail for the horses! *Rattlesnakes!* My heart thumped fiercely and I hung on for my life.

As my horse picked its way up a treacherous, rocky incline through the bush, I clutched the saddle with all my strength. I was not having fun. Ahead of me Joan and the cowboy laughed and bantered back and forth to each other. Then I heard Joan say, "let's go," and to my horror their horses began galloping. No! My legs and my bum already rebelled at the painful contact with the saddle. Galloping would be insane, if not extremely dangerous.

Joan and the guide left me in the dust, where rattlesnakes lay in long, golden grass beside the trail, waiting.

But Joan hadn't deserted me and soon we were on the highest plateau, where the massive gnarled pine tree—the lone pine—owned the wind and the view. The tree appeared more dramatic because its top had been blown off several times by lightning. I couldn't believe the sight below me. I was on top of the world. The tree and the view of the lakes far below—blue jewels in the vast Okanagan valley bottom—made me forget about the tension and pain in my body briefly.

Back at home, after what seemed like an odyssey I'd barely survived, I thought about how the fantasy I had of horseback riding didn't live up to the reality. How on earth had this happened to me? I had no fear of such things when I was younger. Had life beat me up that bad?

I thought about Joan and wondered what it was going to take for me to get my stamina back. I still didn't know what was wrong with me. Patience, I told myself, after what I thought of as my horseback-riding failure. I wasn't happy. Ill health reined me in when my natural inclination was to explore new territories. Next to Joan, I felt like the one who had a disability, but then she must have had an intense period of emotional and physical healing—if not a heap of grief—after the accident. Somehow, she had transcended all barriers; body, mind, and spirit aligned as one, and she fostered no ill will toward her brother, the driver who had fallen asleep at the wheel.

9: River Song

I continued working on my book, checking back in my journals for details, and I finally came up with an idea to make money. While working toward an English degree at Simon Fraser University, I'd cleaned houses and offices. I can do that, I thought. No stress. *I'll use eco-friendly cleaning products. No harsh chemicals for this cleaning lady!*

When I told Joan that I was starting a cleaning business she said, "You're not going to call it something dumb like Kay's Kleaning I hope."

"Well, yes as a matter of fact I am." We both chuckled at that. I went ahead and put notices up and sent ads to the newspapers.

The Gardom Lake News ran an article about keeping septic systems happy and preventing contamination of the lake and ground water by using phosphate free and biodegradable cleaning products. My conscience was clear. Sarah and I had rowed around the lake one cool fall day taking water samples to send to a lab, something she did on a regular basis.

Meanwhile, Mom had been having more troubling episodes of vertigo. It was horrible to see how much she suffered. I'd often driven to Sorrento to help her when she was in trouble. There wasn't much I could do except to be there with her while she retched for hour upon hour, unable to move from the basin she clutched.

Then things took an even worse turn. While gardening a vertebra collapsed, leaving mother incapacitated and in crippling pain. That was the end of gardening for her. My sister, Marilyn, and I found her an apartment to rent in Salmon Arm and Mom put her manufactured home up for sale. Marilyn and her family lived in Salmon Arm and I would be much closer, too. Luckily, our mother liked the spacious two-bedroom apartment. It even had a gas fireplace. She couldn't wait to move in. The United Church was only a block away and her sister Marge could walk over and call for her. She liked that idea.

I knew she would miss certain aspects of living in Sorrento Place, and a friend or two. And who could forget the flavour of her strawberries growing just steps from the back door, that juicy berry warmed by the sun and enjoyed by everyone who visited during the summer. Visiting family and friends also gorged themselves on the abundance of dark plump cherries and there was an apricot tree, raspberry canes, and a vegetable garden.

I didn't think Mom would miss moving the sprinkler around the back and front lawns and gardens during those scorching summer days, not that she'd be able to do that anymore. At her new apartment a pleasant elderly man looked after the lawns, and the automatic sprinklers took care of watering. The attractive, white apartment building looked more like a private mansion landscaped with shrubs, a Ponderosa Pine tree, and two Japanese Maples hung with dark wine-coloured leaves. A wide porch ran the length of her apartment at ground level at the front. Out back another spacious porch overlooked the alley. Back or front were both great places for people watching. The traffic noise along 3rd Street and Okanagan Avenue might take some getting used to, but Mom didn't think it would be a problem, but then her hearing was already in decline.

It took some time to get the apartment just how our mother wanted it, but once that was done and she was settled, Marilyn, her husband John and I breathed a sigh of relief. Meanwhile, at Gardom Lake I played with Bridgey, watered the colourful hanging baskets at each of the cabins for Joan, earning me the name "the flower lady," a name bestowed on me by the tourists. I took care of my housecleaning jobs, but above all, I continued to work on my book.

My favourite place to clean was on the way to Hidden Lake. After a long drive to get there, cleaning was a whole day affair. The house was three stories, a massive place with a self-contained guest house overlooking the Shuswap River. I drove the long dirt driveway to the main house, with its wide porch for sitting, and old man river rolling by. It wouldn't have surprised me to see Tom Sawyer drift by on his raft. Time ceased to exist at the river house, maybe because of the dense dark forest as far as I could see, the silent horses in the corral, the absence of people or cars.

Song lyrics by Robbie Robertson seemed to rise up in me ...

somewhere down the crazy river .... reminding me of a lonely time in Vancouver when that song played on my car radio every morning as I drove to a job I wasn't suited for ... *catch the blue train*. The song stirred something in me, a great longing to be far away doing something other than managing a furniture showroom.

Inside the house, a variety of rescued cats scattered to find hiding places when I dragged my vacuum into the spacious, tiled entrance. Long John Silver, the three-legged cat, was especially fast at disappearing.

One day, as I was dusting the wall of bookshelves in the den, a book caught my attention. Totem Poles: An Illustrated Guide was a book I had carried in my bookstore and was the book that kept falling off the shelf for no apparent reason. I took the book down from the shelf and looked at it. That book may have held the key to the mystery I was trying to unravel about my days and nights spent in my bookstore, Reflections. Opening the book, I stared again at the photo of the Bill Reid carving "Raven and the First People". I remembered seeing that monumental sculpture in the museum at UBC when I was a student there. The stunning sculpture depicted Raven, peering over the edge of a giant clamshell that held frightened little men; Raven: mischievous Trickster, creator of the world. I was still trying to work out the significance that ravens and totem poles had for me. Maybe it was nothing, although I began to believe there was more to it. I wanted to make the connection. Ever since moving to Salmon Arm to open a bookstore, ravens had become symbols of joy for me, despite their maligned reputation in history as harbingers of death.

Ironically, ravens brought light to my sometimes burdened soul, these larger than life black birds; larger than life myth makers.

I thought about the ravens, as I took my sandwich and thermos of tea out to the front porch at the river house. The solitude and the river's song settled my soul. I pondered how the energy was different from Gardom Lake as I took another bite of my peanut butter and banana sandwich.

I watched a ghost train of mist roll along behind a ridge. I admired small garnet-coloured apples clumped tightly along the branches of the apple trees in the yard. Two ravens chatted back and forth near the river, adding to my feeling of contentment. With the cup of tea raised to my lips, I stopped as two deer walked up the driveway, then up the stone walkway, munching grass as they went. They didn't seem to notice me, their white tails flicking. Unconcerned by my presence, the deer nibbled grass right in front of the porch where I sat. *It's so peaceful here.* I breathed in air that smelled like dried leaves mingled with river scent. Listening to the river song, any worries I had about the future flowed downstream with the current.

Something else was working in my life, too. I was in therapy. The Doctor and I discussed many things, including what he called my phobic reaction to the limelight. Dr. H., I'll call him, was shocked that I'd jumped into the herbal business so soon after what I'd been through with the bookstore. I now realized that that decision hadn't done my mental health any favours and likely prolonged my recovery from burnout.

Visiting Dr. H. helped me put my emotions in perspective, especially if I'd had a rough day. He was sensitive, intelligent, and soft-spoken, and I appreciated those things about him—and especially that he encouraged my writing.

I took out a small notebook and jotted down a few notes before going back to washing floors and scrubbing the many bathrooms.

10: Mindful Kitten

I had trouble keeping my word about not letting Bridgey out. My rebellion began on a beautiful spring day, the kind of day where everything in the world sings in harmony. My heart expanded in the warm morning sunshine as I listened to bird song and breathed in air as fresh as the newly unfurled season, as fresh and innocent as any newborn baby.

I carried my baby, Bridgey, out to the porch to sit on my lap. She had never been outside before as she had spent her first six or so weeks in a windowless basement, then inside Mom's house for a week. I felt compelled to share this spring bliss with my bright-eyed little friend.

She sat very still, taking it all in. The planters filled with bright red geraniums, purple petunias and blue lobelia, exotic smelling marigold, scent of trees and flowers, buzz of insects, and the powerful fir branches swaying above us. Showing Bridgey the natural world for the first time, with all its sights, sounds and smells, filled me with wonder as well.

After a while—and I knew I was crossing a line—I set Bridgey down on the wooden deck. Sun warmed planks under her paws.

With an air of mindfulness, soft kitten steps led her to the closest pot of flowers, where she poked her black nose into a purple petunia. This was all done with considerable presence and quiet deliberation, a beautiful thing to watch.

That's as far as exploration of the great outdoors went that day but of course something had shifted in our universe. I had a feeling there might be no stopping it now. I'd say the devil made me do it, if I could get away with it—or if I believed in the devil.

I bought a harness for Bridgey, which I would attach to the porch on a long leash. I knew she would love the soil and grass beneath her paws. I'd sit on the porch steps, watching her leap in the air after a passing blue dragonfly.

When Joan and the cleaning crew of young women arrived every Saturday to clean cabins in preparation for the next wave of Alberta tourists, every one of them fell in love with Bridgey. They all stopped to talk and play with her as they walked back and forth carrying fresh sheets and towels.

At one point, I began letting Bridgey out without her leash. I couldn't control my urge to give her a taste of real freedom. Freedom was something I valued above all else, so how could I deprive my little friend of the experience.

The day she ran through the open door carrying a garter snake, which she dropped in the middle of the carpet, I recoiled and shrieked, "Bridgey, take that out of here!" I wasn't afraid of garter snakes but this motionless creature in my living room freaked me out. I wasn't sure why but I couldn't make myself pick it up.

I ran to the cabin next door and asked a tourist if he would mind helping. He obliged by returning the hapless snake to the tall grass and purple lupins on the bank. After that Bridgey became a hunter of voles. Unfortunately, they were very cute. She ate them, leaving behind a tail and two back legs. I never quite got used to seeing the remains of the little creatures.

One day I looked out to see Bridgey and a magpie facing off near the bottom step. The magpie strutted toward my cat and stopped about a foot from her. Bridgey stood very still, their eyes locked. The magpie chuckled as she flew off, at least that's what it sounded like. Two black and white creatures, one feathered, one furred. That was the first and last time I saw a magpie at the lake. Never a day went by without something unusual or beautiful to marvel at when I lived there.

I wrote, read, walked, played with Bridgey, and cleaned houses. It seemed to be a balance I could maintain. The only thing missing was a connection to like-minded people. But then nothing ever stays the same forever, as I was about to find out.

Part Two

Moving On

11: Six Lessons

Mom was distraught and disoriented when I found her. I'd never seen her like that. She said she'd staggered around the apartment not knowing what was happening to her.

She'd had a TIA, known as a mini-stroke, where a blood clot blocks blood flow in the brain temporarily. A TIA acts as a warning sign for risk of a stroke, so Mom was prescribed blood thinners, and also medication for her atrial fibrillation, or irregular heartbeat.

Although there was no visible change in her appearance, she was different after that. The front porch door was left open, inviting anyone to walk in. The rotting bowl of fruit played host to a cloud of fruit flies. A burner was left on. She dropped things. It wasn't long before she couldn't make it up the small incline on the walk back from town. None of this bode well for my mother living on her own. Something had to be done.

Curious symptoms affected me as well. I began losing strength and along with shortness of breath, I found it tough to go for my walks. Even the incline to reach my car and Gardom Lake Road produced laboured breath. I didn't know what those symptoms meant, but carried on as well as I could. I was also getting to a place where I realized that more human contact, other than Alberta tourists during the summer, would be a good thing.

Bridgey and I moved in with Mom. I thought I'd give it a try for six months, not sure if I'd be able to live with my mother. She is solid, grounded, and in her mind at least, always right, whereas I'm more mercurial, or to put it another way, I didn't get my restless, rebel gene from my mother. Her need for control drove me a bit nuts sometimes, but then if I'm honest, I probably have control issues, too.

I put my furniture in storage and made the small bedroom with a single bed my own, setting up bookshelves and hanging my artwork. The room had a small desk that I set my computer on. As long as I had my books, my artwork, and a place to write, I would be okay, I told myself.

The lessons came on fast, and relentless lessons they were.

Lesson # 1: Never ever be in a hurry when you are dealing with an elderly parent.

Mom was slowing down but at least she was still mobile. She took my arm when we walked downtown. Slow and easy does it. Very slow. Very easy.

Lesson #2: Never underestimate the power of control that your ageing mother has over you.

In the spring I enjoyed planting pots and hanging baskets for the porches. Our eyes and noses enjoyed the scented yellow, royal purple, and tangerine pansies. The lilac tree in the front yard sent its powerful dark purple fragrance to us on the porch. Hanging over the back porch white lilac clusters perfumed the air where I sat, sending me into something of a poetic swoon. I began writing poetry and continued to work on my book.

This was a time of great change, for as an adult child moving in with her mother there were adjustments to make. Adjustments. Yes, well. Take one very stubborn mother who is used to doing things her way. Then take one very stubborn eldest daughter who is used to running her own life and who doesn't like being told what to do and how to do it. Mom had the annoying habit of leaning over me, watching me do whatever it was I was doing. She probably didn't mean anything by it, but I'd feel myself bristle with her breathing down my neck.

Lesson #3: Never argue with your ageing mother. You'll never win.
    It all began innocently enough, although before long seismic rumblings threatened. I probably should have taken into consideration that I was still unwell, although I didn't understand what was wrong with me.
    My dear little mother was shrinking, unwell, and not at all compliant. Did I inherit the non-compliant gene from her? I began to wonder. Advice to drink more water or do her stretching exercises went unheeded no matter how much I nagged. She did what she wanted to do and nothing more.
    I don't think giving up control in one's late seventies would be an easy transition, but her need to be in charge didn't make the job of looking after her any easier. Her physical and mental health slid downhill faster than I could keep up with.

Lesson #4: Get used to back seat driving when you find yourself chauffeuring your mother around.
    The day she lost her driver's license was a heartbreaking blow for a woman who had always been independent. I became her chauffeur, although I never got used to her stomping on nonexistent brakes half a block or more before an intersection. I drove more and more slowly, but it didn't make any difference. She told me where to go, how to get there, pointed out the speed signs—for the hundredth time. I started to lose my mind …. but I never yelled at her. Would this count if we gain points to enter the pearly gates one day?

Lesson #5: No matter how irritating your mother is, do not spray her with water.

Bridgey didn't make things any easier. "She's trying to trip me up," Mom would cry when our feline friend would leap from behind furniture to grab her ankles. Now that Bridgey wasn't hunting for voles in the tall grass and woods at Gardom Lake, she was hunting us instead. Sharp claws. Arrrgh! She wasn't winning any points with Mom, although I was used to her rough way of playing. When a visitor came to see me at the lake, Bridgey hid under the couch and grabbed the unsuspecting guest's ankles. She was irritating that way, but I adored her. I had to break Bridgey of that habit, using a spray bottle of water.

Lesson #6: Mom's way is the right way.

Every morning I draped the quilt over the old bed chesterfield in the living room, smoothed it out just so. Every day Mom came along after me and changed it so the pattern went the other way.

"Mom, why do you turn the quilt around every day?" I heard the peevishness in my tone. "Because that's the way it should be," she said, quite sure of herself. She pointed to one design in the overall pattern. Okay, I got it. The abstract leaf. I could see where she was coming from. After that I always did it the right way, her way. In the end it didn't matter to me which way the pattern went.

From upside down to right side up. Which is which? Give it up. My mother's quiet, persistent changing the quilt around would always win in the end. I thought of this as an example of how differently we each saw the world.

12: Too Sharp the Day

    Mom and I both enjoyed porch sitting, so it wasn't like we didn't have anything in common. People watching came easily to us. After a while we noticed many of the same people walking by every day, both on 3rd Street and in the alley. One of the men who walked by used to come into my bookstore now and then asking for a rosary. I'd tell him I didn't have any, but the next time he wandered in the request was the same. And there he was, walking on the far side of the street. Short and stocky, he had gained more weight around his middle since I had last seen him.

    We watched a regular flow of people from further down our street, who set themselves apart by the way they walked or talked. One woman kept up a steady stream of dialogue in a booming male voice with whatever characters lived in her head

    An apartment a few blocks away housed people with various mental illnesses. A few of the same people had wandered into Reflections, as the Mental Health workshop was in the building next to my bookstore. I remember little Harley with the big cigar, who was said to be schizophrenic, although it was usually my employee, Kristie, who talked to him. Everybody was medicated and well behaved. Almost daily a wide variety of people from different walks of life visited the bookstore, making my job most interesting, and sometimes challenging.

    And now I was caring for my mother, a different kind of challenge. Before long, my health began to suffer even more than it had before. Back pain and headaches mostly. What I didn't know then was that the symptoms of depression and anxiety can be physical as well as emotional.

    All was not well. When I got "the look" from Mom whenever I was on the phone, I had to do something, or go crazy. I had my own phone line installed in my bedroom. Dad did the same thing to her whenever she was on the phone and she hated it. She developed a phobia about using the phone, probably as a result, but here she was doing the same thing to me.

    Dr. H. helped me put things into perspective. He once called her my crazy-making mother. I began to understand that Mom suffered from anxiety. She was mostly fine as long as she was at home and everything was under her control. He also suggested that I should have her tested for dementia. The word shocked me.

I read that dementia is a loss of brain function that occurs with certain diseases. It affects memory, thinking, language, judgement, and behaviour and is almost always not reversible. My mother's dementia, if that's what it was, may have been caused by the stroke. I read that Alzheimer's disease is the most common type of dementia and what could be worse than losing all memory and therefore losing your loved ones. My grandmother, Annie Eliza McCracken, entered a long- term care facility after my grandfather passed away. She had developed Alzheimer's disease and didn't recognize my father, or anyone else. The other weird part of that disease was that Grams thought her reflection in the mirror was a stranger who was stealing from her. The disease had stolen my grandmother's reason, along with all her memories.

My mother didn't have Alzheimer's, but she did have another stroke. The ambulance came and when she was sent for a brain scan in Vernon, the doctor found that she'd had a series of small strokes. After that, I noticed the visible signs of dementia became more obvious and troubling. Words were gone. Thinking was muddled. Her short-term memory was even worse.

I researched and found that there are many types of dementia, and that setbacks, either emotional or physical, can bring on the symptoms. It's also known that people can pass the test for dementia—a very crude test—and still have it, and that they can fool many people into thinking they don't have it. Mom had normal conversations with people; she didn't forget things in her past or anyone's names and yet she could forget an important conversation five minutes later. What a strange and tricky disease. Symptoms can remain stable for a long time if one isn't abusing alcohol or sleeping pills, and if the person doesn't smoke, have diabetes or high blood pressure. Since my mother didn't have any of those habits or conditions the possibility for her maintaining at that level looked promising. For some unfortunate soles an obvious change in their personality is a sign of dementia. Luckily, my mother remained much the same in temperament.

    I kept writing, like a woman possessed, and I think that's what kept me sane, or at least some version of sane. In the morning, I'd write on the front porch. Afternoon, I wrote on the back porch in the privacy and shade of the white lilac tree, my sanctuary. I'd print out a copy to edit, or I'd write a poem. When I was writing, pain, anger and sadness vanished. The only thing that existed was my pen moving across the paper and the pictures in my head. I found that writing poetry was a way to break through and get to the heart of a matter.

    Graham Greene, English author of fifty-four books over seven decades, said he sometimes wondered how all those who don't write managed to escape the madness. He was bi polar, and often suicidal except when he was working on a book. He spoke of his restlessness, his boredom, his depressive episodes. I could relate to the restlessness, which always felt like I should be somewhere else, doing something else. My mother certainly wasn't like that.

    I'd heard several writers say that they write to get to the truth of things. Another author, can't remember who, said she writes to know what she thinks. Both these ideas resonated with me.

    However, even with the writing, the scent of the lilacs, or watching Bridgey play with a leaf in the dappled sunlight on the porch, I knew all was not well. Dr. H. prescribed medication for depression and anxiety. I was spiraling down.

Too Sharp the Day

somewhere between the first light of dawn
and the dream that follows me
for one quivering second
I'm in two worlds

I try to recapture the shadows of the night
to gather them to me

but as one world fades
the other intrudes
like knives of light

my eyelids flutter open, then close
as I sink back
into the comfort of my blankets

rock me back to sleep gentle night
far too sharp the day, too soon.

13: Dorothy and the Writers' Group

Dorothy was persistent and I'm thankful for that. We ran into each other downtown and decided to go for coffee to catch up. I'd seen her a few times since closing Reflections. She was the force behind the Shuswap Writers' Group, a small group of men and women who met twice a month to do writing exercises and to share whatever they were working on.

The Writers' Group also sponsored the Shuswap Writers' Coffee House once a month, which gave writers a chance to read their work to an audience. I was familiar with the coffee house, as I had hosted the event in Reflections for a season, and I always enjoyed meeting the many writers who attended. The evening was always entertaining, and often hilarious. We never knew what to expect from the eclectic mix of writers who showed up to share a poem, a chapter of a novel, an essay, or a song.

"You should join our Writers' Group," Dorothy said. A warm spring breeze reached us at the outdoor table as traffic rumbled by. Dorothy had fixed her big blue eyes and warm smile on me. She knew I was working on a book.

"We'd love to have you." She has more than a touch of the Irish in her, I thought, noticing the sparkle in her eyes.

"I don't know," I said, stalling, as I didn't want to be pressed into anything. I was feeling better on medication, but I was cautious about jumping into anything all the same. The thought of sharing my writing in a group still made my stomach tighten.

"It's a small, friendly group."

"Well." I paused. "Maybe." There was no way that I was going to tell Dorothy that I was somewhat unhinged in the mental health department and that I was on medication for it. People are suspicious of people with mental illness. I knew that. The stigma of having a mental illness, as opposed to a physical illness meant that I must keep that problem to myself.

"You could read a from your book and get feedback." The anxiety caused another flutter in my stomach, but how was she to know. Maybe she was one of those people who thought you just have to pull yourself up by your bootstraps. How many times had I done that in my life? I felt that I didn't have any bootstraps left to pull up.

The afternoon sun brought out the chestnut highlights in her dark hair. She must be about my age, although I felt a lot older than she looked. She seemed to know many people walking by and acknowledged each person with a wave, a smile, and a word or two.

I reflected on how Dorothy was an example of all that was good about living in a small community. She didn't gossip or appear to judge people, but instead chose to put her energy into creating something positive for her community, and I admired her for that.

"When's the next meeting?"

"Next Wednesday. We meet in a room in the Baptist Church from 1 until 3 pm. There's a $2.00 drop in fee." She said hello to a woman strolling by and then leaned back in her chair. "I'll pick you up if you like."

Whoa! Several fearful thoughts collided in my brain and then I heard myself say okay. Okay! I said okay? Boy, this woman was good. There didn't seem to be a way to say no to her.

Sunlight on her blouse. Dazzling. Blue like the Steller's jay I had seen at Gardom Lake. Dorothy favoured vibrant colours, and I reflected on the obvious, that I didn't wear the very colours I found so attractive. I knew that was because I liked to fade into the background. God forbid I should stand out and be noticed. I remember being at Kits beach with my brother Michael once when I was a lot younger and feeling too shy to walk to the washroom without covering myself up.

"What are you doing?" Michael asked.

"I don't like people looking at me," I said.

"They're looking at you because you're a good-looking woman. They're admiring you. Stand tall and take it in." That was a revelation, coming from one of my younger brothers.

Why was I hiding? Growing up in an alcoholic household, you never wanted the attention of the one in a foul mood. Not that my father ever beat us, but the angry shouting and door slamming scared me.

There might have been another reason I didn't like to attract attention to myself that had nothing to do with my father. As a pretty little girl of five or so the teenage boys in the neighbourhood cornered me, talking about inappropriate sexual things. I became prey as I wandered our rural neighbourhood alone—a target for their confusing attention—and a tempting sexual plaything for the teenage boy who I hung out with. I wasn't hurt physically, but may have developed an aversion to being noticed, especially because my mother went ballistic on her neighbour's son when she found out. Why was I allowed to wander by myself all day? No one noticed the boy and his intentions, because no one was there. He rolled out of a speeding car sometime after my mother tore a strip off him. He died. *Did I cause his death?* Cause and effect may have become confused in my mind.

Before I crashed, just like the computer system in Reflections did, I had enjoyed bringing people together for events in my bookstore, just as my house in Kits had been the focal point for many gatherings: birthday parties, summer barbecues, dinner parties, special occasions. I recognized the same tendency in Dorothy.

Was there a way to retrieve that lost part of me? It would take more than money, which I didn't have, or sending my brain to Toronto to the retrieval company, as I'd done with the computer after it crashed. They were only able to retrieve part of the data. That doesn't bode well for me if there's a parallel here. I had retreated so far into myself, into fearfulness, that it might take more than medication and Dr. H to retrieve what I'd lost.

I was ready and waiting when Dorothy pulled up outside our apartment. Just like the first day of school, I clutched my pen and notebook in anticipation. I also tucked a chapter inside a folder, just in case. I reminded myself that I'd talked and read to people at Deanna's. I'd lived, hadn't I?

When we entered the room in the back of the church, my antennae were up, scanning for anything that might make me uncomfortable. No, just a half a dozen ordinary-looking people chatting as Dorothy started a pot of coffee, sending the rich aroma throughout the room. I eventually discovered that there's nothing ordinary about people who write.

The writing exercises were fun and people shared various pieces of writing they were working on. I decided not to read a chapter at that time, but all in all, when the two hours were up, I felt happy for having been there.

I realized that if I never took a chance to overcome my anxiety, I would never know what I was capable of. I'd spent a lot of my life avoiding situations that would make me uncomfortable, yet something seemed to be pulling me through the knothole of my own fear.

14: Upward Spiral

 I continued to write and it felt good to be in town and part of a writing community. My life was looking up. I took long walks to the wharf and along the foreshore known locally as the bird sanctuary. I enjoyed inhaling the marshy scent of the lake and mud flats, which at times mingled with wood smoke drifting down from a house on the cliffs. It was a joyful place with many birds, including the wondrous great blue herons, and the osprey family, who lived in a huge nest of twigs on top of a pole near the wharf. Watching an osprey dive into the lake and emerge carrying a fish in his talons was breathtaking.

 I looked up the names of many of the trees and shrubs that bordered the path. Among the ones I could identify were the red ozier dogwood, alder, paper birch, a young grove of trembling aspen, a couple of small maple bushes whose flame-like leaves turned a stunning deep apricot, tangerine and crimson in the fall. Along one part of the footpath tall cottonwood trees created a tunnel of exquisite, pale green light.

 I noticed soft pussy willow, heard the clear tinkling sound of the spring fed stream next to the path, partially hidden by lush foliage. The stream fed a pond where ducks enjoyed the peaceful oasis cradled in the arms of pacific willow trees. Red-winged blackbirds clung to cattails, singing love songs carried on the wind. Two-dozen or more yellow-headed blackbirds—larger and brighter than their red-winged cousins—lit up a solitary tree in the marsh. My stamina was returning, due in part to my connection with people, my writing, the balm of healing that these walks provided and perhaps the medication helped, too.

 The library became an important resource of books on the craft of writing, along with inspiring memoirs by various well-known writers. Dr. H advised me to read about the lives of authors. That happened after discouraging feedback on something I was working on. He said all authors have had their work rejected at one time or another, and pointed out that

J.R.R. Tolkien's writers' group told him that The Hobbit was unpublishable.

I read several books on the craft of writing by Natalie Goldberg, starting with *Writing Down the Bones*, and including *Thunder and Lightning: Cracking Open the Writer's Craft* and *Old Friend From Far Away: The Practice of Writing Memoir*. Goldberg is a respected writing teacher, painter, and writer, who believes in the power of timed writings that teach writers to trust their first thoughts. She advises losing control in the timed writings. If we censor our thoughts, she says, we may never get to the good stuff, the original material. Outsmart the inner critic by not crossing out or worrying about spelling and punctuation.

I picked up a book on writing from the library called *Steering the Craft* by Ursula K. LeGuin, a prolific, award-winning science fiction author and poet from Portland, Oregon. I tried one of the exercises, writing a page without adjectives or adverbs. LeGuin once wrote that writers know that words are their way to truth and freedom.

In the beginning of LeGuin's writing career, her agent received a rejection letter from the editor at a publishing house, stating that LeGuin's first book *The Left Hand of Darkness* was dry, airless, and unreadable. LeGuin now has enough writing awards, including for that rejected book, to paper the Taj Mahal. I guess Dr. H knew what he was talking about when he said don't listen to the critics, especially the inner critic, and move on.

I read a lot of non-fiction in the form of literary non-fiction, creative non-fiction, and narrative non-fiction, which are different terms for the same thing. I fed my ravenous mind and subconscious with wonderful images and ideas.

I found the inspiring little book *If You Want to Write: A Book about Art, Independence and Spirit*, by Brenda Ueland, first printed in 1938, and reprinted in 1987. I'd seen it in Banyen Books when I worked there. One of Ueland's chapters "Why Women who do too much housework should neglect it for their writing" made me laugh. She also maintains that everyone is original and has something to say. All the reading I did was inspiring me. I felt I was on the right path.

Moving to town, joining the Shuswap Writers' Group, while continuing to work on my book, set something in motion; an upward spiral. I was still cleaning houses, making new friends and renewing old friendships when I was invited to join another writers' group. About eight or so highly creative women—a journalist, artists, photographers and musicians—met regularly to write. Blair Borden and I would go together after I'd spent hours cleaning her old farmhouse.

I loved Blair's gardens and the discarded running shoes nailed to an old shed in her yard, as if someone had run up the wall, leaving their shoes behind. Poetry in motion.

As president of the recycling society, Blair didn't believe in creating garbage. She was a creative soul who wrote clever, funny limericks, played the tuba in the community band, gardened and enjoyed photography.

My favourite writing exercise in that group was writing a chapter for a fictional story the group created. That opened me up to a new experience of working in a different genre, and I loved it! Eventually, the stress of sharing my writing in the group became too much and I quit going. Neurosis is a pain in the ass, I told myself, but recognizing that didn't change anything.

Sometime after that, friends Miranda, Bonnie and I would get together to write. It wasn't as intimidating, because we shared what we were working on over Chinese food at Yan's, and went to a movie afterwards. We always met on Tuesday, cheap movie night in Salmon Arm. Before long, we invited a local poet and rancher, John Vivian, to join us. We stopped going to dinner and a movie and got down to some serious writing for a couple of hours a week. We called our group the Cheap Tuesday Writers' Group. Eventually, Karen Bissenden, another local poet, joined us. The creativity that flowed from those minds, those pens, was impressive. John's life was a poem, for even while working on his tractor he had to scribble down a poem when the muse struck.

All the writing I did with the various groups stimulated my writer's gene, my imagination, which I hadn't exercised much. Or so I thought. I was sure I'd inherited a few of my father's traits, so why not his imagination, too? He would spin stories from that place. Dad was prone to exaggerate to make a story more exciting, which annoyed my mother. "Oh, Bill, that's not how it happened," she would cry in frustration.

    I picked up a paperback called *On Writing: A Memoir of the Craft* by Stephen King. King says writing is about the day job and it's about the language. He writes full time, every day, except Christmas Day. He possessed the tenacity to keep writing, even after all the initial rejections, and even after a drunk driver all but killed him.

15: Little Blue Monkey

Our mother read *Old Yeller* to us in the Hotel Vancouver while we waited to move into a house. The book, written in 1956 by American author Fred Gipson became a classic, and it may have been that book that fostered our love of animals and that taught us another valuable lesson: don't judge a mangy stray dog by his looks, for he might be the one that saves the family.

I'll never forget the grandness of the hotel that felt like a castle to my twelve-year-old self. My mother and the five of us children lived up high, looking out across the kingdom of Vancouver, while we waited for the Canadian Pacific Railway to find us a house. I don't remember our father being there. Mom would take the five of us to the posh dining room, where little brother Michael would run amok through the white-clothed tables, his black curls flying. He escaped one day and got into an elevator and God knows how my mother survived all that. He was maybe four years old, wild and uncontrollable. A little devil with a sparkle in his blue eyes and an irrepressible spirit.

One detail that stands out more than any other is the blue monkey. He was about the size of my thumb and made of hard blue plastic. I can't recall where it came from but that little monkey comforted me, or maybe he was my talisman, my lucky charm. I was a superstitious child. Was I nervous about our move to the big city of Vancouver, after another short stint in Medicine Hat, Alberta?

Green. Everything is green. But it's winter. Maybe I'm dreaming, or like Alice, I've fallen down the rabbit hole.

I could hardly believe my eyes when I saw a tree sprouting large pink and white tulips. The branches of another tree, called a monkey tree, looked like giant pipe cleaners. Flowers bloomed in gardens. Sunlight illuminated a magical world hung with sparkling rain drops.

In Toronto, Calgary, or Medicine Hat we would be building snowmen and skating on outdoor rinks and streams. But the prospect of beginning another new school part way through grade seven made me anxious.

I don't know where the little blue monkey got to, but that wasn't what saved me when I had seven months of work to learn in the three months left in the school year. The British Columbia school curriculum was completely different from that of Alberta. Lucky for me, Grandma English had come to stay with us for a while. Having been a teacher, she helped me study and catch up.

16: The Blue Room

After several years in Vancouver I went through a transformation from shy, ugly duckling to someone who attracted boys and girlfriends who were far more experienced than I was. As sixteen-year-olds, my girlfriends and I created "The Blue Room" in a basement bedroom of my parents' house on Angus Drive. We put a blue light bulb in the overhead socket, which cast an otherworldly hue—sort of like being under water or like being on the moon, the blue moon. That room was our private clubhouse without parents, teachers, or even other students judging us. In the blue room one night I drank lemon gin straight from the bottle with one of my girlfriends. Forever after, even the mention of lemon gin made me want to wretch violently.

But high school was difficult for me. I couldn't concentrate and my marks reflected that. The only subject I liked was English.

My two best friends went to a different school. Karen, my *best* best friend told me about a guy in her class.

"He's so funny, Kay. He cracks everyone up—even the teacher—and he's really cute. A lot of girls want to be his girlfriend."

I took this information in but didn't think much about it, or him, until I met him at one of the parties on the other side of town. Karen was right, he was cute, a little shorter than me, but he had chutzpah. When he pulled out his guitar and sang *House of the Rising Sun* by The Animals, I felt irresistibly drawn into his orbit. He was the sun around which everything revolved, including all the other girls.

Terry lived with his mother in a basement suite. Her distinctive facial features, especially the sculpted nose and high cheekbones of the plains Indians, hadn't shown up in him, but he had her dark eyes lit with that spark of intelligence. It wasn't long before we were going steady.

My first boyfriend, and I was fifteen years old.

The relationship filled me with a sense of belonging, and longing. Terry, my girlfriends, and the Blue Room saved me from an unhappy home life that I escaped from as often as I could. Dad was drinking heavily by then and Mom was deeply unhappy. I found her crying in the kitchen a few times.

My friends and I began sneaking out at night. Mostly we just roamed the streets, feeling the excitement and freedom of the night. I began skipping school, not something Terry would have done, so I can't blame him for that behaviour. I could be found in a café far from home, a hangout for other kids skipping out. The day my mother walked in to find me sitting in a booth with three guys she didn't know was devastating. Poor Mom. She was ashen as she drove me back to school in silence and deposited me at the principal's office.

The vice principal, a 6 ft.5 heavy-set, sadistic brute wearing a black suit, came at me with his mean black eyes, wielding a lethal-looking strap. I smelled fear.

He lifted himself up higher to get better leverage, brought the strap down hard, striking my virgin flesh with such violence, and the pain, I'd never felt pain like that and before I could breathe down it came again. Three assaults on each hand. He did his best to do damage, to make a point, to teach me a lesson. To punish me.

Mom didn't tell Dad, thank God, but that night at the dinner table I had trouble holding my knife and fork with aching, swollen hands. The dinner ritual was painful enough with my father always scowling at the far end of the table if my mother tried to say something of interest. He had two moods: angry and sullen when sober, overly friendly and boastful when drunk. I didn't understand that he had an illness known as alcoholism, and that he probably didn't like himself very much. Was he loved as a child? Who knew. My upper-class grandparents were remote, at least in my memory of them. My father was the middle child, the lost boy. I'm not sure how my poor mother, one of six kids raised by a single mother, related to her in-laws, so different in every way possible from her own mother. My grandmother worked hard to support her children, and you can be sure there weren't any entitled kids in that bunch.

I ran away with my other best friend, Cheryl. She lived with her older sister and husband after her mother hung herself in the basement home. We had skipped school and had been found out. We knew that meant the strap, and we'd be grounded pretty much forever.

We high-tailed it out of town using our thumbs after spending a chilly night in a park!

In Kamloops we met a couple of young guys who let us sleep in their car for the night. In the morning those sweet boys dropped by and gave us their lunches on their way to work. So far, so good, but we didn't have a plan.

The next men we met were older, maybe in their mid to late twenties. They told us we could stay at their house that night. We found ourselves entering a house on the north shore of Kamloops. When my eyes adjusted to the darkness inside I stumbled past empty beer cases and liquor bottles, a discarded child's toy, and in the kitchen dirty dishes cluttered the counter and filled the sink. The thin man's wife had left him, leaving behind despair so thick that it sucked all life and light from the house. The house reeked of death.

Too afraid to go to sleep I sat in front of the eerie glow of the TV all night, with the big guy in another chair doing the same. He didn't talk to me, or even look at me. Cheryl was in a bedroom with the thin man.

Afraid, barely able to breathe. Can't fall asleep. What's happening to Cheryl? What happened in this house to leave behind such a creepy, sinister feeling?

The wife showed up in the morning to collect something. That poor woman, finding two teenage runaways in her house, one in bed with her husband!

Cheryl and I ran, leaving the shouting behind. We hitch-hiked home, where I went straight to Terry's place. He said Mom didn't look well when he'd gone to see her. Pangs of guilt.

Apprehension and an ill feeling filled me as Terry and I stood at the door waiting for my mother to answer. I didn't want to be back there in that confusing house. Held breath.

Inside, facing Mom, the house seemed to echo her quiet despair, her face drained of emotion, except for maybe sadness. Ashamed is what I felt for putting my mother through that. *What was wrong with me anyway?*

17: Did Father Know Best?

My teenage running away didn't end with Cheryl. I kept trying to escape, but why and from what?

I saw the other side of life when I left again and hung out in a Granville Street bowling alley, eating hot dogs, courtesy of the old man who owned the place. A young prostitute took me in and tried to protect me from the life she lived. One day she left for Victoria to make money and died a mysterious death. I found out there was a code of ethics on the street. Street people, hustlers of all kinds, watch out for each other. What did I find there that I didn't find at home?

When I became pregnant at seventeen, after much discussion of the options—from which I was excluded—Mom and I boarded a train for Calgary where my parents had booked me into a Salvation Army Unwed Mothers' Home. Lying in my bunk on the train, I felt numb, staring into the black night as I sped toward an uncertain future.

The glint of the diamond engagement ring on my left hand reminded me of all that I had left behind. I had quit school after grade eleven, but had a job I enjoyed, working with Elizabeth Gordon, the dear seventy-five-year-old woman who managed her own successful business. I had signed up for an English night school course that ignited my imagination and love of reading. To round out the perfect life I'd created for myself, I was enrolled in the Blanche McDonald School of Modeling to work on my posture and poise.

After about a week in the unwed mothers' home, where I discovered farm girls who had been too friendly with the hired help, and sharing a room with a girl who never spoke, but who stole from me, I was placed with a family in the suburbs, on a street devoid of trees or any kind of character. I was free labour, a babysitter for the couple's two young boys, while the mother and father went to work every day. The mother was stressed and unhappy, the father thin and haggard. The oldest boy in his neediness clung to me for emotional support.

Terry followed me to Calgary, got a job, and visited me. He'd always been resourceful. I wore the engagement ring proudly, a symbol of Terry's love and commitment. He was everything in my eyes.

Sometime after putting the boys down for their nap one day a neighbour rapped on the front door. She had the youngest boy, who had apparently escaped from an open window next to the top bunk bed where he was supposed to be asleep. She'd apprehended the boy running down the street. This didn't bode well and sure enough when the mother arrived home she stormed into my bedroom yelling at me. She slapped me across the face, something I'd never experienced before. Still in shock I called Terry and asked him to pick me up. In a hotel that night, I slept blissfully in the arms of my lover, my fiancé, my saviour. He put me on a plane for Vancouver the next day, while he stayed to work.

Terry's mother picked me up at the airport and drove me back to her place in Kits, where I phoned my mother to let her know I was back. She cried. My poor mother. But when I told her that Terry and I wanted to marry and keep our baby she threw herself into the new plan with gusto. She liked Terry, unlike my father, who, although he kept his opinions to himself, it became obvious this wedding wasn't going to happen if he had anything to do with it.

My uncommunicative father suddenly became quite involved in trying to talk me out of marrying Terry. He drove over every evening to my best friend's house where I stayed with Karen and her parents. We drove around, talking. It didn't work. Too little guidance too late? Terry and I married against my father's wishes.

My mother did her best to create an impromptu wedding reception at our home on Angus Drive. A Justice of the Peace had married us in a brief, unromantic service, and from there we drove to the reception.

It was a gorgeous June day. Yellow, pink and red roses bloomed in the front garden, as purple clematis climbed the lattice on the wall to the left of the front door. All was sunlight, rose-scented breeze and joy for the newlyweds, except Dad was drunk and Terry's mother wore black. Her high cheek-boned features and classic Native American nose appeared even more severe that day.

The poor woman must have felt terribly out of place, but I didn't realize that then. She and her son lived in a basement suite a long way from Shaughnessy and her son had married a rich girl, or so she thought. We were a long way from rich, living in a rented CPR house, but it must have looked like a mansion to Helen with its light-filled sun room, piano, dining room, spacious living room with a grand fireplace, it's five bedrooms, three bathrooms and large sunny kitchen.

    I wore a pink maternity dress, and on my head a white bow with a bit of a veil attached. Terry looked smart in a dark suit, white shirt and tie, his polished shoes gleaming. The relatives arrived, doing their best to smile and offer congratulations to the young couple. I had turned eighteen in April and Terry wouldn't be eighteen until August. He was thin, and almost two inches shorter than me, so in my pregnant condition I must have looked something of a pink whale beside him. The photo of him carrying me across the threshold of my parents' home is funny; my brave new husband doing his best not to show the strain of hoisting up his smiling new bride.

    We ate cold cuts and salads from the deli, and my mother had managed to find a modest wedding cake. She looked so pretty in her pink pleated skirt and white blouse. My younger siblings threw confetti at us when we left for a weekend honeymoon at uncle Jack McCracken's cabin.

    After the honeymoon, we lived in a huge house in North Vancouver with Terry's boss and his four motherless children. The story was that their mother had jumped off a bridge. I did my best as a pregnant teenager to look after everyone, but I wasn't their mother. When the father began drinking heavily, Terry and I found a tiny apartment above an elderly couple a long way from either of our parents, or any friends. I was isolated, but it didn't matter because I had a beautiful baby girl and my husband. He went to work every day, while I rinsed poopy diapers in the toilet, loaded them into the buggy with my baby and headed for the nearest laundromat. I enjoyed planning and cooking meals, and keeping baby Teri-Ann clean and happy.

    Sadly, Terry and I did not live happily ever after. Given the odds, our young ages and the high divorce rate in general, that shouldn't have come as a big surprise. He was gone by the time Teri-Ann was seven months old. Did my father know best after all?

18: Writers' Soirée

Now here I am in Salmon Arm, living with my mother, my bookstore long gone, and no blue room to hide away in. Not even a blue monkey or a blue stone to give me courage. But things were going well. I'd joined the Federation of BC Writers, an organization based in Vancouver that had representatives in each area of the province.

While I still lived at Gardom Lake after Reflections closed, Deanna Kawatski, our area representative for the Federation of BC Writers, invited local writers to her farm, including authors from Penticton, Vernon, Sorrento, Salmon Arm, and Kamloops. She also invited the executive director and an assistant executive director from The Federation's main office in Vancouver. I was asked to bring something to read.

We sat around Deanna's spacious table in the yellow kitchen. One by one everyone shared a piece of writing. Nerves played havoc with my stomach. I swallowed the pain and shared a piece from my work in progress, which must have okay because Brad Cran, the executive director, asked me to organize a reading in Salmon Arm with two well-known Vancouver poets.

My aching stomach relaxed later with a glass of red wine out on the lawn in the dimming light. Twilight came quietly, blurring the stark lines of daylight, transforming the barn, the raspberry canes in the garden, and the tall cedar trees into sculpted silhouettes.

As the scent of the night stole in, the feeling of well-being and accomplishment stayed with me, as I chatted and drank wine with published authors and poets, filled my plate with Deanna's lovingly prepared feast of chili, potato salad, green salad and of course her wonderful raspberry pie with ice cream. Nice life they have here, I mused, as I watched thousands of stars blossom in the blue-black heavens.

19: Two Spirals Clash

Marilyn had stayed with Mom and when I came home. I shared my excitement with Mom, but she wasn't doing well. Aside from taking care of what I could for her I had to get on with organizing the poetry evening. I booked Impressions Café—a funky place that trained young people to cook, make espresso coffees, and deal with cash and customers. They had bought my espresso machine and I provided training. We held the monthly Shuswap Writers' Coffee House there at that time.

This was a big deal. Esta Spalding, Canadian author, screenwriter and poet had won the Pat Lowther award for a poetry book in 2000 and at that time was writing for DeVinci's Inquest, a popular TV series shot in Vancouver. Her mother Linda Spalding, a Canadian writer, teacher, and editor had won awards for her writing, and Esta's stepfather, Michael Ondaatje, won the Booker prize for his novel *The English Patient,* that was made into a movie. Miranda Pearson had poems published in many literary journals and was poetry editor for Prism International, UBC's literary magazine.

After all the promotion, and word of mouth got around, when Miranda and Esta arrived I met them for dinner at Impressions. People kept arriving and the excitement was palpable as performance hour approached. The cavernous room in the back reminded me of something out of the sixties with its dark walls, old mismatched couches and colourful abstract art on the walls. After my introduction a wonderful evening of poetry inspired the crowd that included my mother and Auntie Marge, her sister. Many poetry books were bought and signed that evening and I was so pleased that Mom was well enough to attend.

Still high from that event, I strolled downtown one day and ran into the editor of the Friday AM. I knew Lorne from my book selling days. I advertised in his weekly paper when we held special events, everything from readings and book signings, live music, the Shuswap Writers' Coffee House, to workshops and speakers.

Lorne asked if I would like to join him for coffee. When he asked what

I was up to I told him about the book I was working on about my experience moving to Salmon Arm from Vancouver to open a bookstore, he surprised me by asking if I would write a column for his paper that would appear in the bigger monthly edition of the AM.

I don't know if I hesitated, but if I did it was only for a nanosecond. My dream of writing appeared to be manifesting in more ways than I expected.

When I got home, I was in an altered state—part disbelief and part elation—although I did wonder what I'd done. What did I know about writing a column? What was I thinking? After calming down, I realized that I could interview authors, cover events, and promote events. I knew I'd give it my best shot no matter how nervous I was about tackling the job. The first column was due in three weeks.

Much to my relief, I heard about an event coming up. A poet was launching his second book of poetry and local musicians would entertain at the Deep Creek Hall between his readings. Deanna and Eric were going. Lorne Dufour, known as Lornie to the locals, had worked at Caravan Farm Theatre, which is why he knew so many musicians and artists in the area. Deanna said that Eric had horse logged with Lorne in the fall and winter of 1980 and '81 at Bear Creek, near Adams Lake.

The old wooden hall was packed with men, women and children, greeting friends with hugs. Silhouettes danced before me until my eyes adjusted to the dark, aside from some light on the stage, and the light pouring through the open door of the brightly lit kitchen at the back. People brought plates of cookies, squares, and other goodies. They set the baking on a long table in the kitchen, where a huge urn of coffee percolated, sending enticing aroma into the air.

Local musicians played throughout the evening, people danced with abandon, and between sets Lorne read poetry from his recent book, *Starting From Promise*, published by Broken Jaw Press in Fredericton, New Brunswick. He won the 2001 Poets' Corner Award for that book, no small feat considering he was picked from a thousand entries. Several of the poems were reminiscent of his days living and working at Mt. Ida, the mountain overlooking Salmon Arm, and in the North Shuswap, while others spoke of his Caravan Farm days as Stage Company Teamster.

The mood of the crowd, festive as it was, felt a bit overwhelming when I discovered that I didn't know most people there. I felt myself withdraw into the shadows. I had never interviewed a poet before, or anyone other than Mrs. Sturt. I confided in Deanna, catching her between dances. She said to come with her and led me into the kitchen to meet Lorne's wife, Diana.

Deanna introduced us and told Diana what my mission was. "Well," she said, "I can tell you that Lornie is always writing poetry, either by a kerosene lamp in a tent, or at the kitchen table any time of night or day."

"That's impressive," I said, as I scribbled in my notebook. She told me they lived off the grid at McLeese Lake, B.C., where Lorne worked at horse logging. I thanked her and because it still looked impossible to get near Lorne, as he was surrounded by friends when he wasn't reading, I decided I had what I needed and slipped quietly into the night and headed for home.

My life was changing and it revolved around writing, and of course my mother. I enjoyed writing my first column. When I emailed Lorne the column, he emailed back, "Good work, fellow writer." He probably had no idea how great it felt to read those words.

As for Mom, our life wasn't as smooth as I would have liked, but I had to learn patience in a whole new way. I needed to draw on every drop of compassion I could for a woman who had been in control her whole life—even during the crazy—making years with our father—and who was now in the awkward position of letting go, maybe in preparation for the big letting go that would come one day. My upward spiral into happiness about my writing and my involvement in community stood out in stark contrast to my mother's downward spiral. She grew pale and despondent. Not a good sign. With my first column in print, I took her to her doctor. Nothing, however, was prescribed for my mother's apparent sadness, her loss of interest in life.

April emerged fresh and glorious with blooming daffodils and tulips, budding trees, and the sweet song of robins. To cheer mother up I organized a birthday party for her with cake, bright daffodils, gifts, and several family members, although even reading the cards, opening the gifts and blowing out the candles took an effort. Mom, the woman who had always reveled in birthday celebrations, struggled to be present.

She improved a little but the physical pain and loss of freedom had dampened her spirit. I made an effort to get her out for walks, for lunch and sometimes shopping for a new outfit.

I didn't mind cooking three meals a day for my mother, or serving afternoon tea with cookies, but I'd never been interested in fussing with anyone's hair. In between her hair appointments at the salon, Mom sometimes wanted me to curl and style her hair. I was chief cook and bottle washer, chauffeur, and many other things, but a hairdresser I was not. My own hair, pretty much a wash and wear routine, was all I could manage.

Something else irritated me. Mom said the same things over and over again. I felt myself losing patience, sometimes blurting out, "You told me that already!" Then I'd feel guilty, not that she noticed, because she would continue telling me the same thing again anyway. She'd always had a tendency to repeat herself, but it was worse now.

20: Deliverance

I was still in constant pain and regularly seeing Dr. H, who I found to be a great source of hope and inspiration. He told me to stop my mother when she continued saying the same thing by asking her if she'd heard me. He was concerned that pain was affecting my sleep, making it more difficult to cope. Despite his sound advice, life was difficult in many ways. The main thing that saved me was my writing. Bridgey and my writing friends were a great help as well, although sometimes I was too exhausted to even go to my Cheap Tuesday writers' group in the evening, or to the Writers' Coffee House.

Bonny and Miranda invited me to join them on a hike one day. I hadn't felt the muse with me recently, burdened by exhaustion and worry about my mother. I felt all dried up.

I wrote a poem when I got home.

Deliverance

the sun burned hot and dry
until we entered the cool green womb of the woods

with its sweet stands of young birch
and gnarled apple trees blackened with age
wearing crowns of pink and white blossoms
the intoxicating perfume
bewitching

I shed years
as we ambled along a meandering path
lept across a spirited stream
that gurgled
with joy

my eyes discovered shapes and textures
too glorious
too intricate
for words that were too clumsy
for the experience of wonder

suddenly we came upon
the lip of mother earth
silver water
gushing from that hidden place

it fanned out over sheer rock
tumbled
gathered
in a hollow momentarily
shimmering spirals of pure energy
being drawn down

we emerged from the woods
to the low rumble
of brooding black clouds
stretched across the sky
like the belly of a creature
mythical in magnitude

then her water broke
birthing inspiration

and I'm delivered
from my dry spell

21: Raven Magic

In her book, *Negotiating With the Dead: a Writer on Writing*, Margaret Atwood maintains that all writers are double, in that the author is not the same as the person who does the living. Atwood uses the story of *Alice Through the Looking Glass* as an example of how a writer's double dissolves. The act of writing takes place at the moment when Alice steps through the mirror. Alice, the real person, and the writer, or art, become one and time ceases to exist, and also stretches out. That's a great description of how it feels to write, or practice any of the arts. In my experience, time and space dissolve, and the "I" who lives in the world ceases to exist when I sit down to write.

Fascinating insights revealed themselves as I worked on my book, but I'll get to that. I missed the ravens when I moved to town. Occasionally, while walking the foreshore and as I neared the subdivision called Raven, the lofty sound of a solitary raven lifted my spirits; it was the sound of wilderness, like ancient trees groaning and creaking in the wind, like the sound of secret forest places that are a mystery to us non-feathered ones. Sometimes raven vocals sounded like a sacred gong. Wing beats as rhythmic as a heartbeat.

Raven had become a symbol of hope for me. I had never thought of myself as anything but ordinary and yet an extraordinary bird had made an appearance in my life. I still had to figure out what that was about.

In mythology, Raven, the great trickster, represents creativity—among his other more notorious traits, such as playing lewd tricks, and thievery. He foretold of death, yet also of birth and illumination. I felt his influence.

Magic danced hand in hand with logic as Raven created a space where diverse ideas coexisted. This sounds illogical, but isn't necessarily so.

In his groundbreaking book *The Act of Creation*, first published in 1964, Arthur Koestler explains the creative process. He advances the theory that all creative activities—the conscious and the unconscious processes underlying artistic originality, scientific discovery, and comic inspiration—

have a basic pattern in common. He calls it "bisociative" thinking—a word he coined to distinguish the various routines of associative thinking from the creative leap which connects previously unconnected frames of reference and makes us experience reality on several planes at once.

Unfortunately, along with the high of creativity comes the low. Manic depression, now known as bipolar disorder, is a condition that many creative people live with and is thought to have a genetic component.

Earlier thinkers believed that poetic inspiration came from the gods, or from a muse. Perhaps Raven was my muse.

When I began writing my story at the cabin at Gardom Lake, it was winter, and I was bundled up in sweaters and blankets. Thick wool socks hugged my feet, as I sat at my computer next to windows clouded with the icy breath of night. After months of writing, I felt that something was trying to get my attention. Then one day it happened. I sensed Raven, or raven energy if you like, perched on my computer monitor, voicing his desire in that croaking persistent way of his to be let into the story.

Of course! When I thought about it, he had been there all along. I had wanted to write a straightforward account of the strange events that held me captive since moving to Salmon Arm from Vancouver to open a bookstore, but I hadn't let Raven in. That would be too weird, or edgy, or, dare I say it, crazy. If there was anything I was afraid of it was being thought of as crazy.

What was that fear about? Looking at it now, I assume it was a fear of being different. Some people actually cultivate that, many artists do, but not me. I'd never had any artist or writer friends while growing up so what did I know about such things? A glimmer of memory breaks through. It's elementary school. An art class I loved that engaged me totally. As an adult, I was stuck in the broken bone ward at Vancouver General Hospital one summer. Being immobile, I occupied myself by sketching everything around me. Did I have an inner creative impulse trying to express itself?

But how could a bird be influencing my life? How could I make that sound plausible? Why couldn't it have been a robin or a chickadee? But no, it had to be the trickster bird with a shady reputation as long as my arm, stretching back into the dark ages.

Never underestimate the power of myth to influence your life. Life would be as dry as toast without imagination, mythology, and storytelling. If I'd been raised in a different culture or religion, it wouldn't be far-fetched to believe that animals talk to us, or teach us, although we've lost the ability to speak the same language, a symbolic language. Dreams speak to us using symbolic language. It's not voodoo. Mystics believed in the connection of all things.

By telling my story, a picture began to form. As time went on, the patchwork of random mishap and joy that made up my life began to transform; it looked more and more like a tapestry, where I glimpsed a pattern emerging. The pattern seemed to speak of meaning, and in that meaning, beauty, and in that beauty, truth. I began each writing day with a meditation, focusing on the words beauty and truth.

Raven, the restless, mischievous, creator of the world—the iridescent black thread woven into my narrative—brought light to the people. Was he illuminating my path? Raven had used his shape shifting ability to free the sun from an old man who was hoarding it.

In another myth, Raven populated the world with human beings when he freed men from a giant clamshell he found on the beach. Then he, in his own tricky, lewd way, created women.

The archetypal energy of Raven was with me, and influencing me in a way I didn't understand. Once I accepted that, more things began to make sense.

I recalled that the first time I encountered Raven was on the camping trip to Meager Springs Hot Springs with Craig, my husband. I'd already shifted my life in the direction of Salmon Arm, but had agreed to the diversion, thinking that time in nature for a few days would be welcome after all the work of setting up a business. I think Craig and I wanted to see if we could rekindle an ember in our dying relationship. Why is it so hard to let go?

Raven

*I stared into the campfire
like an ancient soothsayer looking for a sign
heart burdened with the pain of unfulfilled longings, midlife disruptions, the angst of being anchored to a life that no longer fit*

*In the morning a sound penetrated the veil of my dreams,
Clear like a bell, yet haunting*

I lifted the tent flap and there soaring in full view in the crisp blue morning a huge black bird—black of beak, eye and feather, shimmering like morning dew

*Like nothing I'd ever heard before
Raven drew me in and we become one within the web of cedar*

Legendary shape shifter. Icon of mystery. I couldn't take my eyes off him for fear he'd vanish.

The gloss of his wing, his startling beauty affected me profoundly as if he's emerged from a deep, holy place few of us know or remember. His sky dance, his song, were for me alone. I had the feeling that this elusive creature had blessed me in some way.

When he flew off, great wings playing the air like a harp, I continued to stare, awestruck, at the place he had been

22: Gentle Souls

I thought a lot about my father who had passed away several years earlier and was buried in a small church graveyard in Sorrento, about half an hour's drive east of Salmon Arm. He may have enjoyed this raven business, as he was a man of imagination, an artist. The paintings he did as a young man hung in several places, including Mom's 3rd Street apartment. After he and my mother moved to Sorrento from Vancouver he quit drinking, and shifted his focus to nature photography. He loved growing roses, reading, bird watching, identifying and cooking wild mushrooms, and walking in nature with his dog, and sometimes the cat. He had a gentle soul.

I had become close friends with a Native man while I had the bookstore. He reminded me of my father. It was more than the raven black hair and the mischievous sparkle of my father's blue eyes, or noticing the same sparkle in George's dark brown eyes. The quiet wisdom was familiar. That friendship meant a lot to me.

When George visited my mother and me, which he did once or twice, or we ran into him somewhere, Mom's persona changed; she radiated a youthful, bright joy that surprised me. It was obvious to me that she liked him.

Both my parents liked and respected Indigenous people and their culture. Dad once told me that when he listened to Native men speak at AA meetings, he had to listen carefully because the wisdom spoken in a quiet, humble manner could be easily missed.

My brother Jim followed in Dad's footsteps briefly. He told me the Native guys who spoke in AA were so honest and intelligent, they made him feel inarticulate—and he's a highly educated teacher. He said it was the same with the Truth and Reconciliation hearings many years later, which he watched and listened to on CBC.

"From Justice Murray Sinclair to the rest of his commission," he said, "they were astounding. Makes me think that we should turn over the running of the country to them and see what happens."

When I moved to the Shuswap my mother told me about the esteemed Secwepemc elder, Mary Thomas. Mary had won the respect of people in the area with her tireless efforts to bring understanding between her people and the white folks. Jack Bowers, of Bowers Funeral Home, once told me that he had gone to the Neskonlith reserve to pick up a deceased man for burial. In those days, white people didn't step foot on the reserve. Fear and mistrust kept the races separate. The next day a tiny woman walked into town to present Jack with a red rose and a thank you note. That tiny woman was Mary Thomas.

I had always wondered what my mother and father had in common. They were such very different people from completely different backgrounds. But it was through my writing about them that I made the connection. My parent's respect for First Nations, other nationalities, animals, and nature may have been the divine thread that linked them to each other. They both loved reading (he non-fiction, she fiction), art, gardens, flowers, a wide variety of ethnic food, and travel. They were both gentle souls and that connection, a spiritual connection, bridged their differences.

It was obvious to us kids that both my parents were open minded and that they didn't think they were above anyone else, even though my father had a prestigious position with the CPR. We all have childhood memories that illustrate how our parents accepted people of different nationalities, backgrounds and social status.

23: Getting to know Mom

I was getting to know my mother in a new way. We shared a love of English crime mysteries on television, especially Inspector Morse, senior CID in Oxford, UK. The day he died was not a good day for Mom and me. At the end of that episode Mom and I looked at each other in silence until I said, "I can't believe that just happened." Mom shook her head, still incredulous.

The Agatha Christie mystery series featuring Belgian detective Hercule Poirot, and another one, Miss Marpole, starring an elderly female detective, were both favourites. We enjoyed the PBS Sherlock Holmes series, and Mom loved Angela Lansbury in "Murder She Wrote".

We both loved art, animals, music of all kinds, flowers and nature, reading, writing in our journals, a good meal, everything from a roast turkey dinner to vegetable curry stir-fry, and daydreaming. I say daydreaming because often now that she couldn't write in her journal she would gaze out her bedroom window at the trees, a man walking down the alley, the clouds and birds, and she would let her mind drift. But then I think she had always been a dreamer; I just hadn't noticed that about her growing up.

Over time, the blows to my mother's health dimmed her spirit. She had more mini-strokes, had cataracts removed from both eyes, suffered more dizzy spells, short term memory loss, and another disc collapsed in her spine. We muddled through the fright and horror of calling ambulances, waiting for hours in the ER, hospital stays, and other indignities.

The first time I had to call an ambulance when Mom was having a stroke, two big men—they were always big, strong men and women—strode into our apartment. As I guided them toward my mother's bedroom, Bridgey ran ahead to block them at the bedroom door. Bridgey`s intense expression told me how worried she was, and that she was prepared to fend off the intruders to save Mom. It surprised me to see my cat's loyalty and determination to keep my mother safe. I had to tell Bridgey it was all right before she stood aside.

Days, weeks, months, and seasons passed. I kept writing and

rewriting, reading and taking walks, visiting Dr. H.

At one point I had to give up the house cleaning when I realized my back couldn't handle the vacuuming any more.

Mom and I continued our journey together. Sometimes, if I wasn't well she would bring me a cup of tea. That gesture was loving, and greatly appreciated. The tea always tasted so much better when she made it. And another thing became apparent. Mom liked my writing, which I would read to her now and then. She encouraged me. We had made it through the difficult transition and were becoming comfortable with each other.

I walked into her bedroom one day and noticed the shine on the walnut furniture and the smell of *Pledge*.

"You polished the dressers, Mom. They look good."

"I can still do little things like that." She smiled at her accomplishment.

The sun slanted through the blinds illuminating the yellow, orange and brown crocheted spread on her bed, where Mom sat, her back resting on the faded brown corduroy bed rest. The oil painting of yellow gladiolas with chestnut-coloured and white chrysanthemums in a turquoise vase hung on the wall above her head, a painting she was very attached to. Someone who had been at her mother's funeral had painted it, she told me.

"I love this room when the sun shines," she said. "It's so cozy."

She said that every time the sun graced her room, a place where she felt safe. The faces of loved ones, both living and long gone, smile at her from the dresser tops: Dad as a young man, her as a young woman, my siblings and their families, her sister, Marge Meier, grandchildren at different ages, and her beloved mother. My grandmother, Irene Matilda English, was dear to Mom. Losing her seventy-three-year-old mother during a simple operation had been devastating.

I pictured the younger Dad, the one in the photo on my mother's dresser, as a version of bad boy actor Errol Flynn, who was popular in earlier times for his romantic adventure films. Flynn had a reputation as quite a boozer, always surrounded by beautiful leading ladies. My father cut a dashing figure with his wavy black hair, his slender, athletic physique, and his bright blue eyes. Mom told me how handsome he was when she took fencing lessons from him, which is where the Errol Flynn fantasy came from. What an extraordinary thing to hear about my father.

Another story fueled the Errol Flynn idea. It was in Mexico where Dad fought off bandits with a machete he'd bought the day before, while my mother stomped out lit matches being thrown through the screen door the bandits had sliced through. Mom and Dad had parked their small trailer at a lagoon where two other couples were parked. When one of those neighbours called out to my father to give up, that the bandits weren't going to kill them, just rob them, Dad finally surrendered. The other couples were already tied up to trees. My valiant, machete-wielding father went to a hospital to get stitches in one hand. What a thrilling tale my parents had to tell when they arrived home. Mom read from her journal to an astonished audience at a family gathering. My parents were lucky because around that time tourists had been murdered by bandits.

Before the incident with the bandits, one of the young couples, perhaps they were from Holland, offered Mom and Dad a puff or two of marijuana. I have a hard time picturing my parents smoking pot with a hippy couple at a secluded lagoon, but there you are. I'm sure there's more to my mother than meets the eye, for on the face of it she's a fairly conservative woman who likes to maintain control.

My father fell for my mother, Marion, when she played the piano for service men at the boarding house where she lived while teaching school in Golden, BC. With everyone crowded around her at the piano singing along, and her with a beautiful singing voice, how could he not fall in love. She had a great figure, pretty green eyes and thick, lovely, light brown hair. She never lost her figure even after giving birth to five children. Maybe the fact that she had been so athletic her entire life is what kept her strong and healthy into her late seventies.

The longer I live with my mother the more I realize that I'm like her, not in looks or musical ability—she played the accordion, the auto harp, piano, and sang in choirs, and I don't play an instrument or sing, except in the car—but I must have inherited her determination to see things through. I don't think there would be anything she couldn't do if she set her mind to it. Thinking back on my book selling days, it took many devastating blows before I was knocked down, and even then Reflections had to be wrestled away from me under protest.

When Mom decided to knit a baby outfit for granddaughter Marlena and her husband Clint's first child, she struggled. This from a woman who had knit her five young children jackets with cowboys or skaters on them, who had knit herself a stunning peacock blue dress, had knit every child, grandchild and now great grandchildren newborn outfits of baby sweaters, bonnets, and booties. She could knit slippers, socks, anything. To see her rip that baby sweater out over and over again, to see her quiet frustration at not being able to do what she had always done, was heartbreaking. But she never complained, and she didn't quit until she finally had a sweater. A less determined person would have given up long before.

She showed the same determination when she went back to school after the kids were grown, to become a preschool teacher. She achieved top marks in every course and became a much sought—after Day Care supervisor in Vancouver. Children adored her and she was crazy about children.

Once a high school dropout, I showed the same determination when I went back to school and earned a BA majoring in English from Simon Fraser University.

One day she'll be gone and in her place another white-haired, pale-faced woman will sit under the yellow glads and the bright afghan and read novels or watch the television she bought for her bedroom. My daughter will bring me special meals and treats when I'm sick, will help me into my faded blue nightie, will bring me a banana and vitamin pills to eat with my breakfast and medications. I will smile and feel happy when the sun warms my room, bringing the colours to life. I'll watch Lawrence Welk reruns every Saturday afternoon. Wait a minute!

Is it possible? I think I *am* becoming my mother. I have to wonder, for I can anticipate her every wish and whim. When I voiced my concerns to my sister Marilyn she laughed. "If I see you tapping your feet to Lawrence Welk I'll know things have gone too far," she said, and we both broke up laughing.

24: April 19th, 2001

Mom's organ stands forlorn against a wall in the spacious living room, except when one of the grandkids plays with it.

"Mom why don't you play something?"

"I can't sit on that bench. It's my back."

"Too bad," I say. "I'd love to hear you play again."

Music feeds my mother's spirit and I try to think of a way for her to sit on the bench with her back supported. Chairs are too low, so the organ sits there gathering dust, a reminder of how musical my mother was. On Angus Drive in Vancouver Mom would play the piano for hours in the bright sun room until the kids came home from school.

My sister Marilyn took after Mom in several ways. She inherited the gene for piano playing, sewing and knitting, and Mom's love of baking. Wholesome pursuits, whereas I modeled myself after my father in my younger years, by drinking, smoking, and other risky behaviours. Funny how things turn out. I'm the one caring for our mother, me in my fifties and her in her seventies, although Mom's eightieth birthday was looming. I decided to organize a surprise party for her.

Mom hadn't been well, but I took a chance and invited all her children, grandkids, her sister, nieces and nephews. Everyone was excited about celebrating the milestone with our mother. Families booked hotels and motels as April 19th drew closer. As the time drew near I felt nervous about keeping the party a secret. What if she wasn't well enough? What if she was overwhelmed by all the attention. She had never had a surprise party before, or been the focus of that much attention.

I booked a large room in the Orchard House, the old mansion that was now an elegant restaurant. I booked a photographer friend. It didn't look like Teri-Ann and Shasta could come. They were living in Texas to be close to Teri-Ann's girls Faith and Melissa, who had moved there with their father and stepmother.

I had moved into my red phase by then. Imagine. Red, the bold, passionate, sexy colour that says: Look at me. I'm here. I exist. The psychology of colour says that red motivates people to take action and instills confidence in those who are shy.

I wrote a poem about red and shared it at a coffee house. Apparently, the poem shocked people. I guess red can do that. Red has power.

I wonder if I used red to express another part of myself. I hid the fact that I was using medication for depression and anxiety, and in hiding that from friends and family I felt like I was lying to them about who I was. In my attempt to propel myself forward was I drawing on the energy and power of the colour red, like an actor who steps into another set of clothes to become a different character? I'm glad that my poem shocked people, because it came from that fiery part of me that wasn't hiding anymore. Unfortunately, the poem disappeared into the black hole of my computer.

In the morning of the birthday luncheon I was a nervous wreck. People had arrived the night before and it was up to me to get Mom to the restaurant. I decided to let her in on the big surprise so she would be somewhat prepared at least. If she was surprised she didn't show it, in fact she seemed unmoved by any emotion that I could detect. Without so much as a word she walked to her bedroom and dressed in her beautiful long burgundy skirt and matching top with a silk accent scarf shimmering with pale green leaves and creamy golden flowers. As flowers go my mother reminded me of the elegant burgundy peonies that I'd always admired, not only for their colour and wonderful perfume, but also for their presence—the tall, gentle matriarchs and quiet heart of any garden.

I dressed in my long red skirt and matching top. Fiery red, like the geraniums that captured the blazing afternoon sun in their petals during the summer on our back porch.

The photographer took the photos outside in the gardens that hadn't yet bloomed, against trees that hadn't yet leafed.

All the excitement may have been responsible for the second glass of wine, which I drank too fast. Or maybe the colour red was to blame. In any case, the slap dash way I cut the cake was, I admit, more of a spectacle than respectable.

    My mother on the other hand conducted herself with grace and dignity, and to my great surprise stood up to address the great length of tables set out before her. About thirty people stopped talking. She thanked everyone for coming and made a few other appropriate comments. I'd never heard my mother speak publicly before, so in the end, I guess the surprise was on me.

    The red phase didn't last long. Maybe it was just too much for me, for I am after all probably more introverted than extroverted. And really how would the great literature of the world have been written if there were no introverts, those of us who can happily spend hours and hours by ourselves writing, and who need to retreat to peace and quiet when we've been over stimulated by people and noise?

25: Writers' Gathering, Summer 2001

Every once in a while, it's like all the stars align. I felt the shift. Is it luck or hard work that brought me to this point? Are the gods and goddesses finally favouring me? Whatever it was I had to accept that I was being offered a gift as the path opened up before me.

Deanna asked the members of the Federation of BC Writers in our region for submissions for a chapbook that she would edit. The idea for the first regional chapbook published by the Federation of BC Writers had been hatched the summer before around Deanna's kitchen table. That was the first-ever regional gathering at Garland Gracesprings Farm, the one where Brad Cran asked me to organize readings for two well-known Vancouver poets. At that time, he suggested the idea of putting together a chapbook that the Federation would publish, and Deanna would edit.

This was a chance for a few of us who may not be in print yet. The chapbook would include poetry, fiction, and non-fiction pieces that had a connection to interior British Columbia. I was working on a short story about a woman named Anne, who was closing her bookstore. Uncertain of what life had in store for her, she turned to the books for answers; oddly, it was a raven that gave her a clue—a story close to my heart. Writing the story as fiction was a great exercise and freeing in many ways.

I struggled to make the piece perfect. I agonized. Deanna edited. One small change and she accepted my story. Deanna and I were becoming close friends, so I knew through our telephone conversations that she had lots of submissions arriving by mail. As the project progressed, Deanna came up with a name for the chapbook: *A Pocketful of Muse: Pieces From Interior BC*, with the cover illustration to be done by her daughter, Natalia, an accomplished artist.

The name had come to her in the wee hours one morning. With each brown envelope, she felt she was reaching into someone's pocket to find the treasure. After careful consideration, Deanna selected twenty-two diverse pieces.

Deanna and I decided to launch the chapbook with a one-day writers' retreat, which we called the Shuswap Writers' Gathering, Summer 2001. As we worked out the details of which presenters to invite and where to hold it, an exciting idea took shape. We would hold it at the heritage hall, known as the North Shuswap Community Hall. The building was well used and well cared for by residents of Celista and the surrounding area, with the advantage of sitting right on the shore of Shuswap Lake. We suggested participants bring bathing suits to cool off in the lake during the lunch break, after all a hot day in August would be a perfect time for a refreshing swim.

We invited Audrey Thomas, author of fifteen books of fiction, and winner of many writing awards, to give a workshop. I had just read her latest historical novel *Isobel Gunn*, a fascinating look at the life of a woman who disguised herself as a man to work at Rupert's Landing (Canada) for the Hudson's Bay Company. She left her depressing, dead-end life in the Orkney Islands in 1806 and managed to hide her identity as a woman for a year and a half until she became pregnant, suspected by some to be the result of rape.

Next, we asked Les Ellenor, the man with the wizard-like eyebrows. He *was* a magician of sorts in that he conjured up stories at a moment's notice. He had recently retired as Professor of English at Okanagan University College in Salmon Arm, where he had taught for thirty-one years. His interests lay in folklore, mythology, and the humanities—and he claimed to be able to tell one thousand stories. I'd once attended a humour-writing workshop he gave at the Sorrento Centre, which is how we became friends.

We also invited children's author Margriet Ruurs, at that time living in Armstrong. Her beautiful books had won awards and she was very keen to be included in our writers' gathering. We asked her to give the keynote address. Her books *Emma's Eggs* and *Mountain Alphabet* had sold well in my bookstore.

The Federation of BC Writers offered to pay Audrey Thomas's travel costs, as she was traveling from one of the gulf islands where she lived. We put the word out to all the writers in the area, used all the contacts we had, and kept the cost low. We designed a brochure, organized food, wine, snacks, and invited people who had a story or poem in *A Pocketful of Muse* to read it at the evening event. We sold tickets to the public for an evening that included a delicious lasagna dinner, dessert, open mic, and live music.

I took care of registrations for the workshops, and with the registrations looking good, we knew that all the writers included in the chapbook were sure to buy at least several copies.

The new Executive Director of the Fed, Merrill Ferron, was in control of the publishing project and she would bring the chapbooks with her.

When Merrill arrived, she took Deanna and me aside in the hall amid the hustle and bustle of volunteers arriving with trays of fresh muffins and home baking.

"I'm afraid the chapbooks weren't ready," she said. We stared at her in disbelief.

"You mean we don't have any chapbooks to sell?"

"I'm sorry, but no. I can get them to you in a week or so."

Deanna and I wandered outside muttering our disappointment. A Pocket Full of Nothing.

Deanna had invited people to her farm for a potluck get together the night before and some of us stayed overnight. I had made a large pasta salad, said goodbye to Mom, who was feeling better and had made her wonderful date squares for me to take to the gathering. My daughter, Teri-Ann, who had come for a visit, stayed with Mom. The two of them had always had a very close, loving relationship. Teri-Ann shone in areas where I fell short: she liked doing hair and nails much to my mother's delight.

Early the next morning, we drove to the hall set in a clearing among huge Ponderosa pine trees that have since blown down in a giant wind storm.

Coffee percolated in a giant urn, sending its rich aroma throughout the hall. I looked at the stage at one end of the hall, and explored the large meeting room behind the stage where Audrey Thomas would conduct her workshop. The kitchen was well-stocked with fridges, stoves, dishes, pots and pans. What impressed me most were the huge, wooden shutters, which we threw open to let the breezes of pine-scented August air waft through the hall.

I managed to introduce Mr. Ellenor, but I was shaky. Lack of sleep together with the noise and excitement played havoc with my nervous system.

We carried on with the excellent morning workshops. During the lunch break, Deanna and I sat on a log, watching several women plunge into the lake. I looked at Deanna and realized that she looked as tired as I felt. We still had an afternoon and an evening event to get through. The heat felt intense and the lake looked refreshing, but I hadn't brought a bathing suit. That wasn't a problem for a couple of women without suits; they wrapped table cloths around themselves as they waded out of the cool water toward the hot beach.

With the help of volunteers, Deanna and I persevered with the evening event, transforming the hall with card tables, tablecloths, candles and fresh flowers on every table. The hall overflowed with wonderful aromas and great camaraderie that evening. I didn't think I would be able to read my story in front of all those writers, musicians, and others, but in a moment of transcendence, I managed it.

Without a chapbook to sell, maybe only half the stars aligned, but it was a start. Merrill snapped a photo of Deanna and me standing under a huge stuffed moose head on the wall at the hall before she returned to Vancouver. The photo was published in the Winter 2001-2002 issue of WordWorks, the Federation's quarterly magazine.

August 11, 2001 had been a long, very long, successful day. The participants and authors praised everything—not only that, but Deanna and I actually made a profit. At least we had a pocket of something to show for our efforts. Back at home I collapsed. It took me a week to recover.

26: September 11, 2001

After her visit on September 10th my daughter flew back to Texas.

The phone rang the next day, September 11th, 2001.

"Mom!" I heard panic in Teri-Ann's voice. "Have you heard what's happening?"

"No." I tensed up for whatever was coming next.

"The U.S. is under attack."

"What! What do you mean?" My heart thumped wildly.

"It's the end of the world." She sobbed, and then blurted out "Turn on the TV. Two planes crashed into the World Trade Center in New York; they're terrorist attacks." She caught her breath. "Mom, it's horrible!"

I could hardly comprehend what she was telling me.

"Where are you?" I heard the panic in my voice.

"I'm in Houston ... I'm scared, Mom. I love you."

"I love you, too."

What about my two granddaughters, Faith and Melissa in Austin, Texas, and Shasta, I wanted to know, but it was too late. Shasta was in Sacramento, California at the time. She woke up that day to find everyone in the house sitting in front of the television, frozen in disbelief at what they saw happening.

Shasta's overwhelming thought was that she didn't want to be in the States anymore. She was the one person in our family with dual American Canadian citizenship, because she was born in Mount Shasta, California to a Canadian mother and an American father.

I turned on the television and like many people I watched a replay in stunned silence as a plane crashed into the North Tower. Nineteen minutes later another plane smashed into the South Tower of the World Trade Center. The scene replayed over and over and over, like being caught in a nightmare of flames, smoke, people running, sirens screaming, and out of the darkened sky thousands of sheets of white paper drifted to earth.

The terrible thud of people landing on the pavement to escape being burned to death sickened me. Many people were trapped above where the planes hit the buildings, with no way of escape. Thousands of men and women were dead or dying as firefighters and police tried to rescue people trapped in stairwells.

Breaking news reported that thirty-four minutes after the South Tower was hit, another plane crashed into the Pentagon in Arlington, Virginia, just outside of Washington, DC. Then more breaking news: twenty-five minutes after that another plane crashed into a field near Shanksville in rural Pennsylvania. No survivors.

Both towers collapsed within two hours of being hit by the planes. Many firefighters and rescuer workers perished that day along with civilians.

I was numb with shock and had to force myself to turn off the TV. I told Mom what had happened, but it didn't seem to register. She carried on as if nothing out of the ordinary had happened when in fact nineteen al-Qaeda terrorists had hijacked four commercial passenger jet airliners and used them as weapons against civilians. Hatred of North American culture and values was at the very core of these attacks. Suspicion, fear, and anxiety affected whole nations after 9/11, as it became known.

Everyone knew the world changed that day, everyone except my mother, apparently. I noticed and puzzled over the latest development: her inability to show emotion when faced with disaster and death. Maybe those circuits in her brain had had enough heart-wrenching ordeals over a lifetime and they finally gave up, or atrophied.

When I talked to Deanna, she said the six farm kids from across the road came to her place to watch the events of 9/11 unfold on TV, as they didn't have television; it was one girl's birthday, one that she'll never forget.

Several months later, Teri-Ann and Shasta arrived in Salmon Arm to make a new life. Melissa and Faith were safe with their father and stepmother in Austin. Teri-Ann said shock, and then depression hit people hard in the days, weeks, and months following 9/11. Every sad and sickening detail was broadcast to us daily on the news. Most of us felt helpless in the face of such violence and hatred.

One of the television channels that sent camera crew into the stairwells and streets during the terrorist's attacks used the version of Leonard Cohen's song "Hallelujah" sung by Jeff Buckley, just him and his guitar, with the images. The song is open to a lot of interpretations, but Buckley's version sounded to most people like it came from one person's broken heart and spirit.

At the heart of it I had to admit that despite moving on in many ways I was still unwell. The broken hearts and spirits of nations over 9/11 echoed my own inner brokenness. When I told Dr. H that my family was coming, he was adamant that rest and writing should remain my highest priority. I didn't know if I'd be able to pull that off, knowing myself and my family as I did. They would have a big adjustment to make and I, after all, was Mom and Grandma. I didn't fully realize that what my mind and body struggled with, mysterious as it was to me, had its own agenda and time frame for healing.

In *The Noonday Demon: an atlas of depression,* author Andrew Soloman says that depression is the flaw in love, and that depression degrades us and eclipses the capacity to give or receive love.

That meant that my condition would have a profound effect on my relationship with my mother and with the rest of the family, who would be looking to me as their touchstone. Worried as I was, there was nothing to do but carry on.

27: Angie

I wandered out to the kitchen to make the morning coffee for Mom and me. The sun shone as it always did in the brilliant Shuswap autumn. I took Mom her coffee in bed, a ritual my father had begun years earlier. Pouring myself a mug I slid into a chair at the table next to the patio door.

From the other side of the patio door the desperate, mournful cry of a cat sent shivers through me. The lament was heartbreaking. I'd never heard anything like it. Out on the porch I called and listened. I waited and scanned the bushes and yard looking for signs of a cat in distress. Nothing. Then I called and listened some more. Puzzled by the lack of response, I eventually went back inside.

That evening, Mom and I watched a program with my sister Karen, the volume on the TV turned up loud as usual. Our mother had grown hard of hearing. Karen had moved to Salmon Arm and lived in the suite below us. Over the blaring sound my ears tuned into a sound from outside, the same loud cry for help that I'd heard that morning, except that now it was dark, chilly, and growing colder by the hour.

With a quick explanation to Karen, we grabbed our jackets and a flashlight and ran out to the front lawn where shrubs and bushes stood along the porch. The lilac tree and row of tall, ornamental cedar trees separated our yard from the house next door. We shone the light around the cedars, called and called, shook the trees. After what seemed like a long time I could feel exhaustion setting in, but I called again. A faint cry came from the shrubs along the porch. I parted the bushes and shone the light in. Two glowing eyes stared at the light.

"Karen, it's a kitten," I shouted.

I dove in to try and catch her but she escaped and disappeared under the bushes along the front porch. She darted under shrubbery and trees, where I finally found her trapped in the corner of the retaining wall. One last plunge on my part and I had her. The tiniest creature I'd ever seen. I held her close, next to my heart, and talked to her. She didn't struggle.

We brought her inside, noticing that she was covered with dirt, but knowing she must be hungry I separated flakes of the salmon we'd baked for dinner and fed them to her one after another as she sat in my hand. She ate and ate.

When she was full, she fell sound asleep in my hand. I found a blanket for her and laid her next to me on my bed to keep her safe. I watched her sleeping until I finally fell asleep. During the night, I fed her milk with an eyedropper. She never made another sound after those that allowed us to find her in the bushes.

Our amazement at finding the tiny creature with a voice that sounded like a full-grown cat kept us wondering about her. How could a kitten sound like that? Lost and alone, she cried for her mother, but how did she get there and where did she come from? We put all our questions aside in the morning as Karen decided a bath was in order. She filled the bathroom sink with warm water, and holding the kitten, gently cleaned her. What a surprise to find that she was actually black and white, and a female, just like Bridgey!

She had the most beautiful markings I'd ever seen on a black and white cat, very symmetrical across her back. She never cried or struggled at being bathed. We made sure Bridgey didn't feel left out by sitting her beside the sink on the counter to watch the proceedings, and she, being Bridgey, watched with keen interest.

Next we made her a litter box of her own in the bathroom away from Bridgey's litter, for the moment at least. Karen took her tiny paw and showed her how to scratch the litter. Well, if she didn't jump right in and use it properly!

When I took her to the veterinarian the next day to get her checked over, he estimated that she was three weeks old. Incredible. She was so smart. She settled in with us right away. She was lovely.

Karen said that an angel must have put her there so we would find her, and that the angel was responsible for making her voice that loud. "She's your angel," my sister said, referring to the kitten who was currently curled up in my mother's hands held next to her heart. We had all fallen in love. The word angel morphed into Angie, and that became her name.

Angie who was saved by an angel.

As Angie grew, the variety of her vocals was astonishing, although I never again heard that loud, mournful lament. She had a different sound for every desire, need, mood, and she was the most playful cat. She provided comic relief, making us laugh out loud often. When she was eventually allowed outside on the front porch, she learned that it was fun to trick us by sitting at the door looking like she was ready to come in and when we opened the sliding door she would dash off. If she could have laughed out loud, she would have. Karen said she was playing knocky-knocky-nine-doors. We always laughed at this trick that she enjoyed playing on us.

Angie grew tall and sleek with a long elegant tail that curled at the end. I called her "the girl with the curl" and sometimes "my sunshine girl" because she brought us such happiness. Another nick name I was fond of was Angie Bo Bangie. Bridgey took all this in her stride, although she wasn't as enamoured with Angie as Mom, Karen and I were. As Angie stretched out, long legs, long tail, beautiful face, Bridgey grew heavier and rounder, which made her tail and her legs seem that much shorter.

Before Angie showed up, Bridgey had suffered a vicious attack. She was on the chaise lounge on the front porch when a neighbourhood cat, the bully, invaded her territory. I saw a flurry of fur, heard a terrible scream and then it was over. When Bridgey came in, I didn't see any wounds, but by the next day I noticed she was sleeping a lot. By the following day, I noticed she wasn't eating or drinking. That night I kept vigil, terrified that she would die during the night. She could barely raise her head. First thing in the morning I took her to the clinic and the veterinarian found a badly infected bite that had to be lanced. Poor Bridgey. After that she had no voice, no meow. She was mute, and even the veterinarian couldn't explain it.

Mom and I began to notice the "talking tail" as we called it. When we talked to her, Bridgey's tail responded with a quick back and forth movement, letting us know that she was paying attention.

She was a clever cat, for she found that opening her mouth and doing "the silent meow" would elicit a heartfelt "Ah" from Mom and I. She began doing the silent meow at the dinner table, looking up at us with her huge, expressive black eyes, which produced the anticipated response from both Mom and me. "Ah, here, Bridgey." Bridgey learned the art of begging in a totally unique way, which didn't do her burgeoning belly any favours. She had made the mute thing work for her.

Another very unusual thing became apparent, this time with Angie. She couldn't purr. A cat that couldn't purr wasn't something we had ever come across before. When Angie tried to purr, it came out as snorting. I think even Angie knew that wasn't quite right, because she didn't do it often, but instead just breathed really fast so that her body vibrated in and out quickly. We were turning into quite the menagerie: a cat that talked with her tail, and another cat that snorted instead of purring.

To round out the family circus, one of Karen's sons, Jackson, moved in with his Mom. Our place became an extension of their apartment. Along with Teri-Ann and Shasta dropping by and occasionally staying overnight, and then Karen's other son Roscoe arriving, we had an ever-expanding extended family—and more personalities to deal with. There were more to come, but I didn't know that then.

Part Three

Getting to Yes

28: Creative Writing with Chris, Winter 2002

In her book, *Bird by Bird: Some instructions on Writing and Life*, well-known American author, Anne Lamott, suggests a way to help when the enormity of the writing project we've taken on feels overwhelming. When her brother was in tears about a school project on birds that was due, his father said, "Bird by bird, buddy. Just take it bird by bird." Lamott draws a parallel to writing, because tackling the dream of writing a novel, memoir or short story can be daunting. She suggests we start by writing a paragraph, a description of an event, or of a person. Bird by bird, scene by scene, that's how it's done.

I began to feel like my recovery was like that, too. As I continued to write, sometimes in a café while sipping a strong cup of coffee, or at the library surrounded by thousands of books, or sitting on a bench far along the foreshore trail with the lake breeze and the cry of a raven to inspire me. I felt myself grow stronger, taking things one day at a time. I always carried my work in my back pack and I'd put down a few words , or paragraphs wherever I happened to be.

People who are driven to write will write anywhere, under any circumstance. Howard White, author, poet, owner of Harbour Publishing, scratched down thoughts, his "gumboot meditations," on a scrap of paper while sitting on a road grade on a spreading machine with rain drip drip dripping off the end of his nose onto the paper.

I still struggled with the structure of the manuscript, and a few unanswered questions, but the story was coming together.

I'd been elected president of the Shuswap Writer's Group, which meant I planned and chaired meetings and acted as the media liaison. I also organized and emceed the monthly Shuswap Writers' Coffee House as part of my responsibilities. My public persona was growing by leaps and bounds.

The Cheap Tuesday Group met regularly and our writing was flourishing and inspiring. Bonnie was a delight, her creative writing always fresh and original. Miranda and John's writing never failed to amaze me, as did Karen's poetry . The result of all this involvement meant more writing and expanding into different kinds of writing. I still worked on the book and wrote poems, but I began to write short stories, too, a welcome change from the manuscript.

Miranda, who worked at the College, had an idea that we, the Cheap Tuesday Writers' group, should sign up for a creative writing course that was being offered for the Winter 2002 session. The new department head, Dr. Chris Castanier, was approachable and down to earth, possibly because his other love was organic farming.

I had never taken a creative writing class at Langara College, where I began my academic studies as a single mother of a fifteen-year-old daughter, or at UBC, where I studied for a year, or at Simon Fraser University, where I graduated with a BA in English Literature.

I could tell from the first meeting with our instructor, Chris, that this was going to be an interesting experience. Aside from Bonnie, John, Miranda and myself, who were all over forty, the class was mostly kids in their first year. I knew that it would be stimulating and I also knew that my undoing would be my nervousness or panic, which hovered too close for comfort, like a gnarly gargoyle—from the French word for throat—who might pop up at an inappropriate moment to choke my words into frightening silence.

The class sat around the perimeter of the room with Dr. Castanier, who was younger than me by at least ten years, at the front of the room. I felt sick about possibly having to talk or read. Wasn't I used to this yet? I could finally lead a meeting and emcee a Coffee House, so why this now? Every new experience that involved me putting myself forward felt like climbing a mountain all over again. Whatever the demons were that lurked on that cold climb to the top were relentless.

Chris showed us some slides and asked us what we noticed, what we liked, and what we would change. We didn't know that the photos of a First Nations graveyard were his, but we had just been taught the three things we were to use in critiquing each other's writing.

He was good-looking in a soft, no hard edges way—earth tones come to mind—and he had a wonderful smile, a pleasing voice. He was friendly, interesting and Intelligent. We were in for a treat.

He gave us guidelines about what he didn't want: children's literature, teen fiction, pornography, slice and dice, misogynist, misanthropic, racist, homophobic or religious writings.

I learnt more about our Dr. Castanier when I interviewed him for my column. From the industrial town of Windsor, Ontario, where he grew up, he went on to complete his PhD at Wayne State University in Detroit. After graduating he moved to Kelowna, where he worked at Okanagan University Campus. That's quite a leap. From the industrial town of his youth to the Okanagan/Shuswap, land of orchards and farms, also known as The Bible Belt. Was Dr. Castanier one of those godless professors that the conservatives and religious fundamentalists despised? I didn't ask about his political or religious beliefs, as that was nobody's business but his own.

He told me he looked forward to relocating to Salmon Arm, where he wanted to combine his love of organic farming, his interest in ecology, with his desire for "rootedness". He told me he already envisioned himself at the Farmer's Market selling his produce, enjoying the people and the conversations.

Spending time with Chris, it was apparent that he liked people and that he was a man of the earth, and dare I say it, a Luddite. He refused to get a computer and preferred to type everything, including his own short stories, on a typewriter, which was unheard of in those days.

29: The Devil and Miss Lolita

Over the winter months I read, wrote, and listened, absorbing everything I could in our creative writing course. I loved it, although I knew the day was coming when my poems and a short story would be critiqued by the class. During our in-class presentation I would be expected to respond with something intelligent about my work. I dreaded that, especially after hearing the smart things people said and knowing how my mind freezes up when I'm nervous.

My mother had that unfortunate affliction as well. When she was attending Al-Anon meetings in an attempt to stay sane while my father was still drinking, she had to write down what she wanted to say and read it when it was her turn to speak. I'd never seen anybody do that in those 12-Step meetings. My poor mother. She was shy in social situations. It's not hard to see where the term "painfully shy" comes from. Shy people are perceived as not having anything to say, because they don't speak up. She enjoyed family gatherings and pot luck events in Sorrento Place, where she and my father lived when they retired, but she always felt more comfortable sitting back and letting other people do most of the talking. That's how I was for most of my life and once again I found myself facing my fears. But was it shyness, or something else?

Canadian author Timothy Findlay wrote that Margaret Lawrence, a Canadian literary icon, suffered from an appalling nervousness that overcame her every time she rose to speak. He said she had what can only be called a debilitating shyness, when it came to public speaking. He didn't understand why because she wasn't a shy or introverted person, and still her nerves tormented her.

One day I walked in the back door of the college, very downhearted as I recall, past Chris's open door. We said hello and before I could continue he said my poems were very good. I was shocked. I didn't think of myself as a poet, I simply wrote poems to express myself differently than was possible in my prose writings. I don't remember what I said to Chris after he praised my poetry, but I floated down the hall in a state of excited euphoria.

One moment I'm stuck in the murky pond depths and the next I've emerged like a blue dragonfly, shimmering with joy and reveling in the sunlight.

When the class gave feedback on my poems and my short story, I was surprised, pleased and flattered, although we did have all kinds in that class. One young man thought my story was about the Devil! The Devil? How he came to his disturbing conclusion I'll never know. Was he one of those people who see the devil's hand in everything? Aside from that one confusing blip, the rest of the feedback was positive and illuminating. I have no idea what I said in response, that part is a blank.

One day it was a young woman's turn. She wrote graphically about vampires, homosexuality and violence. Why she chose that occasion to wear a low cut, blue blouse, I'll never know. Our little Lolita's prominent cleavage dominated the room as she defended her explicit material. Normally she was all buttoned up and plain looking, beige comes to mind, and someone I hardly noticed. Honestly, all that protruding flesh. it was hard not to stare. Chris looked disturbed, used a tone of voice I hadn't heard from him before, as the rest of us gratefully turned our attention to the next student when Lolita was finished.

I submitted the poem I wrote for Miranda on her birthday.

The Pearl

for Mira
with eyes so blue
they reflect a cool mountain lake
on a hot summer day

she's a Pearl
by any other name
the soft hues in her hair
like wisps of silken thread
that will not be contained
by hair bands
or barrettes

Mira Many Names
as real as the sunbeams
that her laughter scatters
as illusive as the moon
partially hidden by clouds

When you discover her true name
the one whispered between snow flakes
or echoed in ancient caves
then she may reveal
the many facets of her love
of her passion
for creating new worlds
with paint
and poem
and song.

Written for Miranda, aka Mira, aka Pearl on her birthday February, 2002.

30: Like Father, Like Daughter

Was I shy, or was there another explanation for my behaviour? I found an answer in the book, *The Highly Sensitive Person: How to Thrive When The World Overwhelms You,* by Elaine N. Aron, a book I sold in Reflections. I recognized my father, and myself. Highly sensitive people (HSP) are that 15 to 20% born with nervous systems that pick up on subtleties, reflecting deeply on everything, and they are easily overwhelmed with too much stimulation, loud noises, and intense situations. This is not a disorder, but an inherited temperament that has not been written about much. I believe that my father's drinking was a form of self-medicating, and I could say the same for myself, having abused alcohol at various times in my life.

My father and I needed more quiet time than other people. He was always off by himself in nature, or with his nose in a book when he wasn't at work, or drinking. His five children overwhelmed him. My mother noticed that I needed more rest and quiet time as a child than the others. One in five people have this innate trait, known in scientific terms as Sensory-Processing Sensitivity. Biologists say that about one hundred species of animals that they know of have this sensitivity too. What it means is that HSPs observe before acting. It's a survival tactic.

One vivid memory I have from childhood illustrates this, although I never understood it until I read the book. Grandma English took me to a park I wasn't familiar with. A bunch of kids were playing on the playground equipment. "Go on," she urged. "Go play with them."

I was horrified, as that was not my way. I didn't rush into things, but liked to watch and appraise situations before doing anything. Grandma was annoyed, but the more she pushed me, the more I refused to budge.

Grandma wasn't an HSP, obviously, and for the 80% of people who are like grandma, and who therefore have no understanding of highly sensitive people, it looks like weakness. For those of us who are raised in cultures where that trait isn't valued, it leads to low self-esteem, because the child feels deficient. I was labelled shy, but Aron says that that isn't shyness. Shyness is learned, not innate. Apparently moving a lot as a highly sensitive child can produce a shy child.

I wasn't sure about my mother; she was a puzzle I had yet to figure out.

Another clue for me was reading that when this processing trait isn't fully conscious, it surfaces as intuition. I shocked people when I knew things they were thinking, and in some cases doing.

Wait a minute! My mother has always known things that on the surface were unknowable. She, like me, also had intuitive dreams. She knew when her children were in trouble, even from a distance. Another piece of my mother that I haven't acknowledged. If Mom is an HSP, I wonder what it was like for her having a non HSP mother. That could have led to low self-esteem.

I noticed that Angie was different from Bridgey. She watched people carefully from a safe distance. She never rushed into anything, unlike Bridgey, her more social stepsister. In lieu of what biologists have noticed, I guess Angie was a highly sensitive cat, just like her highly sensitive adopted mother.

Many writers are shy, highly sensitive, and they are introverts. The paradox is that writers want to be both visible and invisible. We want to be heard, but perhaps not seen. Book tours and public readings ask a lot of people who spend most of their time alone in a room writing, and indeed most writers would prefer to leave the promotion of their book up to someone else.

31: The Red-haired Boy

I tried to understand why I aligned myself with my father, rather than with my mother. A memory pops up. We lived in Vancouver then, and that's when I had a crush on the red-haired boy in high school, but didn't know what to do about it.

Mom was at the stove, adding a dash of Worcestershire sauce, her secret ingredient, to her beef stew when I walked up to her.

"Mom, can I talk to you about something?"

"Oh, no, now what!" She sounded so angry that I walked away without asking her advice about the red-haired boy. I wanted to tell her about my feelings for him and get her advice. That was the first and last time I asked my mother for advice on anything.

A girl I knew at school decided to throw a party the weekend her parents went away for the weekend. She invited the boy of my dreams. Nerves took hold before he arrived and I asked my friend if there was any alcohol in the house. Turns out her father had a liquor cabinet, and after a couple of shots of whiskey to loosen my tongue, to give me courage, I felt ready.

I sauntered over to the red-head standing at the bar in the dimly lit rec room. I said hi. He nodded. I asked whose class he was in. Big red didn't have anything to say after his one-word answer and I couldn't think of anything else to say. Perhaps he was just a pretty face, or he suffered from shyness, or he was highly sensitive, too. I never found out. It may have been the end of my fantasy about the red-haired boy, but it wasn't the end of me using alcohol in social situations. One day, years later, I realized what I was doing and stopped drinking for that reason.

I began to wonder if the ambivalence toward my mother began with her brushing me off, or did it begin much earlier?

32: Unloved

I was eight years old I think when we moved to Calgary for two years. That's were my youngest sister, Karen, was born. Mom already had four other children, two of them toddlers that were driving her crazy. Dad, who had a new pressure-filled promotion, was drinking heavily when Mom's mother came to visit. She didn't have a home of her own, but made the rounds, staying with her various children when they needed her, although mostly she stayed at auntie Marge's house, as it was probably less stressful than our place.

One tragic day, Grandma tumbled off a curb, breaking both her ankles. After she was released from the hospital she convalesced with us. Mom had her hands full with a new baby and the other kids, and with our father. Dad looked bloated and overweight, not my mother's ideal husband. He never came home one New Year's Eve and the following day she shouted at him, "Whose wife where you kissing New Year's Eve?"

She relived that hurt often over the years. My mother used us, at least her two oldest children, as her confidants, I assume because we moved so often she didn't have time to form any close friendships. Or maybe she just felt too crazy. Her lamentations about our father were the basis of the talks, and the tears. In Mom's mind he was the devil incarnate. I felt a kinship with Dad, so that probably set up some kind of conflict.

I may have been lost in the shuffle, not a surprise considering everything going on. I do remember running away once as a kid, sitting at the tennis courts in a miserable state for hours, then dragging my sorry ass home.

I may have still sucked my thumb then, or it was something else that prompted my parents to take me to a doctor. I have no memory of that meeting, but he told my parents that I didn't think that my mother loved me. Ah-ha, so there we have it! An overwhelmed mother and wife was the problem. I doubt that there were any parents who weren't struggling to maintain some kind of sanity, although no one talked about such things back in the fifties. Poor Mom. Maybe she had low grade depression. Or perhaps, more to the point, she didn't feel loved either.

33: The Strange & the Baffling

Joining the Federation of BC Writers connected me to the larger writing community throughout the province. When my name was put forward for Regional Rep, because the position was becoming vacant, I said yes. I had a lot of encouragement and threw myself into the role with enthusiasm. As the Representative for the Shuswap, Thompson-Nicola, and Okanagan areas, I wrote reports for our region that appeared in the quarterly magazine WordWorks. I'd always enjoyed reading everything in the magazine when it arrived in the mail. The magazine offered opportunities for submitting articles, too.

Saying yes was becoming easier. At Gardom Lake after my bookstore closed, I shut the world out, or maybe just people and responsibilities. I needed to heal and to come back to myself.

The experience of owning a bookstore and all that involved taught me that I had strengths and talents I didn't know existed. I enjoyed marketing and promotion, and hosting many different events in the bookstore. Helping a customer find the right book was a joy in itself.

My weakness was filing, still is; I became a hoarder of paperwork, magazines, and catalogues, and even little scraps of paper with notes scribbled on them. Once things went beyond a certain point, it felt impossible to control, although oddly I still knew where everything was, unless anybody moved anything, then I was lost. A friend who worked across the street at the school board office offered to come in on Saturday, her day off, and file catalogues for me. She asked for nothing in return. Another lovely woman, an artist, volunteered her time on Saturdays for a while. She had four toddlers at home that she needed a break from.

Building the bookstore had been the highlight. I'll always remember the exciting time with my brother Jim, husband Craig, and friend Marvin, as we built bookshelves in record time—eight days. It's hard to believe now. My mother looked after Jim's young children, her grandchildren Kristie and Nick, while we worked, putting in long days. As a grandmother my mother excelled. She also pitched in to help stain the shelves when my work crew left us to get back to family and jobs. Mom always pitched in to help her children whenever they needed her.

Writing about the experiences of owning the bookstore helped me relive the five and a half years. The joy, the strange and baffling in terms of books popping off the shelves in the First Nation section, and other odd occurrences that we attributed to the mischievous bookstore ghost. Thankfully I'd kept a journal for years, for without those daily entries I may have lost many of the details of that extraordinary experience. I also knew I was taking a risk writing about the darker side of the town I had chosen to live in. I was so naive. I should have done my homework before moving to Salmon Arm, where active white supremacists looked like anyone else waiting in the Post office line-up.

On the other hand, I discovered there was so much to love about the place, for compassionate, creative, intelligent people far outweighed the hateful few.

I admit the revelation about the town I'd adopted scared me, especially when my bookstore became a target. Me, a woman from Vancouver where the diversity of races, lifestyles, customs, and sexual preferences covered just about everything under the sun, and then some. Not that there weren't prejudices and problems in the city, but for the most part people found neighbourhoods where they were comfortable. Psychologists tell us how important a sense of belonging is to our well-being. When I discovered white crosses painted across my bookstore windows after I opened Reflections, the message was clear: YOU'RE NOT WELCOME HERE. I was staying with my mother at the time. My poor church-going mother who never did anything to attract negative attention to herself. But her eldest daughter seemed to attract the strangest situations and people without even trying.

In the West End of Vancouver where I lived in an older brick apartment building while attending Simon Fraser University, poverty, homelessness, and mental illness brushed shoulders with well-dressed, well-fed men and women dining and shopping on Robson Street. I recall drinking a lot of red wine during that period of my life and still, somehow, managed to pull off good grades at university, and that no doubt was because I loved everything I was learning. I drank socially by that time, and not for the reasons that I had started using alcohol.

I couldn't quite believe that I was a university student, a girl who hadn't done well in school, who had no faith in her ability to learn, and who dropped out of school after grade eleven. I felt blessed to be a Canadian, where higher education was available to me, no matter how old, or how poor I was—and more importantly, what gender I was. I must have looked quite the sight wandering about SFU campus, my thick dark hair flowing almost to my waist, a backpack full of books, a tall slender woman who was older than most of her classmates.

I was fortunate to have several award-winning Canadian authors/poets for several of my English classes. Roy Miki, after reading a paper I'd written, told me that I could write. When I said I'm not good at spelling he said don't worry about that, that's why there are editors. That kind, soft-spoken professor, poet, critic, editor, activist, and Third-Generation Japanese Canadian worked for the Redress Movement and was honoured with many awards over the years. He wrote, *A Record of Writing: An Annotated and Illustrated Bibliography of George Bowering,* that explored the writing career of Bowering, another one of my professors, and a larger than life character who became Canada's first poet laureate. Bowering had written so many books, in every genre, it would take a book to list them all.

Poet, essayist, editor Robin Blazer taught several English courses I count myself fortunate to have attended. To study the Black Mountain poets with a man who had been friends with them was an illuminating experience. The mid-twentieth century American avant-garde or postmodern poetry that emerged from the Black Mountain school became connected to the Beat poets in San Francisco in 1957. Blazer helped spark the Berkeley Poetry Renaissance in the 1940's that preceded the San

Francisco Renaissance of the 50's and 60's.

Blazer said the real business of poetry is cosmology. I studied Dante Alighieri's *Inferno*, the first part of his 14th century epic poem *Divine Comedy* with Blazer. Dante is midway through the journey of his life when he finds himself lost in the dark woods. That's a great metaphor for how many people feel in midlife, and maybe that's why I could relate. I loved the poem.

Blazer and another professor brought Beat poet Alan Ginsberg in for a poetry reading held at Kitsilano High School. Hearing Ginsberg read his most famous poem, *Howl*, gave me goosebumps.

I saw the best of minds of my generation destroyed by madness, starving hysterical naked, dragging themselves through the negro streets at dawn looking for an angry fix .... and so the long poem begins.

Before I began my academic career, I knew next to nothing about poetry and I wasn't particularly well read either. Most of my education to that point had been by watching people, and from direct experience. Attending Langara College and then university opened me to new ideas, thoughts, and the wonderful world of literature. I decided to major in English after transferring from UBC to SFU. It took me three buses and one and a half hours to reach SFU from where I lived in the West End, but I never found that a hardship.

The building on Cardero Street where I lived housed artists, dancers, students, waiters, a stand-up comic, and my gay male friends across the hall, who adopted me as their sister. They poured out their love problems to me, cooked me dinner, and once or twice I went dancing at a gay club with them. I was just one of the girls. I had many friends in that building, including the young straight men sharing an apartment on the second floor. I cleaned their apartment for them on a regular basis, vacuuming around the Harley motorcycle parts strewn about on the living room floor. After carting all the pizza boxes out to the garbage, and washing piles of dishes, I felt like I'd really accomplished something. As a student at Simon Fraser University, I needed the money. On the weekends, I cleaned my doctor's offices and another apartment in False Creek.

One of my neighbours from upstairs, the tall, dark-haired Harley motorcycle rider from Newfoundland, waited tables in an upscale Italian restaurant in Dunbar. He could have leaped right off the cover of a romance novel with those swarthy good looks. When he invited me to join him for a ride on his Harley, I went of course, breathing in the heady scent of his black leather jacket as I clung to him, with the wind whipping my long hair into a frenzy. He was perhaps in his late twenties, while I was in my late thirties. We became lovers briefly, but that's another story. Warren wasn't just another pretty face, for he made delicious muffins. Whenever he made a batch, he'd phone me.

"Muffins are out of the oven. Get 'em while they're hot." I ran to the second floor in my housecoat more than once after such a call, which was okay, as only my friends used that staircase, including a beautiful young dancer on the third floor; she also regaled me with her love problems. One evening I enjoyed one of her dance performances at a theatre at False Creek.

I should have hung out a sign: Tell Momma Your Love Problems. We were one big family of oddballs. That period of my life was long before book selling in Salmon Arm. That's where I lived when I finished my B.A. in English Literature at Simon Fraser University. I turned thirty-nine the day I wrote my last exam and had just become a grandmother. With exams behind me, Mom and I traveled by bus to Mt. Shasta in northern California to visit Teri-Ann, her husband Larry, and our brand-new granddaughter and great granddaughter, Shasta Dawn. Traveling with my mother was crazy making, as her anxiety, which I knew nothing about at the time, kicked in. I saw it as control issues, but the woman was a mess coming and going. Relentless micro managing. I enjoyed her, my daughter and new baby Shasta once we were settled in. Babies draw love to themselves without even trying.

Bookstore ownership, where every day felt like a creative adventure, was a journey of a different kind. The call to be a bookseller was strong and the thrill of creating a place that people enjoyed, that challenged me in many ways, engaged me totally for quite some time, although I do recall a period of painful depression.

When Reflections closed, Lorne, editor of the *Friday AM* wrote a tribute to my bookstore in his newspaper, saying my bookstore felt like a country general store, where people met, chatted, and shared stories around the pot-bellied stove—an image I was very fond of. I'd seen photos of the early days in the Squilax General Store that had captured my imagination.

The paradox is that even though I enjoyed owning and running the bookstore, it was the passion I had for the enterprise that probably ruined me. Too much fire; too little control? Or maybe I just tried too hard to prove myself—me with no business experience. In the end I was all used up, burned up, and how ironic that the massive out-of-control fire of 1998 was the beginning of the end for both me and Reflections.

I came away from the experience richer—not in money—but in so many other ways. I had a story to tell, but it took time to appreciate that. When the bookstore closed, I felt empty and numb with grief. Every day was a struggle to find a reason to go on. Prolonged stress, such as I experienced during the last several years trying to keep my business going, when circumstances beyond my control threw me off balance, led to depression with a predisposition to anxiety.

34: The Ryga Centre, 2002

Miranda, Bonnie and I set out from Salmon Arm on an adventure one beautiful morning in June. We drove the long winding road to Summerland, on the west side of Okanagan Lake. Where once fruit trees grew in abundance, now vineyards stretched down to the lake in every direction in an area now renowned for its wineries. Deanna Kawatski greeted us when we stopped in the driveway. She had accepted the writer-in-residence position at the Ryga Centre for six months. We made the trek to spend the weekend writing with her. As part of her commitment, Deanna was accepting a number of pages from manuscripts of local writers for evaluation.

Deanna told us that the George Ryga Centre Society, a non-profit charitable organization, fund raised the down-payment to buy the Rygas' former home. That was in 1996 and the unique heritage home became a cultural centre/retreat, hosting an author reading series, and song writing workshops among other cultural events.

I knew that Ryga made a name for himself in the history of Canadian theatre with his two-act play *The Ecstasy of Rita Joe*, the story of a young Native girl who goes to the city. What I didn't know was that the play premiered at the Vancouver Playhouse in 1967, or that Ryga wrote novels, essays, short stories, poetry, film scripts, and songs. He produced a great body of work during his short life (1932-1987). Considering he didn't continue his education past grade six, where he began life near Athabasca, Alberta—born to poor Ukrainian parents—his success and literary outpourings are astonishing.

The Centre supports the annual George Ryga Award for Social Awareness in Literature, which is granted to a B.C. writer who has achieved an outstanding degree of social awareness in a new book publication.

Over a glass of red wine before supper, Deanna told us how The Ryga Centre was more than a job for her. The place held memories. She went on to tell us that as a young writer she had taken a workshop from Ryga. He was impressed enough with the novel she had written in Paris to invite her home, where she met his wife Norma. He was known to mentor writers at that time.

Deanna was hard at work on a different novel during her writer-in-residence stay at the Centre. After the success of *Clara and Me*, a creative non-fiction book published in 1996, a Hubert Evans Award nominee and her second book to be a Book-of-the-Month Club selection after *Wilderness Mother*, Deanna wanted to try her hand at fiction again.

The following day, we retreated to various corners of the house to write. Later that afternoon, Susan McIver arrived from Penticton at Deanna's invitation. As a coroner, Susan knew things. Her book, *Medical Nightmares: The Human Face of Errors*, had been recently published. Leonard Cohen's "10 New Songs" played in the background as we chatted in the living room. The glow of the fire in the fireplace added warmth to the dark room.

I talked to Susan about the sudden death of my father in the Kamloops hospital after he fell and his leg snapped in three places. My siblings and I were horrified and perplexed that he should die of cardiac arrest in the hospital.

Back at home, I had to buy Leonard Cohen's CD, the one with his face on the blue CD cover, reminiscent of the Blue album that Joni Mitchell recorded, her face overlaid by the same sultry blue colour. Maybe not so odd, considering she and Leonard had been more than just friends at one time. What is it about the colour blue that conjures up such different emotions? Having the blues transports me to a more reflective, somber place, yet when I hear the blues I feel oddly joyful like whenever I heard Jim Byrnes, Vancouver blues musician and actor, sing the blues. I'd heard him in person many times and knew that he'd lost both his legs when he was twenty-three years old in an accident on the Malahat Highway on Vancouver Island. He went through a rough time after that, but kept playing the music he loved. He didn't become bitter or give up.

The haunting melodies and lyrics on Cohen's latest CD spun a cocoon around me. Such beauty in the sadness, in the plight of being human. In Leonard's ragged voice. Cohen recorded that album in 2001 after living in a Zen monastery for seven years. He said that a lengthy depression had lifted two years earlier. Mom surprised me. She liked the CD as much as I did.

I thought I knew who my mother was. I knew she was tender-hearted, and yet she could be fierce if pushed. She was both vulnerable and extremely strong, fun-loving, dreamy and thoughtful, and sometimes filled with sadness. I wonder if these traits were a legacy from her Irish father, Daniel? The absent father. What I didn't know was that she had an inner life that not many knew about.

She performed the practical things like running her household so well that no one suspected that she was really a moon goddess in the thrall of the full moon. I only became aware of this when a woman from the Shuswap Writers' Group offered to read our palms. Surprised, but willing to see what would come of it, the woman came to our apartment. My sister Karen joined us. Looking at my mother's palm, Eliza said "You were a moon goddess in another life." My mother smiled knowingly. Eliza continued. "You feel drawn to the full moon and are enchanted by it."

"Yes," my mother said. She looked so serene, sitting in her comfy easy chair in the living room, the light from the lamp beside her casting a golden glow over her and her crown of white hair.

I stared at my mother, realizing that I'd never really seen her, or into the depths of her before that moment. *Moon goddess. Imagine.*

35: Whyte and his Passion to Write

I sat among thirty-five men and women, in a semi-circle, around the star celebrity, Jack Whyte, author of the *Dream of Eagles* series, *Uther*, and the mini-series, *The Golden Eagle*. Fran Kay organized the workshop. She'd been trying to get Whyte for years and had finally succeeded. She had been putting on these one-day workshops at the Sorrento Centre for many years, followed by a writing contest based on the genre featured that year.

The Sorrento Centre Retreat & Conference Centre was beautiful in June with spring flowers blooming, Shuswap Lake shimmering through the trees, and a variety of birds singing—a peaceful and lovely spot to hold any gathering. I recalled Mom saying that my father had attended a silent retreat at the Centre once, as part of his healing journey after he quit drinking.

When Jack spoke, his Scottish brogue—softened by several decades living in Canada—still gave him an edge, that of a swashbuckling, pen wielding man of letters. He exuded confidence, spoke frankly, and it was obvious to me that he felt right at home in the spotlight.

Jack lived up to and beyond our expectations as a writer of historical fiction. He was part entertainer, part comedian, with an extraordinary grasp of history. In his retelling of the Arthurian legend, there's a twist, for Whyte believed that Arthur removed the sword from the stone without the help of magic. "I figured it out," he said. "There's a logical explanation for the spectacle."

With that conviction in mind, he would descend to the basement every night to write. That was in 1977. Many years and three manuscripts later, his wife wandered downstairs, wondering perhaps what was ruining their sex life. When she read the work, she insisted he send it to a publisher. Penguin picked him up immediately—hardly the route to getting published that most writers find themselves on. Jack makes a respectable living with his writing, although he cautioned new writers that the odds were not in their favour for doing so.

Whyte threw out another note of caution. According to Oscar Wilde, showing your unfinished manuscript to friends is like showing them your soiled handkerchief. He added, "Your friend is never your editor, however, an editor is your friend." Along with other tips about writing, research and submitting manuscripts, Mr. Whyte insisted one must be impassioned to be a good writer.

The workshop ended and we moved to another room where wine, cheese and crackers were spread out for us. Fran had been talking to Jack about coming back the following year. He was all for it if she would make it a two-day event and Jack promised to bring some of his favourite writers with him. We knew that popular author Diana Gabaldon was a close friend of his and that they often presented together at the Surrey Writers' Conference. Fran was a huge fan of both Jack and of Diana's books.

While Jack held court, a glass of red wine in one hand, surrounded by admiring fans, Fran and her assistant, Blair Borden, approached me with a proposal. Blair gave Fran her notice as she no longer had time to assist her with annual workshops and suggested me as her replacement. I hesitated, as I didn't know Fran, although I knew Blair and trusted her. What gave me pause was that I had taken on many commitments recently, and my health was still shaky. More symptoms, including heart palpitations and irregular heartbeat, should have been a clue that something wasn't right in my life. Dr. H. changed my prescription and wanted to see me every two weeks.

Even with my doubts, I said yes, that I would help her put on the next two-day writers event the following year.

Dorothy and I had come together and we had our photo taken with Jack. "He's quite comfortable surrounded by all those women, isn't he," Dorothy said, as she turned her car onto the highway. I laughed and then told her what I'd taken on for the coming year.

Perhaps getting to "yes" was becoming a bit too easy. Work on the Shuswap Lake International Writers' Festival, the name Fran and I came up with, began almost right away. The first thing Fran and I did was sign up for the Surrey Writers' Conference in October. We wanted to find out how the hugely successful Surrey Conference did it, and maybe scoop a few authors and literary agents in the process. We knew that the long running Conference drew over six hundred participants from the United States, Canada, and elsewhere. We were also aware that besides drawing big name authors every year, men and women had a chance to get feedback on their work from a wide variety of publishers, editors, and agents at the blue pencil appointments.

36: Surrey Conference, October 2002

Journal entry:

October 5th

"I've had my anti-depressants increased by 25 milligrams as of Wednesday. This week has been a breeze compared to last week, and having Karen here, even though Mom was sick and dizzy yesterday and I had to cancel her hair appointment, has been a relief."

"Been trying to keep up the walking along the lake cause that feels like such a calming, yet energizing thing to do."

Friday, Oct. 18, 02, 2:12 p.m.

Teri-Ann's Birthday, born 37 years ago.

here I sit in the Chilliwack bus depot
on my daughter's birthday,
waiting for the Surrey bus

outside the pale sun offers no warmth
the pollution stinks and it's windy

an old man in a blue turban
wearing his grey beard long
leans on his cane

the fat Chinese postman
with dark moles on his face
he waits, too

they're been here as long as I have ... coke machine humming
machine in the coffee kiosk buzzing

the sky has turned milky and
a violent wind shakes the young Japanese maple tree
and the mountains are consumed
by a murky brown haze

    I left behind my beautiful Angie, the abandoned kitten I rescued 9 days ago. I tried to make this addition to our family as kind a transition as I could for Bridgey, but I'm afraid she's not herself.

    Finally, on the bus. Just another two hours to Surrey where Fran Kay will pick me up. The Surrey Writers' Conference started yesterday. We are just going for Saturday and half of Sunday. Fran has a discount on the hotel room because she travels for her job as owner/editor of Agri Digest, an agricultural digest she publishes.

    I had the flu for three days before leaving and don't even know how I've got this far. What am I doing? Brother Michael, Gloria, Heather and James arrived for the Thanksgiving long weekend right after Angie joined our household. No time to write. Angie finally got rid of her diarrhea yesterday. The vet said to take her off milk, and the problem cleared up. It was very hard to leave little Angie."

Saturday evening, I took the claustrophobic elevator down about fourteen floors to the Convention floor. Fran said to save her a place for dinner. I bought a glass of red wine and talked to a woman who was set up with books in the hallway. She was playing Emily Carr in one of the Vancouver theatres and she gave me Emily's blessing, saying that Emily's spirit is so strong that she was present. How unusual. I have a garage sale print of one of Emily's paintings that draws me in whenever I look at it. Emily Carr had even found a place in my book.

When I wandered into the dining room to find a table, I saw that they were all full except for one table against a far wall where a man sat by himself. I made my way through the tables, sat down, and introduced myself. The man, in his forties I guessed, with shoulder length blond hair, neatly trimmed beard, and glasses told me he was here to see if there was any interest in his novel, which sounded like a dark tale of vampires, murder, and mayhem. He didn't look like someone who would write that kind of novel but then neither did the young woman in Chris's creative writing class.

Before long, three other men joined us. They were with the Surrey School Board, one of the sponsors of the annual event. Fran never did appear but I had a great time talking to the men, especially the nice-looking man sitting beside me. I wore my long red skirt with a blue paisley border at the bottom, with slits up the side, and a baby blue sweater. Makeup made me look healthier than I felt, and wearing red made me bolder than usual—well, that and the glass of red wine. The day had been fascinating, but now I was having fun.

I found Fran after dinner. After freshening up, we went down to the bar, as she was still trying to track down Jack Whyte and we knew that was the most likely place to find him. As a non-drinker, Fran wasn't exactly in her element, but when the blond man from my dinner table waved me over, she followed reluctantly. Over the noise of the crowded bar, he had to shout, regaling us with stories about his twelve years as a reporter, covering rock groups, about the drugs and out-of-control behaviour. Fran's expression told me how uncomfortable she felt. She excused herself and made a bee-line for Jack, who she spotted talking to a couple of men in a corner of the bar.

A funny thing happened next when I mentioned the kitten I left at home. The man who wrote horror crumbled as I related the story of how I found Angie abandoned and desperate. With tears in his eyes, he told me he'd become a better person after a cat came into his life. His stepson had a cat that had been hit by a car and he and his wife spent $900.00 trying to patch up the cat's crushed pelvis. Finally, the decision was made to put the cat down rather than spend more money. He said that was the worst decision of his life and that they should have spent any amount to save the cat. He'd written a short cat story that he wanted to show me.

I can relate to an animal having that kind of effect. I've heard that before. In many ways, Bridgey saved me. The healing power of animals is very real, and hadn't the ravens lifted my spirits.

At a Wise Woman conference in Naramata I heard an author talk about how a cat saved her. It was a low point for her, as she'd been in a car accident and needed a pair of canes to walk with. Despondent, she went down to the ocean one day absorbed in negative thoughts, when she heard a cat meowing frantically. The woman saw a kitten hanging onto a log drifting away from shore, whereupon she threw down her canes and rushed into the water to rescue the frightened animal. She has never used the canes since and credits the little creature, who was still with her, with bringing love and healing into her life.

The day had been full of workshops, a couple of interviews with agents, and a wonderful lunch with Elizabeth Lyon, an American editor and author. She gave each of the people sitting at the table valuable advice about their writing projects. I was encouraged by her words.

One of the American agents I met in a line-up for breakfast, a young woman who worked at her mother's literary agency, joined Fran and me at my request. She asked me to send her an outline of my book along with fifty pages. We asked Ashley Kraas if she would like to come to our writers' festival the following June. She accepted with enthusiasm.

I discovered that to pitch a non-fiction book to any agent or publisher I needed a synopsis and an outline that involved writing a summary of every chapter. Another American agent I talked to that day had also requested that I send her an outline with a couple of chapters.

The next morning, I waited in line for a breakfast table and began chatting to the man behind me. He introduced himself as Matt Hughes and he lived in Courtenay, on Vancouver Island. I was exhausted by then so when we sat down I let Fran and him do most of the talking. He told us he wrote speeches for all the political candidates and that he'd written a biography of Len Marchand, the first Native MP in Canada. He was at the conference to give workshops and he wrote both science fiction—using the name Matthew Hughes—and crime fiction using the name Matt Hughes. Fran invited him to give a workshop at our writers' festival, which he accepted.

Fran said she had invited publisher Barbara Gislason, owner of Blue Raven Press, "a publishing house devoted to other animals". Barbara said that everything their publishing house did sprang from her love of animals. She was drawn to the image of the raven as creator.

"To some First People, blue is the colour of communication," she said. "Necklaces are often designed with blue stones at the throat. The combination of raven with the colour blue was a fitting symbol for my publishing company." I found this fascinating, as I was in thrall of ravens at the time, and perhaps the colour blue without realizing it.

Fran's boldness surprised me when at the Sunday luncheon she hopped over to the next table to ask Diana Gabaldon if she would come to our Writers' Festival in the spring. Diana said yes. Diana said yes! I had listened to Jack Whyte and Diana give a reading and talk together the night before. She said Gabaldon rhymed with stone, something I was glad to have cleared up. I'd had no idea how to pronounce her name when I carried her books in my bookstore. The first book in her Outlander series came out in 1991.

Diana's Mexican and English ancestry had produced a dark-haired beauty of exceeding warmth. Diana was blessed with brains as well as beauty and talent, for she held degrees in Zoology, Marine Biology, and a PhD in Behavioural Ecology. Her NY Times best-selling series crossed genres of science fiction, fantasy, historical fiction, romance and adventure, and featured a kilt-wearing Scott named Jamie Fraser, who lived in the mid-nineteenth century. An English woman named Claire, living in the twentieth century, time travels to his world.

By the time Fran and I left after lunch, I was ready to go home. For a day and a half, nothing but non-stop excitement, taking notes in workshops, listening to authors speak about their experiences, meeting new people, and having a page critiqued by several professionals.

One thing worried me. Fran had married and moved to the States since we made the agreement to work together. She was now Fran Kay-Bach. On the car ride home with Fran driving, I began to see a side of Fran I wasn't sure I knew how to relate to, although I didn't know how to put my finger on what it was. I'd seen it during the Conference, too. Perhaps it was that Fran had an aggressive, pushy side. On one hand, those are the kind of people who make things happen. I was taking medication for depression and anxiety, but was still vulnerable and I wondered if this would be a good match.

37: Busy

Journal Entry:

October 24th, 2002.

The cats are having fun chasing each other this morning which is a good thing to see—it's the closest thing to play I've noticed between Angie and Bridgey so far. They both seem healthy and happy (working on Bridgey, whose nose has been a little out of joint). Shasta said, "Her nose is out of joint?" I laughed and explained the expression. I love having Shasta and Teri-Ann here even though it's hectic and crowded at times. And I love having Karen here too. And the new addition to the family—Angie the Angel. Mom seems to be doing okay at the moment and she loves having family around.

I suggested to Fran that if we were going to grow the Writers' Festival, as we'd discussed, that maybe we should move it to Salmon Arm, into the Prestige Harbourfront Resort and Convention Centre. It was a handsome new hotel near the Salmon Arm wharf, close to the bird sanctuary and trail along the lake shore, and it had enough large meeting rooms to accommodate at least four workshops simultaneously.

Journal Entries

October 26 /02

Tomorrow Fran will be here to talk to people at the Prestige Inn with me. I have some research to do for that meeting.

Nov. 5 /02

Talked to Fran last night and have a list of things to do ... check with the Chamber of Commerce, see about a web site etc.

Sent 6 poems and 2 short pieces off to a contest. Should start my synopsis and outline tomorrow.

Sat. Nov. 29/02
CBC radio North by Northwest. Sheryl MacKay asked for a holiday snapshot, an anecdote, 300 words max If they read the piece, they'll send one of the new fall books. Due in 2 weeks, by Dec. 14 & 15th.

Got a fair amount of work done on the writers' festival but not enough. Yesterday was the day I was going to devote to my writing! Nada! Started to file the piles of paper and magazines on the floor in my bedroom—it's growing to unbelievable proportions—and that's all I got done for the day.

Hard to believe I can't remember one Christmas anecdote. There has to be something. Emailed my column off to Lorne yesterday.

We're planning to do Christmas baking, and a luncheon for Uncle Dick on his 89th birthday. Uncle Dick (Mom's oldest brother) is a favourite uncle. He loves kidding people and he remembers everything. Still got all his marbles. Too bad auntie Jean passed on, leaving Dick alone, although he's still his usual jovial self.

Dr. H. gave me a plan to map how I'm feeling and to see how much I've taken on is affecting my physical, emotional & spiritual health (my categories). I was telling him how overwhelmed I am at times by all the things on my plate. Sometimes I feel resentful and on the verge of quitting and then I rationalize how I need to keep doing this. Can't let people down.

He mentioned "my authentic self" and how writing feeds that. I haven't touched any of my own writing for a while. No wonder I'm suffering.

Just had an "aha" moment! After getting the dish washer going and tidying up it came to me: the Christmas in Mexico when I went in search of a chicken for our Christmas meal.

Journal Entry

Sunday, Dec. 8/02.

Up before 5 a.m. in a good mood, cheerful even after getting up at 4 to ice my neck—seems to have done the trick after a couple of days of extreme back and neck pain & headaches. Despite that I met Deanna yesterday at Kindred Spirits, a new café on Lakeshore Drive, to discuss the festival. She agreed to act as a consultant for free and gave me suggestions for authors, and information about the Public Lending Right Commission, Cancopy, and reading programs. Fran and I still had a lot to learn and it would be great to work with Deanna again. She agreed to give three workshops at the festival. We're on a roll!

I read a fascinating book until near midnight. "The Writer's Journey: Mythic Structure for Writers", based on Joseph Campbell's writings. I'm amazed that I've unconsciously followed the hero's journey—just have to tighten up here and there. Want to finish the synopsis ... maybe after I finish calling and emailing authors and others to take part in our Writers' Festival.

I learned that a synopsis must be tightly focused to reveal the goals & stakes, the turning points, and the carrying thread of the theme throughout.

Journal Entry

Friday, Dec. 13/02

up at 5 a.m. rewriting and rewriting

9 a.m. Just emailed CBC my piece called "Christmas Sardines".

Saturday, Dec. 14/02

 Listening to North by Northwest on CBC Radio

Just before the 6:30 a.m. news, Sheryl MacKay said she would read a holiday snapshot from Kay McCracken! AND SHE READ MY STORY! This is a first. How thrilling. I've got the bug now. See if anything can stop me … write, write, write. Send material off …

Christmas Sardines

The trailer park in Guadalajara, Mexico has been home to my mom and dad, my eight-year-old daughter and me for five days, but oddly, we've neglected to buy food for Christmas dinner.

After gifts are exchanged Christmas morning I set out to buy a chicken. My rudimentary Spanish skills are tested, however, when I come upon a small market. When my request for "poulet" brings no response, I resort to flapping my arms and scratching the earth with my feet in a brave attempt to procure dinner.

"Pollo!" exclaims the man as he disappears through a door in the back and returns with a squawking chicken tucked under his arm.

"No, gracias," I say shaking my head vigorously. The flustered chicken drops to the ground, does an imitation of me imitating him. That's when I decide to settle for several tins of sardines, a handful of fresh tomatoes, some beans, and a little rice. The gratitude I feel for the tiny tinned fish rises rapidly in relation to the imagined horror of killing and plucking my own dinner.

At our table that evening my daughter pokes a tentative fork at the silvery fish on her plate while dad lifts his glass to toast the Christmas sardines, and to give thanks that I hadn't brought home a live chicken. The laughter and clinking of glasses rings with merriment as we anticipate fresh pineapple for dessert, and perhaps another dip in the pool.

My life became even busier than usual. The email load between Fran and I took precedence, but in the meantime, I organized the monthly coffee houses. I moved the event to the Saga Public Art Gallery, a brick building covered in Virginia creeper not far from where my bookstore used to be. Holding the coffee house in the gallery meant a lot more work on my part, but it was a gorgeous venue.

Richard, a friend from the Writers' Group, helped me. He had MS, but it didn't slow him down in the enthusiasm department. I asked him to get the serve-it-right papers and we picked up wine from one of the local wineries and other things we needed. I arranged for someone else to make the coffee and tea. My sister Karen helped me set up the Gallery with chairs and tables. I invited local musicians to join us as usual and there were no shortage of writers and poets wanting to read. The Coffee Houses were packed with people enjoying themselves.

Journal Entry

Sunday, Dec. 15/02

Wrote a poem about love yesterday. Ah, elusive love. The lilac perfume on the back porch inspired me.

A love poem

With each new day
the lilac bush swells
watered by the rain
showered with love's sunlight

But I deny
my feelings for you
only feed you glimpses of my love
like a shaft of sunlight escaping overcast skies

and still my love grows

The mall was crazy, noisy, packed with Christmas shoppers. Bought Garry Gottfriedson's poetry book "Glass Teepee". Just read several poems and I like where he's coming from. I wish I knew how to pronounce Secwepemc! Gary studied with Allen Ginsberg. Maybe I can interview him at his ranch.

Fran asked me to fill out a loan application. She applied for a loan on our behalf to cover our expenses for the festival. What had I got myself into? I had just signed on to help with this year's writers' festival and here I was signing my life away, and working my ass off. Fran drew up papers to make me her official partner. This was all way too much for me. I didn't have any money, was living with and caring for my mother, was on medication for depression and anxiety. I felt stressed and anxious when Fran threw that into the mix, but it caught me by surprise, so instead of questioning her, I filled out applications, filed documents, thinking that she must know what she was doing. Why was I so trusting? I began to wonder about Fran, however. She, unlike me, didn't have any qualms about getting what she wanted from people. I'd already noticed that at the Surrey Writers' Conference. I already knew that we were very different people. She probably had me figured out right from the beginning.

Thank God our loan application was turned down.

38: Reluctant Chrysalis

I already had three local writers signed up to attend the Writers' Festival. I was overseeing registrations, the writing contest, website submissions from authors, and the printing of brochures. The phone in my bedroom became Festival Central. Contest entries were mailed to me, which I numbered, sorted into categories, and found judges for each age group and genre. I recruited Chris Castanier to judge one category, and Creative Writing Professor, author and poet, John Lent, from Okanagan College in Vernon, to judge another. Andrea Deacon, children's book reviewer, agreed to judge the youth submissions.

Karen and I drove to Kamloops to meet poet Garry Gottfriedson at Starbucks. I'd seen a review of his book *Glass Tepee* in BC Bookworld and understood that he lived near Kamloops. The cover of his book featured a beautiful young man, Garry I supposed, wearing his hair in long braids, adorned with feathers and bead work; the tepee in the foreground appeared transparent. When I contacted him, he had agreed to give a workshop at the inaugural Shuswap Lake International Writers' Festival, now called Word on the Lake Writers' Festival. We were meeting to discuss the details. The author photo on the back of the book featured an older Garry, wearing a white cowboy hat on a head of short black hair.

I read and re-read Garry's poems, a fascinating mixture of contemporary political insight and cultural awareness as it affected the First Nations People.

I laid his poetry book on the table so he'd know who I was when he came in. We spotted each other right away in the crowded coffee shop. *Smooth brown youthful skin, probably in his late forties, but he looks younger. Although maybe everyone looks young now that I'm in my fifties.*

His black hair was cut short, his dark eyes intelligent. Eyes that didn't miss a thing. Quiet, thoughtful, well-spoken, although come to think of it, I'd never met any loud extroverts in the Native community. Beneath his skin, behind those eyes, I sensed an intensity that came through in his work.

He told us he was working as a Counselor for the Kamloops Indian Band, but I also knew that he was a self-employed rancher. What he didn't mention was that he held a Masters Degree in Education from Simon Fraser University, that he taught at the University College of the Cariboo, and that he'd been awarded the Gerald Red Elk Creative Writing Scholarship by the Naropa Institute in Boulder, Colorado, where he studied with Allen Ginsberg and Anne Waldman. He also didn't mention that he'd read from his work across North America and Europe and that his writings had been anthologized and published nationally and internationally. He had two other books published, but this was his first book of poetry, as far as I knew.

When the band chief walked through the door and saw Garry, he came right over and spoke to him in hushed tones. Solemn faces. Trouble on the reserve. A tragedy had occurred. For me, it was an unexpected glimpse into Garry's life, a mysterious world away from my life in Salmon Arm.

Karen and I chatted with Garry for an hour or so. We talked about his poems and I asked about the appearance of Koyoti in several poems, known to us as coyote. He said that Koyoti is like Jesus to his people and that he teaches humility. He added that Koyoti has a powerful purpose and is at work during transitional times.

"That's what Raven is to the coastal and northern peoples," I said. "I only know that because I've been deeply immersed in Raven and First Nations mythology for a book I'm working on."

Garry responded with interest and we chatted about that, too.

Karen and I left Kamloops feeling good about our meeting with Garry, for like me my sister liked and respected First Nations people and their culture. Fran and I both felt strongly about having an Indigenous voice among the presenters at the Writers' Festival, and I felt honoured to find someone from the Secwepemc (Shuswap) Nation with Garry's talent and qualifications.

It was thrilling to find the authors and poets who agreed to attend our Writers' Festival. Deanna suggested we invite poet and artist bill bissett, who lived half time in Toronto and the other half in Vancouver. Deanna had met bissett at the Young Authors' Conference in Kamloops, where they both had taught many times. Before I knew it, he was on board. Bill was known for his anti-conventional style, his concrete and sound poems, his art work, for launching *blewointment press* in Vancouver, and for not using capital letters in his name or his poetry. In the Paris Review, Jack Kerouac called bill bissett the greatest living poet.

    Ann Walsh and her husband would pick bissett up from 100 Mile House and drive to Salmon Arm, where she would give workshops at the festival. She had seven novels for young readers published, mostly set in Barkerville, during the gold rush. But aside from her YA novels set in B.C.'s past, she wrote short stories for adults, poetry, and articles for magazines.

    I talked to Howard White, owner of Harbour Publishing located on the Sunshine Coast. He had an impressive list of authors and poets to draw from. His *Raincoast Chronicles* had sold well in my bookstore. Howard's own book about the life and culture of logging on the coast *Writing in the Rain: Stories, Essays & Poems* won the Stephen Leacock Medal for Humour. Howard had grown up in logging camps. I mentioned that I'd worked at Banyen Books in Vancouver before moving to the Shuswap to start my own bookstore. "Banyen Books didn't order from us. We were too much about logging for their liking," he said. I commiserated, knowing that Harbour Publishing was about much more than logging, for it was regional history of the Pacific Northwest at its best.

    Aside from the interesting people I talked to I continued to struggle with grant applications and handled much of the promotion, calling on businesses, bank managers, booksellers, and others, looking for sponsors. I was pushed way beyond my comfort level when I addressed two separate Rotary Clubs, the breakfast club and the lunch club. There wasn't even time to give it much thought. I had to prepare my talk and jump in. I felt like a reluctant chrysalis, being dragged into harsh daylight, wings still bedraggled, and still in a vulnerable state.

    Mom seemed almost excited about what I was doing, at least she was very supportive. The woman was full of surprises, and sister Karen was helpful in many ways.

Journal Entry

Saturday, December 12, 2002.

Can't seem to get going today. Little Angie, who's very long & thin & tall, sits on my lap as I write this, pricking my green, badly pilled housecoat. She got squirted twice with water this morning, part of her basic training: no jumping on the kitchen table 101; and no eating flowers in vases 102.

More registrations poured in. As festival time drew closer, I was getting less sleep. I had so much on my mind, so many details to take care of and I was running as fast as I could. Is it any wonder I lost weight, not that I needed to. But that could only mean one thing; I had to shop for a new outfit for the gala event Fran and I had planned for opening night of the festival.

39: Butterfly Blues

I thought everything was covered, the folders a team of us had put together were ready to hand out when people checked in, volunteers had been designated for the various tasks, and my June column in the Friday AM was a full page with photos of the authors, poets and other presenters. I had time to eat a late lunch on the back porch, just a moment to catch my breath, relax in the shade of the lilac tree, and more importantly—to paint my toenails, before heading off to the hotel. I'd been up since 4 a.m. The phone at Festival Central had been ringing all day and there were many last-minute details to take care of. Fran had booked into the Prestige that afternoon.

One unexpected call threw me into damage control. A Vancouver literary agent was stranded at the wrong airport—Kamloops instead of Kelowna. My call to Garry Gottfriedson at his ranch in the vicinity of Kamloops saved the day. He'd hired a crew to bring in his hay that day, yet without hesitation he left them to pick up Kathryn Mulders. They arrived together in time for the Gala evening event.

Shelley, a trusted volunteer, appeared, as I was about to take advantage of my porch time to get grounded and paint my toenails. Something needed my attention right away. Off I went, naked toenails and all.

When I stepped inside the lobby of the hotel, it was pandemonium. Frightening even. A crush of people overwhelmed a couple of volunteers at the registration desk and at the blue pencil sign up desk. A woman, her face scrunched in anger, yelled at me. She demanded to know why she hadn't received the information that Ashley Kraas, a literary agent from the United States, wanted the first page of a manuscript handed in before her session.

It looked like an Army and Navy sale with customers fighting over the last pair of size ten shoes. But no, these fans of the written word were trying to get the best interview time with authors and poets, publishers and literary agents.

I phoned Fran from the front desk. "We've got a problem. Get down here right now," I shouted to be heard over the racket in the lobby.

One volunteer hadn't shown up, or had run away, leaving two very confused women to face all the people who had arrived an hour early to register in person. Fran grabbed a stranger coming for the festival and made her an instant volunteer. Fran was great at thinking on her feet, I'll give her that.

After the chaos, I wanted to freshen up in the room that Deanna, Fran, her granddaughter and I would share. The elevator wasn't working! I headed for the stairs right behind Gail Anderson-Dargatz, her husband Floyd, and their young son.

"Shit! What a disaster. I can't believe it," I muttered, trudging up three flights in the insufferably hot stairwell. I knew Gail well enough by then. The stress had finally gotten to me, but I had to get ready for the gala event, which would begin all too soon.

"Don't worry, all festival registrations are like that," Gail said. She sounded calm and didn't even complain about the three flights of stairs to get to their suite.

I hadn't painted my toenails and Fran didn't have time to have her hair done as she'd planned, but the show had to go on.

I should never have underestimated the power that pretty new clothes have to lift my spirits. When I emerged to help set up the ballroom, I wore my beautiful new long skirt and top, dazzling turquoise and blues, my dark hair flowing freely past my shoulders, a touch of pink on my lips. The butterfly was out. She was flying. She caught the sunlight in her wings. I'd moved beyond tired and distraught to happiness, and a kind of euphoria. Fran and I, with the help of Deanna, had pulled off something extraordinary.

As the readings began I took a deep breath, sat back, sipping my glass of red wine. *Ah, the nectar of the gods, or of writers at least ... no wonder creative people drink—too much stimulation is overwhelming.*

40: A Festival to be Proud of

The Friday Evening Gala had put a smile on my face. Jack Whyte's entertaining keynote address reminded us why we had come together. He was a great advocate of schmoozing, something, in his mind at least, best done in the bar, although he didn't say that. He said that's why festivals like ours were a good idea. Writers work in isolation and when they have the opportunity to get out, mingle, and share ideas with other writers it's a good thing. Who can argue with that, although I have to say that Jack is the exception to the notion of writer as a shy introvert. I glanced over at Fran, who was beaming.

Jack's friend Diana Gabaldon had a previous commitment and was unable to attend our festival, but that wasn't much of a setback. As many as twenty authors, editors, agents and publishers gave short readings from their latest work, or talked about the publishing industry and its expectations. When John Weier from Can Copy read his poetry, I sensed the women in the audience, or maybe it was just me, succumbing to his sensual images. *Whew. Another glass of wine please.* I looked at John, the man with a shaved head, tall and well-built with a rough, distinctly unromantic face, and saw him with different eyes after that. When for the rest of the festival, I noticed Fran's daughter schmoozing with him, I felt a twinge of something like envy.

Outrageous, funny, bill bissett may just be from another planet. Blue hat, straw-coloured hair, glasses perched down on his nose. He read his poetry, leaving us breathless from laughing; and his chanting left us just plain breathless. An unexpected joy. Slow carrots, indeed!

Playwright and performer Caitlin Hicks stunned us with her performance of a handicapped woman's plea for acceptance. Having so much talent in one room thrilled all who were present.

But it was Garry Gottfriedson's powerful welcome in his first language, Secwepemc, and again in English, that gave me goose bumps. Fran and I exchanged meaningful glances, and I could see that she felt the same. We had no idea he would do that, but it felt so right.

Deanna, Gail, and all the others were great, too. I felt like I was bursting with happiness at how well the evening was going.

That night, I awoke when someone got up to use the bathroom and couldn't get back to sleep. Sleep deprived and shaky in the morning, nothing felt solid, least of all me. Lack of sleep can do strange things to people and I guess I'd been pushing myself hard for some time. I remember once my father had to drive the trains when the C.P.R. engineers went on strike. He went days without sleep, telling me how disorienting that was. He indicated that lack of sleep can derange the mind.

My mother once told me how terrified and incapacitated my father was when he developed delirium tremens (Latin for "shaking frenzy"), known as *The DTs*. Only 5% of alcoholics will get The DTs, caused by withdrawal from alcohol. The long list of symptoms is horrifying and 15% of people, even with treatment, will die. Without treatment the mortality rate is as high as 35%. A few of the symptoms—severe anxiety, panic attacks, and paranoia—are things I've struggled with, although not from alcohol withdrawal, and indeed I struggled with those symptoms in a milder form that morning after too little sleep several nights in a row.

If the percentage of alcoholics who get The DTs is so low I wonder if my father had a propensity to these conditions. His highly sensitive nature, I'm sure, was to blame. I'd also heard that drunk people don't dream and that our dreams are necessary to process all the things we've heard, seen, and experienced throughout the day. They keep us sane. No wonder alcoholics suffer DTs. I guess the lack of sleep and dream time contributed to how I felt that morning.

Many artists drink to tone down symptoms of high sensitivity, anxiety and other mental illnesses. I find that a glass or two of wine—depending on how stressful the social situation is—helps to soothe the nerves. I also know that I need to be vigilant about the use of alcohol because of the alcoholism in our family.

"If you get into the ring with John Barleycorn often enough he'll eventually beat you," Dad said. He became wise and peaceful working the 12-Step AA program, attending meetings, helping alcoholics in crises, reading, and taking long meditative walks in nature with his German Shepherd named Girl. She'd either been abandoned or lost before adopting my parents.

Fran, Deanna and Fran's granddaughter got ready to go down for breakfast, but feeling fragile in the extreme, I told Fran I wasn't doing well. She said to have a relaxing bath and she'd send breakfast to the room for me. Did she see that I was falling apart? I hope not. In my mind there was nothing worse than someone seeing how vulnerable I was.

I never liked the term "mental illness", because of the stigma. For me, and indeed most people, it's all but impossible to admit to having such problems. The public fear the mentally ill, and who can blame them with the news reports on murders and other horrors committed by a mentally ill person. And there I was having what could be considered a mini breakdown of sorts. Having put so much effort into appearing "normal" most of my life, the fear that I wasn't, and not knowing where that fear came from, it was the fear that threatened me.

Who was I when my strength and determination, my fun-loving, creative self was under the spell of what could only be described as extreme anxiety? How could I face anyone downstairs?

Fortunately, I got my balance back after the warm bath and breakfast and headed downstairs to join the festival. I had wonderful memories of the Gala evening, although we ran out of food almost immediately because I'd miscalculated the number of people. The other thing that happened was the talented band I'd hired was ready to play for hours but people left after the first set. Most of the band had driven from Kamloops. Festival attendees had travelled far and wide to get to the festival and wanted to get to bed in preparation for the day of workshops beginning early the next morning.

Our Blue Pencil appointments were fully booked for Saturday.

Attendees signed up for a ten-minute interview with one of the authors, publishers, literary agents, or editors to have a few pages of their work evaluated. A blue pencil is a pencil traditionally used by an editor to show corrections to a written copy. The colour is used specifically because it will not show in some lithographic or photographic reproduction processes. I hadn't even considered signing up for a blue pencil session, but after a casual conversation with Jonathan Webb, Associate Publisher, Non-Fiction, and Managing Editor with McClelland & Stewart, he invited me to show him what I had.

Mr. Webb and his wife had come to the festival from Toronto. All I had with me was the first page of my manuscript with a couple of things crossed-out and some scribbling in the margins. How I had the nerve to show that to Mr. Webb, I don't know. He showed a keen interest and asked me questions. We chatted. He asked me to send him a section of the book with an outline. I don't think the reality of that request really sank in, and once I re-entered the stream of festival excitement I filed it under the heading, "Did that really just happen?"

My sister Karen worked the book table all weekend for Lloyd, owner of Bookingham Palace Bookstore. She even carted the boxes of books back and forth to his bookstore. She did an amazing job, as did so many of the volunteers. At the end of the final day, Sunday, Karen, Deanna, Dorothy and I retired to the sunny patio at Spirits Bar and Grill, part of the Prestige Hotel. The shimmering lake stretched out before us, and we gasped as an osprey, a large fish hawk, flew over us carrying a big fish in his talons. We all raised a glass of red wine to toast the success of the writers' festival and shared our memories of the last couple of days. Fran was driving one of the authors to the Kelowna airport at the time.

One thing disturbed me, however. Fran seemed to have mentioned my little melt down to people. I felt betrayed, and angry. The seed of mistrust had been planted.

After a meeting with Fran the next day, I had a lot of details and loose ends to tie up. I sent letters and books to all the winners of the writing competition. We already began planning for the next festival, although I wasn't sure if I wanted to work with Fran again. A sense of duty pushed me to finish what we had started. Fran returned home and we continued our email correspondence. In the meantime, the feedback we got from festival participants, including authors, agents and publishers, was outstanding.

I put my book and the request by Jonathan Webb aside, as there was still so much to do regarding the writers' festival, and with Mom and my family. I left my book to languish, or perhaps it was simply coalescing in the cellar of my mind, to become full bodied with time, like a good wine. I could only hope that was the case.

Journal Entry:

Thursday, July 10, 2003.

Up early and working on my book. Phoned Chris Castanier and he said he would look over the 1st 50 pages for me, but not the synopsis. He'll come by next week with the packaged organic lamb for us.

But today there's still stuff to deal with. Big mix up with American and Canadian cheques that for some reason I had to sort out by running around, back & forth to the banks etc. Giant headache. What was Fran thinking?

Saw Dr. H. yesterday and as usual he put things in perspective for me. He said to put the outline down and email off my 50 pages 1st! Then I can focus on everybody else's stuff. He told me that I put other people's needs before my own and to honour that about myself, but to find some balance in that. Something else Dr. H. said stunned me: he acknowledged my qualities of compassion, devotion and bravery. Never having heard such things before, it felt strange.

And yesterday I ran into a woman who said much the same thing ... that I create beautiful places and events for others (she'd heard what a huge success the Writers' Festival had been and wasn't surprised because she remembered how I created my beloved bookstore with such care and attention). She said that my attention to detail and ambiance creates places where people feel good, and that I'm wonderful with people. That's a lot to take in.

Right now, the world is looking a lot happier and friendlier. I'm happy with my revisions so far. Just have to find out what's involved in an outline. Emailed Jonathan Webb.

Saturday, July 12/03
It is beautiful out here on the porch. I'm in my housecoat because it's early—no people, no cars ... enjoying the way the light is shinning through the olive coloured leaves of the Japanese maple trees, the red seed pods, the light and shadow playing on the deck, the crow who lives in the tall fir trees across the street chattering, and the mauve and pink petunias luminous as they greet the glorious day.

Bad night though ... had to phone the police once ... people howling in the streets and in our alley. Was awakened around 2 a.m. again.

I'm so looking forward to working on my book and outline.

The air is fresh and cool this morning, unlike the stifling heat in our apartment last night, and that with all 3 fans going all day. Patrick, the deejay across the hall installed a ceiling fan in Mom's room the day before. Mom adores Patrick and listens to him on her radio.

41: Xcellent Birds

With blackbirds, ravens, magpies, red tailed hawks, great blue herons and other birds appearing in the book I was working on, what happened next is somewhat hard to explain. Take one very quirky poet named bill bissett, a river, a hot summer day and me, and my journey veers off into the mystic again. My tombstone will read: She sailed into the mystic … Van Morrison.

At the writers' festival, bill, the court jester, teetered down the vast courtly halls of the Prestige, blue hat perched on his head, chanting "excellent, excellent, excellent" because everything in bill's world *is* excellent. Laughter bubbled up in me as I watched him and I'd shout "excellent" after him. He'd retort "excellent", then I would echo him, and back and forth it went like that … transforming the landscape of the writers' festival … a pied piper, leading poetry enthusiasts into a magic place made of sound and words.

That summer bill visited Salmon Arm and brought his friend Helen from Vancouver. They stayed with Shelley and Ronn, and I was invited to join them at the Art Gallery. From there we had lunch sitting on the spacious deck of the Prestige Hotel, literally a stone's throw from the Shuswap Lake. The next day we drove to Enderby, crossed the bridge, parked under the tall river trees, and walked down a bank to the river's sandy shore.

When bill threw off his shirt, I was startled at the sight of his stomach, which was a mass of thick scar tissue. I'd never seen anything like it, and averted my eyes, not knowing what to say.

After the book *radiant danse uv being: a poetic portrait of bill bissett* was published I read that bill had wanted to be a ballet dancer and a figure skater. Those dreams were dashed when as a ten-year-old boy he began two years of abdominal operations for peritonitis. It occurred to him that he could write and paint and that would be his way of letting words and images "danse" on the paper or canvas.

bill and I took our time wading into the cool river, chatting while standing knee deep and then waist deep under the blazing sun. We finally swam to an island, where we marveled over wild strawberry plants next to wild animal paw prints hidden amid the foliage.

After dragging ourselves out of the Shuswap River, bill and I, along with Shelley, Ronn, and Helen walked back up the embankment. Standing stock—still at the top of the bank and overlooking the river were four unusual birds. They didn't fly away from us or make a sound. Dumbfounded, we pondered the situation. These birds weren't acting birdlike at all.

At any rate it was time to leave and the gang dropped me off at home. My clothes were heavy with sand and water logged. I could barely move after exerting the energy to swim in the river.

I lay in a warm bath for a long time. It took ages to get warm and gain my strength back. That night I was inspired to write a poem about the swim in the river with bill. When he dropped by in the morning to say goodbye, I let him read the poem, which he graciously acknowledged. After chatting with Mom, who was pleased to meet bill and Helen, they left. Mom enjoyed company, no matter who it was, and especially, I noticed, if one of the visitors was male.

Xcellent Birds

half our clothes off
bill, Helen, and i follow Ronn
under Enderby Bridge
into Shuswap River

bill says he and i are
easy going gradualists
because of the way
we approach the river

we have become river gods
and goddesses, now transformed
by river smell and penetrating sun
that drives us into cool water

bill and i swim to an island
where everything is different
a wolf print lingers among wild
strawberry plants

when we leave the river
soggy clothes heavy with sand
we come across four silent
grounded birds

they stand poised on a cliff

while we cluck and coo over them
wondering our human questions
but these silent birds are a mystery

they may be doves, i say
there are 4 of us and 4 doves, offers Helen
doves are love, says Ronn
xcellent beautiful xcellent, says bill

we all agree but later when i search
my bird books, unable to identify them,
i'm mystified maybe it was a group
      hallucination, says bill, or maybe

      it was the way we approached the river.

(Edited version that appeared in *radiant danse of being, a poetic portrait of bill bissett.* Nightwood Editions, 2006)

Part Four

It's Never Too Late to Reinvent Your Life

> "Our mistakes make the best stories,
> and that's why we should not think of them as failures."
> Susan Musgrave
>
> (BC BookWorld, Spring 2015)

42: Timing is Everything!

When I did resume working on my book, I did so with a vengeance. By the time I had the outline and the book ready, it was almost a year later, June 4th, 2004. I sent everything off to Mr. Webb at McClelland & Stewart with a cover letter. I had kept in touch with him by email, so he knew my manuscript was still coming his way and he was still very much interested.

My writing buddies in my Cheap Tuesday writers group were appalled. Miranda couldn't believe that I would set aside something as potentially life changing as a request to send my work to McClelland Stewart Publishers in order to continue working on the writers' festival. I had to admit that she was right, but when I take on a commitment nothing can shake me loose. Remembering the dying days of my bookstore Reflections and how I went down with the ship, so to speak, all because of the pit bull grip I bring to projects. I wonder what that's about? Dedication? Stubbornness? Stupidity? Or was it simply a driving need to prove to myself and others that I could succeed?

Even with my reservations about Fran, I found myself pressured into becoming president of SAW, the Shuswap Association of Writers, the non-profit organization created by Fran to take advantage of grant money. She needed a board of directors. She called a meeting. Dave Harper presented a slide show meant to inspire us. An awkward silence followed when no one stepped forward to fill the board positions. Dave said "We have great parties." That broke the ice.

Dave had set up our festival website the year before, and designed the posters and brochure, something he did on a freelance basis, as well as teaching courses for Continuing Education at our local College. We were becoming friends in the process of working together and Fran gave him steady work on her Agri Digest. I figured if Dave could take on a board position, then so could I. How's that for rational thinking?

So it came to pass that we now had a board of directors, with Fran as the self-appointed festival coordinator. My buddy, Deanna, became a director at large. She couldn't come to meetings because of the distance she would have to travel, complicated by the fact that she didn't drive.

The excitement had been building for the June Writers' Festival. We had another outrageous line up of great authors, agents, editors, and publishers: Robert Sawyer, Terry Brooks, Gregory Schofield, Audrey Thomas, Kathryn Cole, Deborah Hodge, Steven Galloway, Sarah Ellis, with literary agents Kathryn Mulders, Carolyn Swayze, Kathryn Cole, and Johanna Bates. Several popular authors from the previous year were invited back, including bill bissett, Garry Gottfrienson, Gail Anderson-Dargatz, Jack Whyte, Ann Walsh, Deanna Kawatski, and a few more. Representatives from publishing houses Heritage House/Touchwood/Rocky Mountain Books and Raincoast Books said they would attend.

Fran convinced another new friend, Bob Beeson, to offer a workshop. Bob wrote and illustrated children's books and worked for a local printer. Fran could never do anything half way. It was over the top, or nothing. We had lost money the first year, so it wasn't prudent to invite so many authors and others who all had to be paid, fed, put up at the Prestige Hotel, as well as paying their travel expenses, but Fran had her way.

I acted as the host to greet our authors at the hotel and walked them a short distance to the boat launch where the Wanda Sue paddle wheeler was waiting to take our guests on a relaxing tour of the Salmon Arm Bay. We asked Dave, who also taught local history at the college, to share his knowledge with the authors as the Wanda Sue paddled serenely through the blue waters of Shuswap Lake to Harold Park and back.

The next morning, Deanna said, "Have you heard the news about Jonathan Webb?"

"No, what?"

"He's been let go."

"Are you serious!"

Deanna affirmed what I could hardly believe.

"Crap, there goes that," I said. "Finished before I even start."

In retrospect, I'd say that Miranda and my Cheap Tuesday Writers' Group were right when they said to put great opportunities before non-paying volunteer work, no matter how noble the cause. I guess my priorities were all mixed up, but I felt passionately about the writers' festival and the importance of the event for the community, and indeed for all writers. I also felt strongly about carrying out my commitment.

43: The Wheel of Fortune Keeps Turning

I received a polite rejection letter from McClelland & Stewart, informing me that Jonathan Webb was no longer with them, but the ramifications of bad decisions and bad luck don't last forever. The wheel of fortune kept turning, stopping on "lucky break".

Karen Bissenden, a local poet who had joined our Cheap Tuesday Writers' Group, called me to say there was a book being put together with poems about bill bissett. She had heard the poem I'd written and encouraged me to send it to the editors, telling me that she sent in the poem she'd written about bill. She took the liberty of sending my name along to the editors, who then contacted me.

Journal Entry:

Tuesday, July 20, 2004

I had a surprise upon opening my emails, after reading one from Fran and one from Deanna—there's one from jeff & rox. It started "dear Kay ... we have narrowed the submissions of poems about bill bissett down to 65 from 127 (I'm still totally calm at this point thinking that they're going to tell me that I didn't make it into the anthology and that's what I was expecting and only sent it because Karen passed my name along to them).

What! They say my poem was accepted! Before reading on I ran shouting into Mom's room and I'm getting goose bumps all over and can hardly believe what I'm reading because I know that submissions came from big-name, award-winning, accomplished poets from all across Canada.

I couldn't believe my good fortune. They edited it but kept the best part of the poem and gave it the title "xcellent birds". Emails were flying back and forth between the editors Jeff Pew, Stephen Roxborough, and me. Then came news of a Vancouver launch for the book. There would also be a Toronto launch, and a Vancouver Island launch. Karen and I were in illustrious company with the likes of Margaret Atwood, George Bowering, Brian Brett, Leonard Cohen, Lorna Crozier, Patrick Lane, Susan Musgrave, bpNichol, P.K. Page, Sharon Thesen, Tom Walmsley, sheri-d wilson and many, many more.

I sent an email saying that I would read my poem at the Vancouver launch of the book radiant danse of being: a poetic portrait of bill bissett.

44: Robbie and Stormy Arrive

My first great grandchild came into the world March 2nd, 2004. Shasta met John in Salmon Arm, became pregnant, and they moved to Whitehorse, where John's mother and sister lived.

Shasta said they would be driving to Salmon Arm, perhaps in September, with Robbie, their Jack Russell Terrier, a kitten, and as much of their belongings as they could stuff in their small car. These kinds of stories are guaranteed to give great grandmothers heart palpitations.

For some time, things had been getting worse for me. My daughter had met someone and they fought constantly, making family dinners unpleasant. Peter was a sweet young man, but out of his depth when he caught the goddess of his dreams—my daughter, a beautiful older woman. Teri-Ann, a.k.a. Nahanni, the name her father had given her when she entered her teen years, was a name she preferred at the time. He had taken the name from his time working in the Nahanni Valley of BC, also known as the headless valley. The headless valley reference had always given me pause. Was it a good idea for Terry to give his daughter a name with such a sinister history, granted Nahanni was a beautiful name, but two men had been found without their heads in the valley, a mystery that had never been solved.

My daughter had been diagnosed with post-traumatic stress disorder, commonly referred to as PTSD. The diagnosis explained some of her behaviour at least. It's not just soldiers who suffer with PTSD, which is a severe anxiety disorder that can develop after exposure to any event that results in psychological trauma. The event may involve the threat of death to oneself or to someone else, or to one's own or someone else's physical, sexual, or psychological integrity, overwhelming the individual's ability to cope. Nothing was going well for my daughter, and I was worried.

Considering how prevalent sexual abuse is, one in three women, and although the number of men may not be as high—the result is just as debilitating—a large number of people cope in whatever way they can, although their quality of life suffers. Self-medicating with drugs and alcohol is all too common in people with PTSD. In the long term those ways of coping make things worse. Suicide starts to look preferable to the living hell for those with broken spirits and deep psychic wounds.

Shasta began having seizures when she and John lived down the block from Mom and I. The childhood car accident that almost killed her had left her susceptible to seizures and other problems. She was on medication for that, and for her panic attacks. Before Shasta met John, she had quit school after being humiliated, bullied and threatened by a few mean girls. Her self-esteem suffered. She began running with the worst crowd in Salmon Arm. She went missing a few times and I drove around looking for her. At one party, a girl threw her down the stairs—not a good thing for a girl with a head injury and prone to seizures. Things kept getting worse.

And into the darkness, a ray of light arrived to spread some joy. We had an unexpected visit from John, Shasta, and little Robbie on a hot afternoon in late August. Robbie's beautiful face and beaming smile outshone the sun that day. Mom and I fell in love. Shasta said he was happy because they were so happy. *Thank God for that.* I'd heard a disturbing report from Teri-Ann who had flown to Whitehorse to help after the birth, but on the surface at least everything seemed fine.

Shasta asked if they could leave their kitten for a couple of days, just until they found a place to live, as they would be staying with John's grandparents, who had a dog. Our furry little guest scampered about the apartment like a wee nymph; she was black and white-part sun beam, part moon beam. Shasta said she named her Stormy because of the way she thundered up and down the hallway of their mobile home.

Shasta and John didn't settle in their own place right away so Mom and I found ourselves inheriting a third cat. She was fun and full of curiosity and she had black toe pads, except for one pink one! I found that oddly endearing, as Bridgey and Angie both had pink toe-pads.

Another black and white female kitten had come into our life. We hadn't asked for any of them. They had asked for us, or so the veterinarian said. A sooth-saying veterinarian, how interesting. I do recall seeing him in my bookstore from time to time. He, like almost any vet I'd ever met, was incredibly kind and gentle, as you would expect an animal lover to be.

I asked Teri-Ann what she thought the significance of all the black and white was. She immediately replied "yin and yang." *Oh, ya. Balance.* The very thing I need to be reminded of constantly, and now I had three sweet little reminders.

I was very surprised that my mother accepted Katie into our household. She wasn't worried about what the owner of the apartment would say, or what anyone thought about us having three cats. This was a side of Mom I hadn't seen before, as she was normally overly concerned about doing things by the book, and never upsetting neighbours. If I were a Freudian, I'd say that her superego—that part of our personality that is highly influenced by society's and parental rules—was normally in charge. It appears my mother's brain had changed in more ways than I realized, or had I missed that part of her. The lovely thing is that we bonded over our love of animals; we had both fallen in love with the newest edition to our family.

45: More Poetry

I enjoyed a poetry course at the college that spring and came out of it with a poem I liked. Without realizing it, I'd written a poem that seemed to create the balance of yin and yang.

March

She blew in like one of the furies this morning
blew in pounding the earth with lashing rain,
rain that pummelled the streets into torrents.

Her gales came blowing down the mountainside
screaming across the valley
shaking trees in her bony fingers.

Full of wild churning energy
like a banshee possessed
she danced our wind chimes into a frenzy.

When she's vented her wrath,
clocks are left blinking
computer screens gaping.

In the wake of that mood
sweet notes heralded a change
a robin sang from his dark dripping branch.

Wait long enough and everything changes, one way or the other. One thing I knew for certain was that when I used my creativity, the world felt like a much happier place.

More poetry emerged in the days and weeks that followed.

Survivors

raucous, comical

ubiquitous

crow

a punk with street smarts

gypsies and outlaws

who find safety in numbers

they come mired in myth

making them bolder yet

not showy like peacock

or sweet of song

like sparrow

at home everywhere

in alleys of asphalt

where garbage bins provide treats

of egg foo young and shrimp fried rice,

where a man slumps, needle still in his arm

neon signs along Hastings Street
shimmer in puddles pooling on dark sidewalks

crow hops and struts
the colours reflected in his bright eye
eyes that find opportunity
everywhere

in Salmon Arm
from my back porch
I watch black sentinels perched in fragrant trees
among the apple blossoms
cawing, cawing

while a single crow,
perched on a clothesline post,
scolds the cat below.

Edited March 11, 2007.

Another birthday and I was having qualms about getting older. The number fifty-seven seemed daunting.

April: a girl lives

April, also known as "budding trees moon"
the month that delivered me

my BIRTH day

wow
never thought
I'd live this long

the words crone, elder, or wisdom years
don't seem to resonate

maybe a walk
along the bird sanctuary
will lift my spirits

the air smells delicious
is alive with flight
and the ecstatic trill
of red wing blackbirds

pussy willows surprise
protruding from bare stalks
a smile

reaches

the daylight of my lips

pale grasses

weave tapestries of distinctive beauty

while new shoots

push forward

  green and glistening

beneath the lines on my face

a girl lives ...

Written April 8th, 2004.

Writing the poem made me feel better. I shared it with Deanna that evening at the Mexican Restaurant where I'd organized a bunch of us with April birthdays to celebrate together.

46: Artistic Personality

Journal Entry:

Sunday August 22, 2004

Angie is most unhappy and is hiding out under Mom's bed growling whenever Stormy comes by. Stormy wants to play with my cats but they won't have anything to do with her. Mom and I didn't feel she was a "Stormy" so we were calling her kitty, which morphed into Katie. Unlike my two, she doesn't use her claws when we play with her. She's Katie One-Pink-Toe, a.k.a. Katie the Cutie. Angie Bo-Bangie (my nickname for her) and Beautiful Bridgey both had adjustments to make.

I worry constantly, only the worry has been dulled somewhat by the anti-anxiety drug I started taking on Thursday.

I talked to my doctor. I had switched to a doctor at the clinic, not because I didn't like my other doctor, but because she was often delivering babies. When he took me on as a patient, he read my entire file, including a letter from Dr. H.

"You have an artistic personality," he said after reading the file. I don't know why I didn't ask him what he meant by that but I imagined it meant something about the emotional ups and downs that artists deal with.

Told him how I'd been feeling worse and worse lately. I said tell me what's wrong with me, doctor. He said, you have "generalized anxiety disorder." Oh great! I am nuts. But the anxiety and tearfulness and constant stressed out feeling had been getting worse for some time—to the point where I knew something was terribly wrong. I felt weighed down and shaky, *had heart palpitations, and was nauseous, which I thought may be a result of the medication.*

Doctor said to persist with the pills for two weeks. I guess the medication knocks you out so you don't have the energy to worry as much. Depression and anxiety go hand in hand.

David Keisey's *Please Understand Me: Character and Temperament Types,* first published in 1978, says that people with an artistic temperament tend to experience a greater range of emotion than other types, and that we can be emotionally reactive. We spend a lot of time alone and have superior powers of concentration.

Keisey also points out that artistic types alternate between the greatest extremes of sociability and social reticence. They possess an instinctive longing for the natural, the pastoral, and are quite at home in the wilds; nature seems to welcome them.

I could see myself in the description of the artistic temperament, but that made me think if that's who I am why did I never recognize that I may be a creative person. No one ever encouraged me in the arts. I didn't do well in school, so I guess people thought I was dumb. These days I think it's generally known that there are different types of intelligence. But the damage had already been done to my self-esteem at a young age. My mother did give me piano lessons, although I didn't continue for long. Of all the things that I did in school, I only remember several art projects that absorbed me, and the writing I did once, and that's about it.

I couldn't understand why I was getting worse. For a while I was doing well, so I had stopped taking the antidepressants that my doctor prescribed. But things started piling up, crashing in on me. It was frightening. I became testy, angry, moody.

Anxiety that doesn't go away gets worse over time. Anxiety disorders include panic disorder, obsessive-compulsive disorder, post-traumatic stress disorder, phobias, social anxiety disorder, and generalized anxiety disorder. By that time, I realized that at least four generations of my family struggled with anxiety issues, resulting in health problems: my mother, me, my daughter, and granddaughter. My daughter had a lot of health issues, my mother had been strong at one time in her life, but had crumbled a few times along the way, and my health had been suffering for some time. On and on it seemed to go, generation after generation.

    As the eldest, I may have been witness to more than the other kids. I doubt if my father noticed that our mother was exhausted and stressed. The two years in Toronto may have been the worst. The poor woman found herself stuck in the suburbs without a friend, or help with her five children. Our father worked in the city and arrived home at the end of the day to the neighbour woman inviting him to have a beer with her.

    I remember my mother screaming and screaming, as she stood on our porch, in ear shot of the woman and my father sitting at an open window, drinking beer. If she lost it, who could blame her? Help for housewives was non-existent in those days. Wives and mothers didn't go to psychologists or psychiatrists back then, well maybe if you were rich or a movie star. My mother didn't take medication and she didn't take to drink. My friend's mother down the street took dishes into the basement and smashed them against the cement floor to release her anger. Poor Mom had no outlet for an unjust life. She had married a drinker.

    Mom told me how after they were married, Dad used to stay out all night gambling and drinking with his single friends. I don't think she ever got over that, as she told that story with great bitterness over and over again. She had babies to look after, a yard, an apple orchard, and pigs to feed.

    Mom had been raised in a tight-knit community in Revelstoke surrounded by family and friends. She enjoyed church, singing in the choir, sports, dances, and a family who never became slaves to alcohol. She had married into a wealthy upper-class family, she who grew up without a father, and very poor. My father's mother, according to Dad, felt superior to many people. He never understood why. His father was a general superintendent with the Canadian Pacific Railway, a lofty position. My poor mother, trying to fit into a family that was so completely different from her upbringing. I don't know how she did it.

In Calgary I may have been ten or eleven my parents sent me to a doctor, something I don't remember. Apparently, I told him I thought my mother didn't love me. I sucked my thumb to an unacceptable age, which may be why they sent me. My mother's mother had come to stay with us, had fallen stepping off a curb, and broken both ankles. So along with looking after her mother, five children (I remember some crazy out-of-control scenes), and dealing with her husband drinking more than ever, is it any wonder she was overwhelmed and a little nutty.

In all probability my mother was depressed and therefore she couldn't nurture the kids properly, and I'm thinking of Toronto, too, when I say that. Strange as it seems, I took my father aside and told him I thought I was going crazy. I was a just a kid, but I had a psychologically absent mother (exhaustion and depression) and father (work and alcohol). I think I muddled along the best I could. My brothers played various sports, but our father never went to any of their games. How strange that seems. Both my brothers are devoted fathers who encourage their children in everything they do.

Some of my best childhood memories spring from that time in Toronto, despite the problems at home. The best of times and the worst of times. In the winter there were frozen streams in the woods to skate on, or the outdoor ice rink in the school yard. In the summer, we built forts in the woods, rode our bikes, and I caught frogs to feed to my pet garter snake. I paid for my own horseback riding lessons by washing neighbour's cars. It was in Toronto that I had my most favourite teacher ever. I can still see her crooked teeth and her faded blue dress stretched so tight over her large bosom that the strained buttons looked as if they might pop open at any moment. But she was kind, and that's all that mattered. I wrote my first story in her class, an experience I shall never forget. I had wonderful friends and we did really interesting things, like taking the bus and then the subway to down town Toronto to visit the museum. I remember being awed by the Egyptian room and the mummies.

47: Writers' Festival, 2005

I was still the president of SAW, still working my butt off for the 3rd festival when it became very apparent that all was not well. The board and Fran were at serious odds over several aspects of the 2005 Writers' Festival.

Fran invited Will Millar, of the Irish Rovers, to give an outdoor concert as part of the festival. This idea of hers had been voted against by the board because of the expense, but that didn't faze Fran. The west coast Celtic band, Tiller's Folly, was also invited. That meant huge set up fees for the stage in a school field, not to mention the fee for Will Millar and Tiller's Folly.

The lineup of presenters, although stellar, was over the top. Friday included a song-writing competition and a story-telling competition at the theatre. Saturday morning, I introduced Arthur Black who gave the keynote address. Saturday and Sunday workshops, interviews, outdoor performances, and readings at venues around town became a nightmare to organize and promote. George Bowering and Deanna Kawatski read to a large crowd at the Art Gallery, although most other venues were not well attended.

Sharon Butala, Kathleen Flaherty, a CBC Radio producer, Alex Forbes, Lee Maracle, Sid Marty, Simon Rose, Gregory Schofield, Dona Sturmanis, Diane Swanson, AlanTwigg, Ann Walsh, Joan Weir, including George Bowering and Deanna offered workshops Saturday and Sunday. Jack Whyte, bill bissett, and Garry Gottfriedson had been brought back, too. Howard White of Harbour Publishing had agreed to judge the storytelling competition.

Salmon Arm's three presenters included Les Ellenor–Making magic worlds: the fantasy of JRR Tolkien, CS Lewis, and JK Rowling, Tom Moen sharing Natalie Goldberg writing skills, and Shirley Tucker, Fine Arts teacher, actress, playwright and author. She won the first annual Heritage Group Writing Prize with her non-fiction book proposal, *The Great*

Transcontinental Hike of 1921. Over the previous ten years, Shirley had written, produced and designed six full-length plays. I always enjoyed her visits to Reflections while she was working on a play at the theatre just around the corner from my bookstore.

    I had to get Alan Twigg and Sid Marty to the Java Jive café as part of the free public readings during Saturday afternoon, and then back to the Prestige Hotel. I had put signs up at the cafe earlier that morning.

    Despite the signs and a program of events in local papers, the handful of people having coffee looked bewildered, but I launched into my introduction anyway.

    "Sid Marty and his family live on an old farm in southwestern Alberta. He's a conservationist, songwriter, musician, non-fiction author, and a poet. His non-fiction book, *Leaning on the Wind: Under the Spell of the Great Chinook,* was a finalist for the 1996 Governor General's literary award. We are excited to have him take part in our Writers' Festival this weekend."

    Sid stepped forward, a big, rugged-looking man with a beard. He wore a brown, wide-brimmed hat, an attractive mountain-man. His pretty wife had come with him to the festival and she sat in the café lending her support.

    Sid talked about his life, his writing, his thoughts and feelings on aging before reading from his book. He said when he reached middle age he noticed that he became invisible to women. That was the first time I'd heard a man say that. Women were familiar with the phenomenon, but it was a revelation to hear a man admit it. But why would it be? Don't we all—no matter how old, or what gender—wish to be acknowledged, admired even? Who wants to be invisible after a certain age?

    Sid finished his reading. Applause. I stood up.

    More people wandered in and I encouraged them to have a seat. I acknowledged a professor from the college with a nod.

    "I'm about to introduce another author, Alan Twigg," I said, competing with the hissing of the espresso machine, the clatter of dishes, the chatter of staff and customers.

    I looked toward Alan, a slender man framed by large windows that allowed the luminous June sunlight in. He smiled. In contrast to Sid, Alan was clean shaven, with dark, curly hair. Younger than Sid and me, attractive.

"Alan Twigg has owned and published BC BookWorld magazine since 1988. You can pick up your free copy of this wonderful resource for readers and writers at any bookstore or library. Alan is a historian, prolific author, photographer, soccer player and musician. And that's not all. He developed a free on-line reference site of over 7,000 authors, and his 10-year project involved the literary history of B.C."

I paused, then added, "Alan read at an outdoor performance at Marine Park last night with Jack Whyte, Arthur Black, Alex Forbes, Tom Moen, Garry Gottfriedson, Dona Sturmanis, and the storyteller competition's top two winners, plus a performance by Howard White of Harbour Publishing, one of the storytelling judges. Please welcome Alan Twigg."

Alan chose to play music and sing instead of reading from one of his books, an enjoyable surprise for all present.

Back at the Prestige Hotel, Alan suggested that we get a glass of wine, so off we headed to Spirits Bar and Grill, overlooking the shimmering Shuswap Lake. With a glass of red wine each, Alan told me about his frightening ordeal with a brain tumor. He woke up one day and didn't remember the names of his sons, and he couldn't write—devastating for a writer. He was rushed into surgery.

After the five-hour operation to remove a large tumor, Alan started writing again in the Intensive Care Unit just a few hours later.

The hand-written notes turned into a small book, *Intensive Care: A Memoir,* an honest and revealing exploration of Alan's year post surgery. The imminence of death can greatly enhance life, wrote Twigg. "Confirmation that one is loved can be exhilarating, more powerful than any drug."

We talked about my granddaughter Shasta and her long journey of recovery after the car accident she somehow survived when she was four years old. She suffered severe head trauma and third degree burns to her body. I didn't often talk about that, as it was too painful, but Alan was so honest about his own struggle to come back that I felt comfortable discussing Shasta's nightmare with him. After the festival, I gave Alan's book to Shasta and she found it just as fascinating as I did.

The performances by Will Millar and Tiller's Folly were rained out. I had to hand it to Fran—she dreamed big, but she didn't dream practical.

After the sparsely attended outdoor concert, an impromptu jam session took place in Spirits Bar and Grill with Tiller's Folly, and a local band called Cats and the Fiddle, a group of talented young women from Salmon Arm. Jack Whyte jumped in, moved by the great music and energy, to sing a song with them.

We were left with a huge debt after that festival, and we discovered that Fran had been putting things on her credit cards. No one had authorized her to do that. I was responsible for organizing the AGM and frankly I was desperate to hand over the job of president to someone else.

48: Divided Loyalties

After Fran delivered her financial report at the AGM, which was unclear and inconclusive, the audience sat in dumbfounded silence. The only thing that was clear was that third festival had left a substantial debt.

A woman from the back of the room spoke up. Everyone turned to see who the husky voice belonged to. Deanna and I sat at the front of the room, facing about twenty-five to thirty people in the meeting room at the Baptist Church.

I peered at the stalky woman of medium height standing at the back of the room asking questions. She seemed quite sure of herself, almost aggressively so. She wore a wide-brimmed, floppy hat. Long dark curls partly veiled her face, and with the light from the windows behind her I didn't have a clear view of her features. What I did have was a feeling about her that I didn't know how to put my finger on.

Who was she and where did she come from?

I had invited Ineke, a woman I knew, to put her name forward as president. I thought she'd be great, but after the disjointed financial report and knowledge of the large debt, nobody stepped forward.

We all agreed that we needed another AGM. Inside I was screaming NO. It had been a lot of work to get this one organized and there was so much tension between the board and Fran at this point that it was painful.

Two AGM's later, Mystery Woman, I'll call her MW—the stranger that spoke up from the back of the room—became president. Ineke had been voted vice-president, and Sally Scales, a newspaper woman in Salmon Arm, took over as Festival Coordinator. The Prestige Inn was represented at that meeting, as the hotel was owed money. The manager offered to let The Shuswap Association of Writers pay down the debt in increments, with assurance that we would be fund raising to do so. He told us that the Prestige was happy to continue hosting the Writers' Festival.

I finally allowed myself to relax after giving my president's report, knowing that now we had a new board in place. I looked toward MW, smiled and gave her the "thumbs up" to show my support, although the look in her eyes as she stared at me wasn't what I expected to see. I didn't know what her cold gaze meant or what was behind it, but it left me feeling uneasy.

As the days passed, I did my best to answer the landslide of email questions from MW. She wanted to be brought up to speed before the first board meeting. I admit I was exhausted and therefore probably short on patience, but I did my best to answer her questions. The curt, almost rude tone of her emails rankled me, although I didn't say anything and persisted in helping her.

A date was set for the first board meeting and Ineke invited me to bring information and files to the meeting. I was looking forward to the gathering of the new board, as I knew everyone and was happy to see them get started. I looked forward to stepping back, way back from the position of president.

That was before I saw the email from MW that I wasn't supposed to see, the email that started a war.

The email addressed to another board member was nasty in its criticism of me. Hurt feelings turned to anger in a flash. The fighting Irish in me felt deeply offended. I sent an email to the board saying that I wouldn't be at the meeting. I didn't want anything more to do with MW and I said so. The worst word I used was "rude" and maybe "dismissive;" other than those words that implied a judgment, I used no vicious personal attacks of any kind, no four-letter words, no slander.

The meeting of the board continued without me. By the end of that meeting, my friend Maureen, who had signed on as secretary, had been reduced to tears and quit the very same night.

Maureen, a professional editor, had edited my manuscript. I had learned a lot from her thorough and thoughtful editing. She said I should send my mss to Sharon Butala. I'm not doing that, I said, completely nonplussed by her suggestion. I'd had dinner with Sharon and her husband—at Chris Castanier's invitation –before she gave a talk that Chris had arranged at the college. We had a lovely time and Sharon enjoyed herself, but she was an award-winning author and I was nobody.

Maureen was persistent. I followed through and received a very favourable response to my writing from Sharon. My shocked response tells me that I didn't yet have confidence in my writing. Sharon's encouragement, and Maureen's, meant of great deal to me.

Poor Maureen, what had MW done to upset her, and why, since she was only there to help. From what I heard about the meeting, I became even more convinced that something bizarre was going on.

This is where my life started to resemble the fantastical world of Alice in Wonderland. MW was the Queen of Hearts. She ruled, and that was clear from the meeting. Her vindictive nature knew no bounds and all her anger focused on me. *Off with her head! Off with her head!* She began sending out emails to everyone in the writing community accusing me of things.

Her words were blows that stunned me, and the emails kept up relentlessly. On top of burning out in my attempt to help, now I was being crucified, each criticism another barb meant to tear down my confidence. After reading about my unkindness, martyrdom, lack of generosity, resistance to change, how I wanted to ride in and rescue the Board, and how I messed with people's lives, I felt sick. *I can't read any more of this.* I stopped reading emails and answering my phone.

What was this really about? The insidious gnawing at my self-image was frightening, there's no denying that. Wasps at a carcass. But I wasn't dead yet. Maybe if I'd been a weaker person. By that time in my journey, I felt strong about who I was at least.

It was the silence that scared me; the silence of all but a couple of people—and even they didn't really know what to say. It added a feeling of alienation to the strange situation. Like Alice, I suddenly found myself alone in an unfamiliar landscape, not quite Wonderland, but more than a little disorienting.

Have I been condemned by my friends? I can handle MW's thoughts about me. They mean nothing because she doesn't know me, but if my writing community feels the same way I'm devastated.

Perhaps board members and others were in shock, much like I was. I, and now they, knew the extent of Mystery Woman's wrath.

In a revealing email to Fran, MW said she understood Fran's frustration in working with the old board. *So that's where she heard about the AGM! All was becoming clear. In an even earlier email, MW had criticized Fran. Curiouser and curiouser.*

It became clear that MW's harsh personal attacks weren't going to stop. No use sticking my head in the sand any longer. I sat down at my computer and wrote a long email to her and to the board, and it was at that point I mentioned I would be contacting a lawyer, which I did. I had printed out the slanderous emails.

"Does she have any money?" the lawyer asked. I had no idea. Soon after, MW, which morphed into Misery Woman in my mind, withdrew as president of SAW, stating personal problems.

Many friends came to my aid, but there was confusion, hurt feelings, misconceptions, and divided loyalties. A few people thought that Fran was being treated badly. It was not the writers' festivals finest hour.

The painful experience that threatened to bring down the festival, that fractured loyalties, that had me questioning who my friends were, allowed me to find my voice in yet another way. When I'd finally had enough of Misery's slanderous emails, I fought back with my writing.

The ordeal taught me many things: I learned that I'm far stronger than I thought, that I have a lot of friends in the community who ultimately stood by me, and that my writing and my sense of humour got me through a tough time. I didn't roll over and play dead. I suggested in the email that if MW was a spiritual healer, which she purported to be, then I was Mother Teresa. That made me laugh out loud as I typed it. I wasn't the one dragging her name and reputation through the mud, as she was doing to me. And all that because I refused to go to a meeting that she hadn't wanted me at anyway.

Far from wanting "power and control", another of MW's accusations, more to the point, I desired to be involved with people I admired and respected, doing something I believed was worthwhile.

Power and control—that's a good one. Me, the person who doesn't like the spotlight, who prefers to work in the background to support others.

Above all, I learned that there was power in words, in speaking my truth, in stepping out of the shadows. I was learning more about myself. My integrity was intact. As stressed as I was, and as hurtful as her words had been, I didn't stoop to her level of personal attacks. I stood up for myself, and I had survived. *I was becoming a better, braver version of myself as I faced each new challenge.*

The fiasco has been good for me in another way, too. It opened my eyes to the truth of things. I had kept the niggling feeling I had about the mystery woman to myself, because I didn't know what it was about. People aren't always who they say they are. Another reason to trust my intuition.

But did I really get it that I had to stop taking on so much? That remained to be seen. Thankfully, my mother had remained oblivious to the turmoil, although maybe she did sense something. If she did she never said anything.

49: The Ups and Downs of Life on 3rd Street

The alley below our apartment, the one I looked down on from the back porch when I took breaks or worked on editing, contributed to my anxiety and stress. New people had moved in across the alley: they were selling crack cocaine. Customers came and went all hours of the day or night. A variety of regular-looking people, male and female, working class for the most part, stopped by for their "fix".

At night the alley became animated with loud voices, fights, drunks coming home from the bars, and the usual crack addicts. I called the police many times but finally gave up and began sleeping on the couch in the living room, which didn't do my back any favours. Mom wasn't affected, because she couldn't hear anything from outside.

When Mom and I moved in, a lovely family lived in the house next door. They kept gardens of flowers looking beautiful. After they moved out, half a dozen young guys settled in, and eventually moved out. They did party occasionally but weren't as bad as the couple with two pit bulls. The pit bulls were chewing their way through the fence in their back yard. My mind reeled, thinking of the consequences.

I'd be sitting on our porch that overlooked their back yard, writing or taking a break when I'd see one of the dog owners throw big hunks of meat into the yard for the ravenous dogs. The sight kind of turned my stomach and I feared for every one of us coming and going in the back door of our building, where our cars were parked. Especially vulnerable was the young mother and her toddler in the ground level suite below Mom and me. Karen had moved to Kamloops for a job by then.

Then it happened. The dogs broke through the fence. Thank God the owners retrieved them before anyone was hurt.

Shasta, John and Robbie moved next door when the place was for rent again. John and my great grandson Robbie, a toddler at the time, were in their front yard, picking apples off the ground the day I crossed our lawn to see Robbie.

All was well until I looked around to see that my mother had made her way across our lawn to see Robbie, too. She was smiling, no doubt proud of herself, for she had never ventured out on her own, had never opened the gate on the porch, or walked out onto the lawn. As surprised as I was, I took her arm and we walked a few steps toward Robbie and John.

In a terrible instant everything changed as John's back was turned. Robbie ran toward the busy road where cars roared by, going far too fast to stop for a little guy dashing out between parked cars. I dropped my mother's arm and sprinted to Robbie, catching him just in time right before he reached the road. With pounding heart, I turned back to see Mom lying on the ground. Horrified, I dashed to her. She wasn't crying, but everything was wrong. Her eyes were closed against the piercing sun. She couldn't move. John stayed with her as I ran to call an ambulance and grabbed a bed sheet to shield her pale face from shards of burning light. *What had I done! I had let go of her!*

It was August 3rd. She was eighty-four. Grief and guilt squeezed my heart.

I knew one of the ambulance attendants, who told me he thought Mom's hip was broken. Consumed with dread, I jumped in my car and followed the ambulance to the hospital. The rest is a bit of a blur, but it was a long road of recovery, as it is for most elderly people who fall and break a hip. The statistics were not in their favour. Some elderly people never recover fully from a broken hip and many more die within a year of falling. With that knowledge, I held myself hostage with worst-case scenarios.

Mom was taken to Vernon for a hip replacement and then back to Salmon Arm Hospital. After that she was moved to Bastion Place for physiotherapy and strength building, where I visited her every day.

"I've got to get out of here," she'd say. "Some of these people are crazy." To be fair she was on the second floor where the patients with Alzheimers lived, and she shared a room with a couple of women who weren't in very good shape. When I took my mother to the dining room for lunch, I was shocked at what I saw. Some patients had to be spoon fed food pablum-like mush. Their blank stares were what frightened me the most. Even the people who could feed themselves looked vacant. They didn't speak, simply ate, and went back to their rooms. *What kind of life is this? Is there no mercy for the horrors of old age? Made me want to start squirreling away pills in case I found myself losing my memories and my functions one day.*

The physiotherapist who worked with Mom was concerned that my mother couldn't seem to grasp, or remember, the concept of how to get her socks on with the sock-putting-on-contraption, and kept forgetting how she was shown to use stairs.

With those concerns dogging me, I bought the special equipment she needed to make our apartment safe and organized a physiotherapist to work with Mom at home.

While Mom was in Bastion, my grandson Ty was born; it was August, 2005. Peter and Teri-Ann had moved to Langley when she became pregnant. Teri-Ann and I went through a sad, strange period of alienation. Awful words had been spoken. It wouldn't have been the first time, or the last, but it seemed to get worse each time.

In the meantime, Shasta had become pregnant again. She, John, and Robbie boarded a plane to Whitehorse for the second time. *Doesn't anybody stay in one place any more ....* a line from a Carol King song reminding me of the time I lived in Whitehorse with my young daughter. *You're so far away ...*

Mom eventually came home and we muddled along. I put her socks on for her, as she still couldn't handle the sock contraption. She was able to walk with help, an arm or a walker, but the stairs were treacherous to navigate even with help. Mom's sister, Marge, would walk over to collect her for church once a week.

On October 16th, 2005, I wrote the following poem.

Early Senility

Too much on my mind
Left the car lights on again
twice in one week
run down batteries

And this morning
when the door shut behind me
after wrestling with mom's
boots, her jacket zipper, and her walker
up the stairs, down the stairs
and out

it was the sound
the finality of that click
that alerted me

me in my slippers
no coat and no keys
ground soggy with brown leaves
and a chill in the air

Now who's the senile one?

Mom took her sister's arm
and waved a cheerful goodbye to me

50: Poetry Launch for bill bissett

> *We dont*
> *know as*
> *much as*
> *r pomes*

- bill bissett (*radiant danse uv being*)

As usual, nothing happens overnight in the publishing world. It was 2006 by the time Nightwood Editions had the book *radiant danse uv being: a poetic portrait of bill bissett* ready. The launch would take place at the Ironworks Gallery in Gastown on May 18th at 8 pm. I made a decision to go. I wasn't going to let this one slip by without at least making the effort to overcome time, space, and nerves. I sent an email saying that I would read my poem at the launch. I let my brother Jim, my friend Carol, and my ex-husband Craig—all in Vancouver—know. I would make arrangements for the care of my mother and our cats and I'd start preparing myself mentally. Mom was supportive of me going to read my poem in Vancouver. She liked my writing and encouraged me to get out into the world with it, something that surprised me. Sometimes when I was too tired to go to the writers' coffee house or the writers group she'd say, "Go, you'll have a good time." Bless her for that, and if I did go, I discovered that she was right.

I'd found another place where my mother and I connected. She who loved writing in her diary every day for as long as I could remember, and she who loved reading.

My copy of the book arrived in the mail. A black and white photo of a much younger bill gazes at me from the cover. He has full lips, dimpled chin, blond hair, and a face as sweet as a cherub. Grey tones and shadows shroud bill's face, which is offset by the faded orange and purple in his shirt and the title. On either side of the photo are the names of the eighty-seven poets included in the anthology. When I saw my own name, alphabetically placed among the others, it felt surreal, yes, with a sense of euphoria.

He's the man Jack Kerouac called "a great poet," James Reaney dubbed "a one-man civilization," Warren Tallman hailed "A brave new spirit" and Margaret Atwood declared "my astral twin." (from the back cover of radiant danse uv being)

I decided to take the greyhound bus so I could relax, read, and meditate on the upcoming event, a huge leap for me. I read *radiant danse uv being* from front to back and practiced reading my poem. Anticipation grew as we pulled into the Vancouver bus depot. I found Craig, who was expecting someone with long dark hair. Mine had since been cut short and I'd coloured it auburn. I thought the red added a little flare. As we drove toward his brother Nelson's house, I reflected on how comfortable it felt to be with Craig. More than my ex-husband, he was a friend, and he was family despite the piece of paper from the court that declared us divorced.

"I've been to a couple of poetry events at the Iron Works Gallery," Craig said, as he drove through the city. It's a great venue. It holds over two hundred people."

"Over two hundred people!" My voice squeaked in fear.

All the calm I thought I'd managed until that moment disappeared. Wrong thing to say to me. Me who had only ever read to a limited audience, the hometown gatherings in Salmon Arm. Oh my god!

I had planned to lie down and close my eyes for an hour or so at Craig's before heading to the Gallery, but instead we were going to Nelson's for a barbecue. I remembered what a friend had told me before I left. Say yes to everything, she said. In other words, stay open to all possibilities.

The trouble with being anxious, which is really just intense fear spread out over a greater period of time, is that I'm sort of out-of-my-mind, in fact, almost out-of-body. I want to shut down, a form of running away, because I've created negative or catastrophic scenarios of what is to come. It's almost like the panic attacks I used to have before getting those somewhat under control with the help of the hippie psychologist, Michael, who worked at Pine Free Clinic on Fourth Avenue in Vancouver. I think Michael actually had more issues than I did—he chain smoked hunched up in a chair across from me—but he knew things, like how to deflect a panic attack when I felt one coming on. I'll never forget him for that, although it was hard to actually see him through all the smoke. But fear being the powerful demon it is, at times I wasn't sure I could deflect anything.

I began repeating every calming mantra I could remember. *Be here now. Be in your body. Breathe. Om.* And then we were in Nelson and Carole's lush back yard (she was on holidays in Mexico), more a fairytale garden of pathways through fantastic shapes, colours, and perfumed flowers, than a yard. Nelson offered beer and laid chicken kabobs on the barbecue. I sipped a beer, which didn't help. Maybe I should have guzzled it. No, no, I was too uptight to loosen the grip that stress had over me. I had to be in control.

What I remember is that during that couple of hours, when Nelson asked about the book I'd been working on, I said I couldn't come up with a title. I'd brainstormed a hundred different titles and nothing would stick. Later, when Nelson was inside preparing the rice and salad, Craig asked me to give him a succinct summary of the book.

When I finished he said, "A Raven in My Heart." I said it over a few times. Yes, that *was* the title. Imagine that. Later, I came up the sub-title *Reflections of a Bookseller,* playing off the name Reflections, the name of my bookstore.

Time to go. I obsessed over what to wear, but had settled on my black cotton skirt, white blouse, and black sandals that I'd borrowed from Teri-Ann. The sandals had a medium high heel, which I wasn't used to, so I kind of wobbled down the sidewalk. My appearance worried me, for even with blush on I looked ashen. But then after a Salmon Arm winter everyone is shockingly white, although I thought my face made porcelain look rosy-hued.

I saw people streaming into the Gallery as we approached. *Oh, shit!* I wanted to turn around, but of course I had to go through with it. I'd let the organizers know that I would read. I had friends and family coming to hear me. *I must be crazy; that's the only explanation I can think that has brought me this far.*

Inside the door I saw editors Jeff and Stephen greeting people. *So many people.* I squeezed through the crowd and introduced myself.

"When do I read?" I asked. An awkward moment followed, as Jeff and Stephen looked at each other.

"We didn't receive an email," one of them said.

"I wondered why I never received a reply to my email," I said. I suddenly felt foolish and out of place, as various thoughts raced through my mind. *Should I leave? What should I do? I'm so embarrassed.*

"Wait here. I'll see what I can do," Jeff said. "I think someone in the first half cancelled." He returned moments later, saying I could take her place.

I saw bill talking to someone in the gallery, where his paintings hung. I went over to say hello and asked him over to the table to meet my brother Jim, niece Kristie, Craig and Nelson. Gracious as always, bill recalled fond memories of meeting Mom, before someone else grabbed his attention.

I sat down. I didn't feel like myself. I was just going through the motions of being there. "Be here now" eluded me.

To me, the country mouse, the stage looked daunting. A young woman ascended the stage to light candles. If I were the throwing up kind, I would have. At least that way I'd spew out the nerves and get rid of them. I'd heard that some entertainers do that.

My friend Carol arrived with Marilyn, another old friend. We had been in a woman's group together. Carol said to give her my nervousness. She had come to Salmon Arm to help me with various aspects of setting up the bookstore and at other times over the years to help me when she was visiting.

Carol and Nelson were married at one time. Things had changed. They were no longer on speaking terms. They ignored each other with me, the silent referee, between them. The large room was dark, filled with men and women and the babble of hundreds of excited voices.

A woman approached me at the table and asked for my autograph! A rush of warmth flooded my body, my heart, as I signed my name beside my poem in her book. That experience left me with an inner glow that was hard to explain. The validation of my talent as a poet gave me a different kind of thrill than anything I was used to.

Other people were getting drinks from the bar, but not me. I had one ativan with me just in case. *It's now or never.* In the washroom I tried to swallow it without water. *Oh dear, this won't work in time to stem the tide of rising anxiety.*

I kicked the sandals off under the table, talked to a daughter of an old friend/roommate of mine, surprised that she was there, although at that point I was finding it difficult to talk to people. Just as the noise level and excitement threatened to overwhelm me, the room became silent, as the first poet ascended the stage. Poet after poet walked to the mic in the middle of the stage and read. The readings, the poets, were magnificent, mesmerizing.

My silent mantra became *"do this for bill, do this for bill, do this for bill ... it's his night."*

When Sheryl MacKay, host of CBC radio's North by Northwest program, announced my name a rush of adrenaline, like a rogue wave, overcame me. I jumped up and wove my way through and around tables and chairs toward the stage—without my shoes!

I heard Sheryl say, "Kay McCracken is the co-founder of the Shuswap Writers' Festival," as I maneuvered through the obstacles. Barefoot, at the mic, I might as well have been naked.

The ativan hadn't worked. I managed a weak "hi bill," directed toward bill, sitting front and centre in the audience. *Country mouse, country mouse.* Felt almost frozen, but managed my short introduction to the poem and then began reading. That's when the magic took over, like the time I read another poem for the first time in my bookstore for the Writers' Coffee House. The words were like an incantation that carried me through to the end.

Praise the Goddess of book launches, for allowing me to live through the experience. Later, I submitted an article to WordWorks magazine about my adventure, which they accepted. I'll tell everyone from now on never underestimate your ability to step into the unknown, with or without your shoes, because if you never take a chance, you'll never know what you're capable of.

51: The Wind Changes Everything

A hot, windy day on the foreshore stirred the poetic impulse. I tried writing about the wind, but wasn't happy with the poem. It wasn't until I heard Tom Wayman read his wind poems during the launch of his new book *high speed through shoaling water* that I became excited.

During the intermission I passed Tom on the stairs and said "I tried to write a poem about the wind and I couldn't do it."

"Yes you can," he said with conviction. "Yes, you can." I went home inspired and worked on the poem, with Tom's words echoing in my head ... *yes you can, yes you can.*

July: Windsong

the wind called me down to the lake
where I sat among swooning willow,
the windsong fuelled by July's sensuous heat.

windsong ruffled the lake's dark surface
exciting two grebes who rode the waves
up and down

the tempo picked up
when the cottonwood took up rattles
and the birch chimed in
drowning out a chorus of gulls
ebb and flow

the wind
the wind changes everything

I wanted those lush air currents to loosen me,
to become my muse

wanted the fullness
and the lightness of it
to fill me and carry me away

wanted my song to merge with the other.

Tom's words reminded of *The Little Engine That Could*, a favourite childhood story about a little blue train that didn't think he could climb the high mountain, but agreed to try when all the bigger engines refused to haul the long train of freight cars. Near the top of the mountain, the little blue engine slowed down and began chanting the words "I think I can, I think I can, I think I can." Coming down the other side he said I thought I could, I thought I could, I thought I could. I was the little engine that could.

The illustrated book first appeared in the early 1900's and was reprinted many times, a favourite pick of teachers.

52: Secwepemc Cowboy

In April 2007, I organized a fund raiser for Word on the Lake Writers' Festival. April is National Poetry Month in Canada and Garry Gottfriedson had a new book of poetry published called *whiskey bullets: Cowboy and Indian Heritage Poems*. The poems explore themes of duality in the parallel worlds of cowboys and Indians. Growing up aboriginal on the Tk'emlups Reserve (Secwepemc) near Kamloops Garry grew up with strong First Nation values and traditions, while remaining immersed in the cowboy and ranching culture of the interior of BC. His poetry doesn't shy away from the tough issues of gender, sexuality, race and politics. No sentimental rhyming poetry for this Secwepemc cowboy. His poems are hard hitting, honest and moving.

I also featured the poet Alex Forbes from Kamloops, who I'd met a couple of years earlier. He'd written a collection of poems about the infamous stagecoach and train robber, Bill Miner, known as Grey Fox, Gentleman Bandit. Originally from Kentucky, Miner was thought to have committed the first train robbery in Canada near Kamloops, BC. He and his cohorts botched the robbery, but his legend endures.

Garry brought a friend of his, who had never read his poetry to an audience before. In the spirit of the event I donned a cowboy hat, a borrowed sheriff's badge and earrings from artist Frieda Martin, cowboy boots and leather vest belonging to my brother-in-law, John, and I wore a long brown skirt that my daughter had given me. I was the organizer, emcee and sheriff all rolled into one. I had never tried on this persona before and found I enjoyed myself enormously once my nerves took a hike. Like an actor I slipped into the role and out my own skin.

A rancher poet friend brought hay bales, an antique rifle and a couple of other ranch props that acted as a backdrop for Garry, his friend, and Alex, who read their poetry to the large, enthusiastic audience. Garry sold many books that night at intermission. Afterwards, local poets stepped up to share their work. I read a poem I'd written for the occasion.

Wild West Revisited

Miss Kitty

I liked her

her life

TV life

Gunsmoke

And me just an impressionable girl

She owned the saloon

was friends with the sheriff

good friends

But that was American television

in the fifties

No lust, sex, or prostitution,

No smoking, spitting, or lewd remarks

A show my mother would like

No Indians. No Indians?

Just Miss Kitty

Her independence

Her calm self-possessed nature

Queen of her realm

So forty years later I revisit the fantasy

Not a saloon, but a bookstore

complete with espresso bar

Not Miss Kitty, but close enough

Not the Wild West, but small-town BC

where just about anything goes

from placard carrying church goes

to an annual biker stomp

Not a sheriff, but a carpenter

who liked his cappuccino strong

whose tool belt slapped his thighs

when he strode through the doors

Good morning, Miss Kay, he'd say

Polite, respectful

So far, so good, I thought

ignoring the hunger in his eyes

But in this Wild West

The cowboys came to read poetry

And the Indians weren't Indians

But First Nations, Shuswap, Secwepemc

with roots deep in the land

We became friends

They weren't going anywhere

while the carpenter

Trickster, Shapeshifter

ravenous for more than just cappuccino

ran off leaving chaos in his dust

I cried, cursed

and closed up shop

prayed that I got the lesson

prayed for a little less wild in my west next time

53: Gracesprings Collective

I met Alex Forbes, a friend of Deanna's, at the 2005 Shuswap Writers' Festival. He was giving a haiku workshop and another poetry workshop, neither of which I attended because I was busy with something on the organizing end of things. I recall that my back was in severe pain during that festival and on meeting Alex—a big bear of a man with white hair and beard, and happy blue eyes—we chatted briefly. He hugged me goodbye. A bear hug. At that moment I thought oh, oh, my back. But low and behold, that hug acted as the chiropractic cure. I was finally pain free after swallowing too many painkillers all weekend, none of which helped much.

During our chat, Alex said something that startled me. He'd purchased a copy of The Shuswap Writers Group latest anthology at the book table and read the poem and a short story of mine included in that issue. "I found your poem and story very moving," he said. I still couldn't call myself a writer, or a poet, so to have Alex's affirmation of my writing meant a lot. He had probably read and graded hundreds of thousands of poems and stories in his time as a professor at Thompson Rivers University in Kamloops, and before that at the University of British Columbia; his poems, essays and reviews appeared in many journals and collections in Canada the United States.

Rumours of Bees: Paintings of Tricia Sellmer; Poems of Alexander Forbes (2003, Red Heifer Press, Beverly Hills, California), is a gorgeous book of poems and art. Sellmer is an internationally acclaimed artist who has done many collaborations with Alex. Their collection of Art Catalogues were produced by Art Galleries for their exhibitions throughout British Columbia. Alex liked collaborating with other artists. A CD of his poems *The Bill Miner Roadshow* featured music by Henry Small & The Shiftless Rounders, with the poems read by Tina Moore.

Alex had an idea that he'd run by Deanna, and now that he'd met me they included me in the great scheme. The year was 2008. As a published poet and English professor, Alex had connections and he really believed the time had come to break out of the long-established hold that publishers had over writers. Gracesprings Collective was born. The name Gracesprings came from Garland Gracesprings, the name of Eric and Deanna's farm on Garland Road. Grace was the name of Eric's aunt, the first female psychiatrist in New York, the woman who had helped Eric and his father buy the farm. The funniest thing is every time I tried to say the name of our collective in the early days it came out of my mouth as Graceland, and I'd sing a few bars of the catchy song Graceland by Paul Simon. *Goin to Graceland ...*

    We held our first meeting at the kitchen table where Mom and I lived. Mom had known Deanna for a while by then and was always pleased to see her. She had enjoyed Deanna's books. Meeting a male friend of mine always put a little sparkle in my mother's eyes, and the fact that Alex was a poet and an author made it even better. Mom discreetly stayed in her bedroom while we hashed out the perimeters of our Gracesprings Collective.

    Alex's manifesto: *In starting Gracesprings Collective, the founding members sought to remedy some of the imbalances in current literary life. For too long, writers whose work had either been dropped or neglected by corporate publishers, had little recourse but to self-publish. While self-publication can be honourable (Whitman self-published all the time), the popular imagination often assumes that work so published must be unprofessional. The writers who started the Collective, who have countless credits to their names in terms of prior publication with major publishers, therefore sought to develop a third way between corporate publishing, and self-publishing: collective publishing, whereby the benefits of corporate publishing (editing, arranging of readings, and marketing support, to name a few) are retained, while power to get their work out is returned to the writers themselves.*

    Caroline Woodward, a published author with deep roots in the Peace River region of British Columbia, and longtime friend of Alex's, joined our group at his request. Deanna also knew her. I'd carried her books *Disturbing the Peace* and *Alaska Highway Two-Step* in my bookstore, although I'd never met her. In 1993, she and her husband Jeff owned Motherlode Bookstore in New Denver, in the Kootnays, the same year I started my bookstore Reflections in Salmon Arm. Most recently she'd been a book rep for a large Vancouver book distribution company, Kate Walker & Company. At the time she joined our collective she lived and worked on Lennard Island with her husband at a Light Station off the west coast near Tofino.

    I volunteered to be the book rep for our group and began making official calls to bookstores from Salmon Arm to Kamloops, Vernon, Kelowna, and beyond. I also set up readings and book signings for Deanna and Alex.

    Life was busy and exciting as my mother and I continued our journey together. Mom supported what I was doing with the Collective and with my writing. I would often read her what I'd written. I could see she loved to be read to. In the mornings, I'd sit with my coffee, writing or staring out at the wintry world, which inspired another poem.

Winter Poem

they glide in
silent as falling snow

settle among grey limbs
etched in white

their coal-black feathers
light up the tree

like beacons
on Winter Solstice

54: Richard Wagamese

As our Gracesprings Collective rep I had been restocking our books at Bookland on the north shore of Kamloops when the manager told me that Richard Wagamese would be there in half an hour to sign books.

"He has a new book of short stories about his life called *One Native Life*," she said, as she walked me to a table piled high with his books. She picked up *One Native Life* to show me.

"This book is included in the Globe and Mail's 2008 Top 100 Books of the Year."

I'd never heard of him, so the manager told me that Richard lived at Paul Lake near Kamloops and that he was a wonderful writer. I decided to stick around.

The little I read of it, I knew I had to buy it. The bio on the flap that told me Richard was an Ojibway from the Wabasseemoong First Nation in northwestern Ontario. He had four novels published: *Keeper'n Me, A Quality of Light, Ragged Company* and the award-winning *Dream Wheels*. His autobiographical book *For Joshua* was published to critical acclaim in 2002. He'd worked as a newspaper reporter and a broadcaster for radio and TV, and his columns for the Calgary Herald won a National Newspaper Award in 1990.

My interest was piqued as I had a keen interest in all things Indigenous.

Several people hung around the coffee stand, waiting to talk to Richard. I stood off to the side near the main counter, making myself inconspicuous. The old shyness was with me still.

Richard arrived, almost as if the wind had blown him in. There was an energy about him, his amused dark eyes behind glasses, his wide grin, and on his head a black hat, known as a pork pie hat, that made him stand out, that and his tall, slim frame, his dark brown skin. Who was this magical being who had suddenly appeared in our midst?

Richard sat down with the people waiting and began to spin stories, and as he did I was drawn in. He cast his spell, like a fisherman using a bright coloured lure, and I was hooked. He told a story of his school days, about not being able to see the blackboard because his eyes were so bad. He said he learned to read upside down over someone's shoulder. Is that possible?

I bought three books: *One Native Life, Ragged Company,* and *Dream Wheels*. When I read Richard's books I wondered why he wasn't more well known.

Another time I wandered into a store on the main Street in Kamloops to ask if they would carry our books. I was surprised to see Richard at a table signing books for people, so we chatted like long lost friends, and laughed about who knows what. Fans stopped by to say hello. I bought *Keeper`n Me*, published back in 1994. On a whim, I bought two small chocolates being sold at the counter. I gave one to Richard, had the book signed, and headed back home.

As I drove down the highway past the sage brush hills and buff coloured clay cliffs I wondered how a kid that had been bounced from foster home to foster home, who had been abused and abandoned as a child, who had lived on the street for years as a teenager, and who had crawled inside a bottle and had used drugs to find solace, how it was that he sat there at all, never mind that he had a prolific outpouring of wonderful books to his credit. How had he overcome the odds that were stacked against him? How did he learn to write like that?

It may have been in an interview with his chosen sister, Shelagh Rogers, host of CBC`s radio program The Next Chapter, or I may have heard Richard talk about it on One Native Life, his weekly commentary on CFJC TV 7, Kamloops. As a scared sixteen year who didn't know where he belonged, the day he wandered into a library was the day he found a haven. It was quiet and warm, he said, and he read so he wouldn't get kicked out. The skinny, unwashed street kid had left school in grade nine. He read everything and it awoke something in him. He felt transported by the words of famous writers like Thomas Wolf, John Steinbeck and others. He carried a small coiled notebook to jot down things he overhead, ideas etc., and eventually began to wonder if he might be able to write.

The next time I saw Richard it was his turn to hang back behind the large crowd that had turned out to hear Deanna Kawatski, Alex Forbes and me read at Chapters in Kamloops. I glimpsed his black hat, his tall figure—almost a shadow—half hidden behind a bookshelf, as I arranged posters and books at our table amid the commotion of people arriving and chairs being set up.

That morning I'd woken up in pain after Deanna and I stayed the night at my sister Karen's apartment, and stupidly, I swallowed a T3 pain pill not long before it was time to leave for Chapters. Lack of sleep, anticipation, and nerves were conspiring against me, too. I'd put a lot of effort into promoting this event, but we didn't know what to expect.

We sat at a table facing about thirty men and women seated and standing, waiting for us to begin. As book rep for our collective I'd managed to get our books into the mega book chain. The manager was supportive of local authors and agreed to have us read and sign books, although as this was our first appearance as Gracesprings Collective I think we were each a little rattled to see so many people. Most authors are lucky if one or two people show up at a book store signing.

My book wasn't published yet, but I would read a passage from the manuscript, take names and email address of anyone wanting to be notified when my book came out.

When I stood up to Introduce Deanna my first halting words told me I was in trouble. I'd heard of this happening to speakers but had never had the experience myself. My mouth was so dry, probably from the pain pill and not enough water to wash it down, that my mouth felt sort of glued together. *Oh my God!* I felt myself panic, but then used every ounce of will power to force the words out. Stress must have been written all over me.

I got through the ordeal and searched the faces before me for the one brown one among all the white faces. He was gone, black hat and all.

After a successful appearance as Gracesprings Collective we were mighty pleased. That was the first of several appearances in Chapters Kamloops and in Chapters Kelowna, and by that time my book was published.

Unfortunately, the next time I saw Richard the old demons he thought he'd left behind had snared him. His wife Debra Powell was in the awkward position of making excuses for him when he didn't follow through on our invitation to present at our Writers' Festival. Addictions are sneaky and powerful, a way to deal with pain and pressure; it's not a moral problem as most people think. The pressure of becoming an award-winning author who people looked up to may have been too much. Richard wouldn't be the first writer to have been destroyed by fame.

55: Lakeland

Marilyn and I had trouble finding 10A Avenue North East but at last we found the street sign, an offshoot of 10th Avenue NE that wasn't even on a map. We turned left onto it just before the defunct Fas Gas—now a used car lot. On the left the sign "Lakeland Mobile Home Park," and another sign: 'Slow' Children At Play.

We turned left on the snow-packed road instead of going straight. An elderly man shoveled a driveway with slow, methodical movements, as birds flitted back and forth to feeders along the front of his mobile home. An almost life size stuffed brown bear appeared to climb a tree trunk in his yard. I felt comforted by the sight, for everything looked normal, well except for the bear, but that was just cute. I'd been searching for a mobile home for Mom and I for over a year but in our price range there wasn't anything we liked—many were dark and dingy—and there were always pet restrictions.

The newspaper listing said "pets welcome," which was an anomaly. My brother-in-law, John, saw the ad and told me to check it out. He had always been helpful. By that time, I was discouraged until one day when Marilyn was free we decided to give it a try. The price was right, but would it be a run-down dump like so many I'd looked at?

When we drove past the man shoveling, a beautiful snow-laden park ringed with graceful-looking trees opened up before us. Across the park sat a pretty white mobile that turned out to be the very one we were looking for. Number ten: black numbers on brand new white siding. Marilyn and I got out of the car, welcomed by silence and deep snow, like a protective blanket laying over the yard. Tall trees were the silent sentinels that sheltered the mobile on three sides. A wooden fence enclosed a large back yard, a camper, and a shed. An empty mobile with new brown siding was the only close neighbour, and it was for sale as well.

"This is too good to be true," I said, turning to Marilyn, who agreed with me. "And there aren't any stairs. I've been worried about Mom and the stairs. Even with my help she can hardly do the stairs at the apartment now. This is exactly what we need."

"When Mom passes on one day, you'll be able to afford this, Kay. John and I have been concerned about you and your deteriorating health."

We peered through the large living room window. New windows, too, I noted. "Marilyn, look," I blurted out. "New laminate floors, an electric fireplace and mantle, pretty curtains." Everything inside looked as new and fresh as it did on the outside. I could barely contain myself.

"Let's call the Realtor," Marilyn said, as she dug her cell phone from her purse.

"Can you come right over?" I asked. Before I knew it, the Realtor was inserting the key in the lock. Inside, the single wide mobile wasn't a disappointment, for it had two bedrooms, and an office for me that looked out into the woods. It was lovely and bright, and it was clean.

I hadn't yet learned that if you think something is too good to be true, it usually is.

56: Too Good To Be True

Mom and I moved in at the end of January with a lot of help from family and friends. During the first week, I worried that moving my mother might have been a mistake. In the morning she'd peer out her bedroom, look down the hall both ways and say, "Which way is the bathroom?" *Oh, oh.* But she got the hang of it within the week and began to feel comfortable in our new home.

A knock at the door changed everything. A woman introduced herself. She was from a mobile home park in Boston Bar and she'd heard that our park was for sale. She was on a mission to buy mobiles and find people that might want to move into her park. I looked at her in disbelief, asked her where she got her information.

"I have it from a reliable source," she said, smiling. I hadn't even unpacked all the boxes yet.

I had hardly recovered from that shock when the manager of the park, the owner's daughter, arrived at our door, introduced herself, and handed me a notice. They were applying for rezoning, from mobile home park to highway commercial.

"Are you fucking kidding!" I shouted. "No one told us that. We wouldn't have bought this place if we'd known. This is criminal!"

She tried to reassure me that nothing would happen right away, but as I shut the door on her, I thought I might be sick. They hadn't even wanted to meet us before we bought our beautiful mobile home. I had used the "f" word, a word that I reserved for times when great anger or emotion required a strong response. It flew out of my mouth before I could stop it. *Trailer park girl ...*

The shock to my mind and emotions disturbed me profoundly. I'd been hit hard by something that I didn't see coming. Blindsided. The threat of loss reverberated through me, echoing the feelings of devastation I experienced when I was forced to give up my bookstore.

How could I tell my mother, who struggled just to maintain as her health deteriorated? If I was that upset, what would it do to her? I felt dangerously close to falling back into the dark, dry well of depression. I'd been doing pretty well, floating on a river of happiness about beginning life in our new home.

I thought back to the idyllic scene Marilyn and I had come upon: pristine snow and graceful trees in a park-like setting, where everything appeared peaceful, blissful and clean. That illusion became even more apparent as the ice disappeared from the road, exposing huge potholes, and when the snow receded a small mountain of junk and rotting garbage lay exposed, was left to fester like a boil full of poison. A neighbour said that it was the remains of a trailer that had been torn down. She told me that the man who had lived there would get drunk and stand outside at night, shouting, and shooting his rifle into the air.

In the gully that lay between the woods I looked out upon from my office, separating us from the next mobile, rusting pieces of machinery stood out like rotten teeth.

What have I done? My poor mother. The realtor's words came back to haunt me. You should pay Kay and Marion to live here, she had told the owner. I didn't understand her comment then, but she obviously knew more about Lakeland than we did. My own words—this is too good to be true—came back to haunt me.

Two weeks went by before I could tell Mom about the rezoning nightmare, but keeping the news to myself felt unbearable.

When I did talk to my mother about what happened, she appeared to take the news in stride, maybe because she could see how upset I was. Mom was definitely becoming less feisty in her ageing, and as she became more peaceful, more accepting, I became more anxious and unsettled, and yes, combative.

Getting angry, I mean *really* angry, helped pull me out of the downward spiral. That happened after I saw what the owner of the park told the newspaper about park residents. She was quoted in the Salmon

Arm Observer as saying the park was home to drug dealers, addicts, and low-income families. We were people on the way down, she said, and did all but call us losers and scum bags. What an underhanded way to get the city to change the zoning. I have to hand it to the city counselors, for they turned down this first application for rezoning, saying the residents would have nowhere to go.

Her words ignited my outrage. My anger at the injustice fueled me to act. I began writing letters, one that I took to every resident in the park and another one to the Salmon Arm Observer newspaper, which they printed. I used my column, too. I wasn't going to crawl away and disappear as I had after Reflections closed. I would stand and fight.

I became "the shit disturber" as one resident put it, which was an affirmation rather than condemnation. I rallied the residents, found a spokesperson for us, studied the Mobile Home Residential Act and looked at what was happening to other mobile home parks in the province. I organized meetings, showed up at City Hall, called lawyers, visited our MLA. I did everything I could to bring awareness to the situation facing park residents. Mobile Home parks everywhere faced a similar fate because land prices had sky rocketed.

The owners of Lakeland offered residents $6,000 to leave. Six thousand dollars to people living on limited and fixed incomes, in some cases with old and crumbling mobile homes, was too good to pass up. Several families accepted the offer and moved out. The exodus of out Lakeland had begun.

That was my first foray into political activism. I threw myself into it with everything I had. I found my voice with the help of my writing. Acting felt a lot better than passively sitting around waiting for the other shoe to drop. I don't know where that saying comes from, but it has an ominous tone.

57: Enchanted Forest

It's tough to be in a fighting mood when spring brings the pleasures of mating birds and blooming flowers. I was thrilled to see a fire pit emerge in the back yard and pictured us enjoying wiener roast with the grandkids on a summer evening. Frilly daffodils poked pretty heads up along the back fence. One glorious red tulip boldly proclaimed her right to exist in the space between the back lawn and the woods. Mom and I ate breakfast, and other meals, sitting at the table that looked out over the lawn and a wall of purple blossoms that sent delirious lilac scent wafting to us through the open window.

Journal entry:

April

A pair of courting ravens arrived again today, one swirling around the other, uttering endearments as they twirled and danced and dipped together. A joy to watch. Everything pulsed with life and the energy of desire. A pair of northern flickers have taken up residence in our woods. Three pairs of Brewers Blackbirds arrived about a week ago and strut about the lawn and underneath the bird feeder, sometimes they sit on the fence or on the wire, extraordinary looking black satin bodies and that yellow bead eye, making their untuneful "chuck" sound. Red-winged Blackbirds visited the feeder, trilling their joy at spring's arrival.

In May pale, beautifully scented wild roses appeared in the woods, their pink blossoms irresistibly delicate. I planted pots on the front and back porches. Pepper plants, oregano, parsley, rosemary and thyme, several varieties of tomatoes, fiery red and bold pink geraniums, marigolds, purple and yellow pansies.

Mom and I sat under the umbrella on the front porch after breakfast, enjoying the balmy morning and saying hello to the neighbours: the short, stout woman holding leashes for her two mincing Chihuahuas, and the elderly couple who stopped to chat, the whiff of wood smoke sailing to us from their home nearby. Everyone who drove by waved and smiled, and we waved at the children playing, their voices mingling with the throngs of chirping, thrilling birds in the trees ringing the park.

Our cats—the "the girls" as my granddaughter Shasta called them—joined us and nibbled on the fresh catnip growing around the porch. The elegant Japanese maple tree in the front garden shared space with an expansive bush of splendid open-faced roses, the dark red of rubies, and orange tiger lilies. Scattered in the lawn, among vibrant spring green grass, tiny purple violets that made my heart sing.

When Deanna arrived, I showed her around the back yard. She was staying with us to take part in the June Writers' Festival. "Look at that. A mountain ladyslipper," she said, pointing to a flowering plant just visible on the outskirts of our woods.

"Isn't it lovely," I said, moving in closer to take a better look. I'd seen these wild orchids before. The delicate white and yellow slippers looked like a perfect fit for a fairy's tiny foot. Deanna had already ventured further into the woods when I heard her exclaim, "Kay! There's dozens more!"

When I followed her into the cottonwood and evergreen thicket, I couldn't believe what I saw, for scattered among the trees in quiet repose, the three slippers on each slender stalk appeared as bright as miniature lanterns on the cool forest floor. The further we waded into the stillness, with the sunlight and shade playing among an infinite variety of shapes and shades of green, with the sweet scent of spring welling up around us, it was those fragile flowers that enchanted us.

I'd been too busy with festival business to walk into the woods recently, so I was stunned by what I saw. Normally, there are only one or two of these exquisite orchids in a wooded patch, but this, this was something beyond imagining. The further I ventured in, the more of them I saw. There must have been at least four dozen plants sprinkled through the woods.

I turned to my copy of Plants of Southern Interior British Columbia, to page 280. "The seeds of orchids are also unusual in that they contain no food reserves. Successful germination and establishment depends on an ideal combination of conditions, often including an association with fungi. These demanding requirements make propagation difficult and rarely successful. Many species are becoming rare due to urban development, cultivation, logging and cattle grazing."

The president of the Naturalist Club and his wife dropped by at my invitation. He had never seen such a profusion of the shy forest flowers. We photographed them. I wanted to know if we could stop development if those plants were on the endangered list. Not yet, he said. Damn, there goes that idea.

It broke my heart to think of the enchanted woods, as I now thought of them, bulldozed to make room for a commercial venture of some kind. The woods were home to many birds and rare orchids, and I thought it sacrilege to destroy any of it. And what about the elderly couple who had lived in the park for thirty years or more, who tended their gardens of bright flowers and their lawns with such care? What will happen to them? And the others?

58: My Book Launch, June 13, 2009

An odd calm had settled over me as I parked my car and walked toward the Art Gallery. I wasn't about to question my current state, surreal as it was, although I felt an inner flutter when the Gallery came into view and I saw all the people gathered outside on the steps and on the sidewalk enjoying the musicians who were entertaining them. I had booked the Dust Puppets, a local group that I enjoyed, to play at my book launch. The lively four-piece acoustic band played a wide variety of folk, blues, gospel and country music. With long-time friend Ken Firth, of the Shuswap Writers Group, on harmonica, vocals, guitar, whistles and percussion, and his wife Elda on the stand-up washtub bass—the "gut bucket"—adding her incredibly powerful voice, there would certainly be a lot of toe tapping and fun.

The June evening was glorious, sunny, full of promise. I carried a bunch of late-blooming lilacs that I'd just cut from a neighbour's tree. My coming-out-as-an-author party was about to begin. The focus of the evening would be on me and my writing, not a place I'd ever pictured myself being comfortable, until recently. I'd had to psyche myself up for this. As I walked up the Gallery steps, saying hello to friends, I was aware that I didn't want to break the spell of composure, even if it was just an illusion, so I kept going. The image that comes to me now is that of a poker player who keeps his or her cards close to the chest, until it's time to lay them down.

It was about 6:45 pm. The event was to begin at 7:00 pm and I didn't want to arrive too early. I'd dropped by the Gallery in the afternoon to check on things. My friend Dorothy was there organizing seating and setting up the gallery. Under Dorothy's supervision my brother Jim, his son, Nick, and my ex-husband, Craig, who had all arrived the night before, set up my bookcase with books, a rug, and wicker chairs. I'd borrowed the chairs from Lyle, my chiropractor, and his wife, Frieda, the artist. My idea was to recreate a scene from Reflections, because the setting for *A Raven in My Heart* was my bookstore.

I'd done the work, finished my book, booked SAGA Public Art Gallery six months earlier, distributed invitations & posters around town, placed an announcement in the papers, organized food, including ordering a cake that was a replica of the beautiful book cover, and volunteers.

Dorothy greeted people as they came through the door, asking them if they had a memory of my bookstore Reflections they would care to write down with the pen and paper she handed them. One of those memories would be drawn later for a signed copy of my book.

My sisters Marilyn and Karen were already seated at the book table spread out with my books, bookmarks, and a brilliant arrangement of red, orange, and yellow flowers that had arrived from my Gracesprings Collective buddies. Clinging like a whisper to the flowers, a pretty green butterfly seemed the perfect symbol for my public emergence as a writer, as someone who was about to share her very personal story with the world. Huge doubts had plagued me about publishing the book, but I'd managed to push them aside. I felt compelled to share certain things I'd seen and heard while managing my bookstore. I clung to the belief that the truth of my experience was more important than my insecurities. Even my trembling ego, my self-conscious, doubting self knew that. Most people had no idea what the book was about. I was going to reveal things about my family, friends, myself, and Salmon Arm that may have consequences. Too late to worry about that now.

I invited Deanna and Alex to read at the launch. Carolyn Woodward couldn't be with us, however she sent a lovely card and an incredible stick-on raven tattoo; the raven was beautifully rendered inside a circle. Just before I left home, Karen helped me stick it on. Raven rested on my left breast over my heart, the black t-shirt just low enough to show him off. *A Raven in My Heart*.

Mom had not been well for weeks, but when the time came, she got out of bed and dressed herself. When she made her mind up, there was no changing it; she was going to be at my book launch no matter what. It was shocking to see how frail she had become and how small and thin she looked sitting beside Jim, my six-foot four brother. Her face was drawn and pale, and I knew it was a struggle for her to be there. Mom had always been strong and capable and now she suffered with a crumbling backbone and atrial fibrillation, making her susceptible to more strokes. Her eye sight and hearing were going, *and* she had COPD, making even breathing difficult for her. But there she was, sitting front and centre, the only thing missing was her beautiful smile.

Dorothy had reserved the front row for my family. Teri-Ann sat on one side of Mom, her beloved grandma, looking stunning in a red dress. Her auburn hair was cut in a stylish bob. Craig had set up his video camera next to one of the pillars along the front row. Nieces, sisters and their husbands took their places in the front row. Behind them Mom's sister Margery, her friend Ellenor, and some cousins. Having my family and friends at the launch of "Raven," filled me with courage.

I stood off to one side at the front as my emcee, Clive Callaway, made moves to start proceedings. Sarah, my friend from Gardom Lake, had recommended her partner, Clive, when I said I was looking for an emcee. We met at their place overlooking Gardom Lake and I was impressed by the enthusiasm and attention to detail that Clive and Sarah brought to the project.

Looking over the crowd, I noticed friends Tim and Laryssa from Vernon, many friends from the Salmon Arm writing community, and even some people I didn't know. Then I saw George standing at the back of the packed gallery; I smiled, acknowledging his presence. I was pleased that he had come, as he was an important character in my book. His friendship meant a great deal to me. Without his endorsement, I would never have published "Raven" in its present form. I had wrestled with my conscience, but my motto to "tell the truth," remained firm. I sensed that if I could tell the truth of my experience perhaps other people would be able to relate. Maybe my experience would even be of help to someone.

As I scanned the back of the crowd, I saw a First Nations man who used to come into Reflections bookstore back in the day. At the time, he was looking for books on Two-Spirit people, those indigenous North Americans who fulfill one of many mixed gender roles. When I studied anthropology, they were known as berdashe, a derogatory term that is no longer used. He wore braids and a skirt, and struck me as crow-like just then, his black eyes searching for something of interest. Too bad the piece I'd written about him didn't make it into my book, for Two-Spirit people are a fascinating phenomenon, and traditionally at least they had an important role to play in their communities.

    By that time, minutes from going on, I began to feel a little strange, like the nerves might hit at any moment. Sarah had brought a raven recording, which she played as a signal for people to be seated. The croaking raven woke me from my dream bubble. I felt wide awake and alert as I listened to Clive's introduction. And then I was walking up to the mic.

    I acknowledged how happy I was to see everyone there. I'd been visualizing this moment. Preparing mentally was as important as all the other preparation I'd done. I thanked my dear mother for being there, reporting that she'd been ill.

    I mentioned that the book had taken me twice as long to write—ten years—as the story had been to live. That got a chuckle. Then I read the first excerpt from the book that I had practiced with Marilyn. She'd been a great help, showing me where I should slow down and then where I should let a punch line, or a funny bit, sink in before continuing. She had also done the final edit before going to print. Alex, Deanna, and Caroline had each read the manuscript, and had contributed valuable editorial input.

    I wasn't sure what to expect when Bonnie Thomas, the youngest daughter of the esteemed First Nations elder, Mary Thomas, took to the stage to speak. Clive announced that Bonnie was now "Raven Friendly" as a result of reading my book and that she would like to pass on some thoughts, having just read it. She hadn't been a fan of ravens, but like so many people had viewed them with suspicion, and in some cases with fear.

    Bonnie, beautiful, Bonnie. She began and I almost fell into a swoon at the power of her words.

    "Your book is beautiful in so many ways and I thank you for honouring

my mother by mentioning her and the work that she was doing toward building bridges between us all.

"There is so much of the book that I could relate to, as a woman, as a mother, and the transformations that we all go through in change, and the importance of taking care of ourselves before we attempt to take care of others.

"You talk about walking in the woods with such passion and I felt like I was with you, listening to you tell your story.

"Storytellers are important people in the community and we respect them. They talk about the history and the lessons. You have a strong gift, Kay. It's been an honour to read about you."

I didn't know whether to cry, laugh, jump up and down, or disappear—and I wanted to do all those things at once. Her validation of my story, my writing, and of me, overwhelmed me with emotion. I stood up to receive the gift that she presented me with: a CBC produced recording of the Shuswap myths that included the voice of her beloved mother.

I was given Bonnie's name by a friend, who had been a close friend of the late Mary Thomas. I had asked her if she knew someone from the local First Nations community who might read my manuscript. There were a couple of scenes with Mary Thomas of the local Neskonlith Band, and as I was getting the book ready for print I thought I'd better make sure I wasn't overstepping any boundaries, cultural or otherwise. When we met, Bonnie agreed to read "Raven," although she was a very busy woman. She worked full time, had children and a partner, and was involved in helping her people much the same way her mother had done. She's smart and articulate, a woman who isn't afraid to take on the government, the judicial system, and the city for what she believes is right.

During the intermission, I rode the high from hearing Bonnie's words of praise, and from the response I got from my own reading. I signed books for a steady stream of people as joy, excitement and happy sunlight streamed through tall, elegant windows. Throughout the room, glowing bouquets of white, pink and purple petals held that sunlight. Friends, family, good food and drink, the scent of peonies and lilacs wafting through the gallery, and me thinking that heaven was right there, right then. Bonnie told me later that the heady scent of lilac transported her to a passage in my book.

The evening was a carnival of readings, laughter, live music, a variety of people of all ages, cake and great finger food, and delicious iced coffee donated by the Shuswap Coffee Company. And me wearing a black t-shirt and black capri pants, wrapped in my daughter's sheer purple scarf that I used as a shawl over bare arms. Black raven tattoo. Silver raven bracelet.

I chose what to wear at the last minute and hadn't given it any thought. That seems odd to me now, but I'd been so busy with so many other details, including making scrambled eggs for Mom and the men in the morning, and answering phone calls. Upon reflection, I see the choice of black with a mist of shimmering purple about me was, I dare say, raven-like.

When I tried on a couple of different things, settling for the casual black clothes and sandals, Craig said, "That's very butch." I ignored him. His comment and my defiance characterized our marriage, but Craig is family, even if he is my ex-husband. I felt honoured that he came to my book launch with his video equipment to film the event for me.

When I wrapped the sheer scarf around myself, it felt right. I'd never given the scarf any thought when she'd left it for me at some point, but there it was, completing my choice of what to wear that special evening. Purple lilacs, purple scarf. Black raven.

Deanna looked beautiful in a purple, knee-length dress, her long dark hair falling over the bright pink pashmina draped around her shoulders. She read from *Stalking the Wild Heart*, an eco-literary novel that U.B.C. professor and novelist Luanne Armstrong called "moving and powerful." Harold Rhenisch, prolific award-winning author and poet said, "The depth of her knowledge of people and place shows in every luminous word." Nancy Holmes, professor and poet, University of British Columbia, Okanagan campus said, "Kawatski's debut novel deals with the damage done to families and the environment, and how such traumas as clear-cutting, extinction, war, and domestic violence are intimately connected." Deanna would launch her novel at the North Shuswap Community Hall in

Celista in September.

Alex Forbes was animated reading from his hilarious, off-the-wall novella *Oranges*, about two puppets who don't know they are puppets. They are on a road trip to the interior of BC, a piece inspired by surrealist Irish playwright Samuel Beckett. Natalia had illustrated *Oranges*, painted the brilliant cover painting, and painted the gorgeous cover painting for *Stalking the Wild Heart*. Alex would launch *Oranges* at Chapters in Kamloops in the fall.

Friend, Patrick Allwood—an actor who was also part of an improv theatre group in Salmon Arm—wrote a short skit set in Reflections bookstore. He and Clive performed it.

Centre stage, hanging against a black backdrop, was the stunning painting of raven against a bold orange sky that local artist, Lee Rawn had painted. I had commissioned her to do the painting and asked her to say a few words at the launch. Lee told a funny story, one of her many talents, about her first art exhibition at Reflections.

There must have been raven magic in the room that evening: the croaking raven calling people back to their seats after intermission, the First Nations presence, the fact that I wasn't nervous or paralyzed by fear.

Lest I forget, there's another aspect of raven, the great Trickster, that I was all too familiar with. Had things been going too well? According to Raven mythology, raven can't abide perfection and he likes to shake things up.

When it was time to pull a memory of Reflections from the fish bowl, Clive wasn't sure who to turn to. I pointed to Teri-Ann, wanting to include her. She slipped her slender hand into the bowl full of folded pieces of paper and withdrew one. She couldn't read the writing. Clive looked at the name on the paper. "Dave Harper," he said. "Would you please come up and read what you wrote?"

So Dave, my no-fear-of-public-speaking bachelor friend, possessor of a keen, dry wit, stood facing the audience of over one hundred people and began to read.

"When Kay first opened Reflections she was having some difficulty with a computer. I was asked to advise her about her problems and I have to admit I found her a bit distracted and somewhat of a complete ding bat."

A ding bat! A ding bat! Someone tell me he didn't just say that! I gasped. Laughter rose around me like the sound of doom.

For a split second, I squirmed in my seat like a gopher trying to find her hole, with the shadow of a raptor passing overhead.

From the pinnacle of praise, I'd plunged to the depths of embarrassment with lightning speed. Dave's words went to the heart of the girl who was easily embarrassed, who often wanted to disappear, the girl who never felt comfortable if the attention might inadvertently turn on her. The invisible girl.

Dave wasn't to blame. Trickster had found the Invisible Girl's hiding place. Just when I thought I was free of her, thinking she had disappeared forever, she'd been outed.

Dave continued. "Fortunately, history has definitely proved me wrong," he said, looking straight at me. He paused for effect. "Completely wrong."

I laughed along with everyone else, because if you don't laugh when Trickster strikes, you'll cry.

I wanted to set the record straight, to explain that he wasn't called in until the final fatal blow had been dealt to me and my bookstore after more than five years. A succession of inexplicable calamities were destroying my business—along with any sense of balance I still possessed—when the computer system crashed and the backup hadn't worked. I lost almost everything. I was more than distracted. Shock and fear threatened to shut me down me if I didn't act fast. I ran in every direction at once, searching for a solution. That's when Dave met me for the first time.

Never mind. I loved the music that Ken and his band played. I'd asked Ken if he knew *Harvest Moon* by Neil Young and he said they had never played it. The song was mentioned in "Raven,`` so I thought I'd ask. Well, if the last song of the evening wasn't *Harvest Moon*. They had learned it, and I was filled with such happiness at hearing the song that I sailed home in a cloud of joy.

All in all, the launch of "Raven" was a huge success, and probably the high point of my life so far, although I wasn't about to take the great number of book sales at the launch for granted. Launching *A Raven in My Heart* was only one leg of an exciting journey. The next year was spent organizing television and radio interviews, doing readings, book signings, and writing articles, and all this from the invisible girl who thought she had nothing to say; from the woman who struggled to find her own voice through the confusing haze of depression, anxiety, feelings of inadequacy and failure, from the woman who rose above being a ding bat!

59: Full Circle

I arranged for Deanna and me to do readings and a book signing at Banyen Books in Vancouver. My brother Jim put posters up in Vancouver. Deanna and I would stay at Jim's house, where he made us comfortable and drove us everywhere. I was struck by the fact that I had come full circle, and that seemed terribly significant to me. I had worked in Banyen as a book clerk, gone on to open a bookstore of my own, closed my bookstore, and I now I had returned to give a reading from my own book!

When my friend Carol showed up, happiness almost obliterated the nerves that were threatening me. We had worked together at Banyen Books. And Tom, my old friend, still worked there and he would be introducing Deanna and me. *This is too perfect.* I acknowledged the woman from the Federation of BC Writers that had brought her daughter. My cousin Barb arrived with a friend, and Jim had brought my niece Kristie and a few friends. More people we knew arrived.

We were set up in a cozy corner of the bookstore, with comfy wicker chairs, cushions on the beautiful Persian carpet, the wall behind us hung with colourful tapestries. I still considered Banyen Books to be one of the most beautiful bookstores anywhere, although this location was a different one than the one I had worked in.

What a surprise when Alan Twigg, publisher of BC Bookworld, arrived to take photos of Deanna and me. He couldn't stay, but was pleased that we were there, as he thought Banyen Books was a wonderful independent bookstore. After our readings, we gathered at Aphrodite's Organic Café and Pie Shop in the next block to visit with our friends and share a few appetizers.

The next evening, I'd arranged for us to read at the Agra Café on Granville Island, as part of the Federation of BC Writers contribution to the Vancouver Writers' Festival. I was the representative for our area. The place was packed! Jim drove us, and Craig joined us. Deanna and I each downed a glass of red wine to steady our nerves. When it was my turn, I stumbled over a word, as I have a habit of doing. I laughed and said maybe I shouldn't have had that glass of wine. Laughter. Sylvia Taylor, president of the Fed at the time, shouted, "Maybe you should have had another one!" More laughter.

The following day, Deanna asked if we could take Alan up on his invitation to her to visit him in his office. In the backyard of his home, among lush foliage and gardens, we found Alan's office and Alan at work. He offered us tea and we chatted. At one point he said that writers were under the mistaken notion that having a book published would change their life.

"It has changed my life," I said. He asked me to write him an article and email it to him about how publishing my book had changed my life. I had no idea at the time that he would publish the article and give it an whole page in BC Bookworld, with a huge photo of me—the one he'd taken at Banyen Books.

Excerpt from BC Bookworld article: Spring 2010.
Lookout, a forum for & about writers #38

In Bold Print: **How ex-bookseller Kay McCracken rescued her uncensored self**

I wasn't hiding anymore. I'd thrown off the cloak of invisibility and everywhere I went after that people stopped to say how much they loved the book or could they buy a copy from me. Emails began flooding in. People I didn't know called me at home. Praise for "Raven" was heady stuff. It was better than any drug I'd ever tried. I basked in feelings of worthiness because it was apparent that I'd written something that was touching people at a deep level.

It's five months since I launched "Raven" and my life has changed. As I go about the business of promoting and distributing my book, I've noticed a trait that wasn't there before. Boldness! Radical boldness! It grows stronger every day. It comes from a willingness to believe in myself, and what I've written. Call me naive, but I'll take it—all the joy that comes from allowing my uncensored self a say. Life dishes up enough heartache; I'll grab joy while I can.

60: Writers Festival 2010

What a thrill to see my name among the list of presenters for the 2010 Shuswap Writers' Festival on the attractive black and red poster designed by my friend Bob Beeson. *Could I have imagined any of this a few years ago when I lost my bookstore, my health, my confidence, and no doubt my mind.*

The poster featured Brian Brett, winner of the 2010 Bill Duthie Booksellers' Choice Award for his recent non-fiction book *Trauma Farm: A Rebel History of Rural Life*, Anne DeGrace, Patricia Donahue, Alex Forbes, Melody Hessing, Deanna Barnhardt Kawatski, Crawford Kilian, Mark Leiren-Young, Kay McCracken, James Murray, Steve Noyes, Lee Rawn, Crystal Stranaghan, Sylvia Taylor, Margaret Thompson, Vici Johnstone, owner of Caitlin Press, Jo Blackmore of Granville Island Publishing, and Ron Smith, Editor at Oolichan Books.

I asked friends Bob Beeson and Shelley Corbin to join me on a Promotion Committee I was putting together for the 2010 festival. Bob had designed posters, brochures and the program for the writers' festival for several years, and Shelley had volunteered at the first festival in 2003 and had volunteered at many more since then. Having once been in business for himself, Bob knew about marketing. He was highly creative and an original thinker, although he wasn't exactly a join-a-committee-kind-of-guy, so he surprised me when he agreed.

That year we had Sophie from the local Radio Station with us and she proved to be a dynamo. Shelley, as a former teacher, had great organizational skills and ideas. Unfortunately, Sophie had to move back east part way through the process of planning the Writers' Festival, which left Sarah Kipp from Gardom Lake to shoulder the responsibility, as she was the president at that time. It was nerve-wracking getting to the finish line, but with Sarah and the rest of the volunteers working flat out, we pulled it off.

It was Sophie, the festival coordinator, who asked if I would present a workshop. I was reluctant, as I was already busy with promotion for the festival and with Gracesprings Collective, and caring for my mother, who seemed to have one health crisis after another. Her hearing had gone downhill drastically. When I raised my voice to make her hear me, after repeating myself for the third time I sounded angry. Angie would run over and circle us crying. She loved Mom. They had a morning ritual they enjoyed. Angie would jump onto the bathroom counter and Mom would pet her, talk to her continuously, as Angie walked back and forth soaking up the love.

I took mother to have her hearing tested and she bought the hearing aids recommended. Mom never did get the hang them: I cleaned them every morning, put in fresh batteries, and put them in the right way, because if I let her put them in, she tried to stuff the wrong end into her ear.

"They plug my ears and I can't hear," she'd say often.

Eventually, we gave up on those things that plugged her ears and I bought a cheap amplifier that attached to her and that seemed a lot more manageable for watching TV, or visiting with guests.

As April 8th drew closer, I tried to prepare for an interview with Sheryl MacKay, host of CBC radio's North by Northwest weekend program that I listened to faithfully. My final strategy was just to stay calm, although I was so busy there wasn't time to get nervous. She had read my book, which I thought was amazing in itself, and wanted to interview me. It was my birthday and I hoped that might bring me luck with the interview, after all, nothing bad ever happened on my birthday.

After stopping in Vernon at Gallery Vertigo to drop off festival fliers and posters, I carried on to Kelowna. I managed to find the CBC office and was surprised at what a modest little studio it was. The interview had to be delayed for twenty minutes while they worked to eliminate an echo in the system. Sheryl was in the Vancouver office, and after the interview I wondered about a couple of things I said. *Oh well, too late to worry about that now.* I was happy that I'd had another chance to promote the Writers' Festival and that I had a great chat with David French, the news editor with the lovely voice. I thought he was so kind to take the time to chat to me after the interview.

I left festival fliers and a poster and walked the four blocks to Mosaic Books to deliver more fliers and posters. I had done a book signing there in November, on the first big snowfall of the season. I was happy to have my friend Dave with me on that occasion. We had put together a big display and I needed help setting up.

Shasta and a friend were coming to stay for several days. Her birthday was five days after mine. Mom's birthday was five days after Shasta's. There were cakes and gifts to buy, people to invite for both events. Income tax to prepare, while trying not to get overwhelmed. Angie got clobbered by a big black male cat. Lots of blood on the steps, although he may have got the worst of it. She only had a nick on one ear. I had to dash off to an appointment and asked Mom to let Angie in, but she forgot. I was angry, but with Mom's short-term memory in tatters, how did I expect her to remember that?

"A fire," Mom said, as she stood looking out our kitchen table window one day. Her tone conveyed nothing of the drama taking place. What I saw shook me. A trailer on the other side of our neighbour was fully engulfed in flames. The twelve-year boy I was friends with lived there with his family, their dogs and cats. People were running, kids were crying. Several people stood silent, stunned expressions on their faces, as flames shot out of every window. I was shaking so bad I could hardly dial 911, although someone had already called. I started crying when I realized that our closest neighbour wasn't home, but her two beloved Chihuahuas were inside. In a frantic state, I yelled at a young man to save the dogs because it looked as if that house would go up, too. He crawled through a window but couldn't find them.

Then came the howl from hell: a roaring, hissing sound like nothing I'd ever heard before as the fire broke through the ceiling and walls. Thick black smoke billowed out windows, flooding the park, transforming a spring day into hades. It sounded like something was about to explode and someone yelled "Run!"

When our neighbour arrived home, the fire chief told her that she couldn't go into her house. The woman, half his size, shouted "fuck you," pushed him aside, and emerged with her beloved Chihuahuas, as the fire scorched the side of her mobile.

    The next day the charred skeleton of the trailer stood as a reminder of the power of fire. The smell of toxic chemicals permeated the air of the park for weeks. What amazed me, was that my mother had been so unmoved by the fire, or so it seemed. I remember when her brothers, Dick, Jack, and Jim each passed away. We lived in town on 3rd Street then. No emotion, no tears, nothing. I thought it odd, but speculated that maybe she had to conserve what little energy she had by not wasting it on useless emotions. Or maybe the reality that death visits us all sooner or later had made her philosophical about it. I will never know because I didn't ask her, and she never spoke about her brothers again after their passing.

    I cleaned up the front garden on April 20, and then on April 22, Earth Day, I headed to the First Nations celebration down by the river. My Secwepemc First Nations friend Bonnie Thomas and her brother Louie talked about the ecology of the river and the land and their connection to it. I wandered down the trail alone afterwards, lingering at the fish drying platform, transported to another time, imagined the salmon drying there. Strolling on to the river bank, I stood soaking in the essence of green living forest and cool river until something caught my eye on the opposite bank. A belted kingfisher flitted through the trees, thrilling me with his silvery blue grey feathers, perky crest, and long sharp beak. I didn't want to leave the river, the sound, the smell, the motion, for it lulled me into a peaceful place.

    "There's a waiting list of six people for your book," the librarian said, with a smile. I felt elated in a way that was still new to me.
    The next thing was to design a workshop, but there were lawns to cut and gardens to prepare and plant even as the festival loomed ever nearer.

    Mom's right eye became irritated. It looked terrible. When her doctor looked at it, I was shocked to hear that my mother's bottom eye lashes had flipped up and were scratching her eyeball. The doctor showed me how to tape the eyelashes down and apply ointment daily. Poor Mom, although she handled this latest indignity well, I wondered how many more insults this aging process could dish out.

Later the eye surgeon began giving her regular botox shots, every five weeks or so, that helped restore the eyelashes to their rightful place. Mom hated getting the painful shots. I sat with her while she endured the ordeal, feeling her pain. My poor little mother was falling apart bit by bit.

As the time grew closer to present my workshop I got jittery. I practiced my material with Lee, who had done the cover painting for my book, and who was also giving a workshop at the Festival. When I began to feel overwhelmed, Shelley helped me put it all into perspective.

At the last moment, Deanna had a family crisis to attend to and couldn't be at the festival. I had suggested that our Collective be featured at the Friday evening Coffee House that kicked off the festival, so now it was just Alex Forbes and me. The place was standing room only and with all those famous authors reading I felt intimidated, but got through it.

The morning of the Writers' Festival I was ready. Brian Brett's keynote address was amazing. Then off to give my first workshop without any idea of what to expect or how many people would attend. Two people I knew were coming to my workshop and I steered them into someone else's out of nervousness, but the room filled up despite that.

Lee, who was introducing me, said "Kay, this is the woman who got the raven tattoo after reading your book." She was from Penticton. I'd forgotten about that. The young woman had phoned me at home to rave about my book, tell me about her tattoo, and that she had asked the local bookstore to order my book. What a surprise to meet her in person, although at that point I was trying my best to stay focused and calm, although I was astonished when she slipped the shirt from her shoulder, unveiling a discrete raven tattoo. She said that she was so moved by my memoir that she went right out and got the raven tattoo. I had the same kind of feeling hearing that as I did when the woman asked for my autograph. There are no words sometimes, only a great rush of pleasant sensation.

The workshop was over, and I had actually enjoyed the experience, well, all except for the woman who wouldn't stop talking when I asked if anyone wanted to read what they wrote in the exercise I gave them. She was quite an elderly woman and she went off on a tangent that had nothing to do with anything. She didn't even take a breath so that I could cut her off. I began to panic, but finally managed to jump in and stop her. If there's one thing I've noticed in this life, there are those who love to hear themselves talk, and those who can't get a word in, the listeners. Extroverts and introverts doesn't quite explain it.

Later, I thought maybe I do have more of my mother than I realize. She had been a teacher and I had just taught people something about writing a memoir.

Right after my presentation I had to cross the hall and introduce Brian and his workshop. After that I introduced Jo Blackmore of Granville Island Publishing.

Taking a chance, publishing my book, saying yes to presenting a workshop and everything else I took on was expanding my self-concept once again. My confidence had expanded and I think that helped me face down my fear of being seen and heard, and ultimately that weakened the demon of anxiety that usually had me in its thrall. I didn't understand how else I could be doing things that used to terrify me.

I can't remember when it was exactly, sometime in the spring or early summer that I wandered into the kitchen, went to the sink to fill the coffee maker with water and stared in complete disbelief at what I saw sitting on the lip of the green bird feeder.

At the time I didn't know what kind of bird it was, because I had never seen anything like it. I didn't want to breathe for fear the small bird that shimmered with bright turquoise feathers would disappear.

Finding the bird book, I looked it up: Lazuli Bunting, male. The illustration didn't do it justice at all, for the bird was truly astonishing. It was the encounters with birds and animals that I treasured above all else about living in Lakeland.

Part Five

The Final Years

Extreme Laughter

Not long after the book launch, I stopped to listen outside Mom's open bedroom door. Curious laughter bubbled up from a deep well somewhere in that tiny shell of a woman. Stepping inside her room I saw Mom laughing so hard that tears streamed down her face. She was sitting up in bed, reading my book.

"Mom, what's so funny?" I'm grinning because I'd never heard my mother laugh like that. She can barely contain her mirth, but eventually managed to say "It's the part about my mother." Then she reads "the look, not quite the evil eye, but close enough." And then she's laughing again.

"You know that look?" I say.

"Oh yes," she said, wiping the tears from her checks.

Coyote

Several days after the launch I prepared to meet Dorothy and Erica in town. I had thank you cards and a bottle of wine for each of them, and a book for Erica's husband Patrick who had written a skit and performed it at my book launch with Clive.

Erica got stuck cleaning up the kitchen at the art gallery after my book launch. I'd been oblivious to her plight, as I was chatting to people and signing books. Jim, Craig and Nick packed up my books and carted the bookcase and other props out to the van. I needed to make amends.

I turned right upon leaving Lakeland Mobile Home Park and headed toward town on 10th Avenue when a coyote trotted across the road in front of me and slipped into the woods behind our mobile. Oh my god. Angie's in the woods. Angie hung out in the cool woods during the day and I was terrified that the coyote would get her. Cats disappeared all the time in the jaws of coyotes, although I'd never seen one during the daylight in our park. I pulled a fast U-turn, then hit the gas pedal hard. Screeching to a stop in our driveway, I jumped out, grabbed a shovel and ran into the woods banging on trees and yelling

"Get out of here, coyote! Get Out!"

"Angie, where are you? Angie!" Yelling and banging trees like mad woman.

Teri-Ann watched this bizarre display with a look that I read as what's my crazy mother doing now? She had come to stay after the book launch. "Angie's in the woods," I yelled at her, "and a coyote ran in there." Tension had been building between us, but I had no idea how to deal with it.

No coyote to be seen. He must have kept on going across the highway on the other side. No Angie either. She was probably cowering under a wild rose bush, terrified to come out.

I called to Teri-Ann, as I jumped back into the car. "Would you call the Java Jive café and let Dorothy know that I'm on my way."

When I walked into Java Jive Dorothy was laughing. "We heard you were chasing a coyote," she said. She and Erica found that terribly amusing, and I felt a little silly.

After the high, the low

Journal:

Sunday, June 21, 2009.

Extreme joy leads to extreme sorrow …. my daughter … what I perceived as hatred in her words and in her eyes … shattered.

My friend Dave helped me through a bad patch after that. Mom remained oblivious to what had happened. The phrase "Don't tell Mom," meaning my mother, was often uttered in hushed tones when anything bad happened. Nobody wanted to burden her. She'd already had enough to deal with in her life and should be able to live out her elder years free from stress and anxiety. At least that was our misguided belief. Our assumptions didn't hold up if we'd looked at the reality. Mom could handle the worst of the worst and not crumble. She was incredibly strong.

Some time later, Deanna told me she sensed my daughter's vulnerability at my book launch. Our relationship was not on solid ground at that time. After the launch of "Raven" I probably should have taken a break, but Teri-Ann wanted to bring Ty, my grandson, for a visit. There was a call from Shasta, stranded at an airport in the States. Things went from bad to worse in a second.

After my daughter left, I kept working …. so much to do … setting up signings, sending out books, doing promotion for Alex's next book Oranges, and for Deanna's book Stalking the Wild Heart, writing thank you notes and buying gifts for people who helped with the launch. The troubles between my daughter and myself had to be put behind me, but I knew that this rift in our relationship wasn't going to be repaired easily.

Journal:

Thursday, July 2/09.

Today I talked to my doctor about what happened with Teri-Ann. I wanted his opinion. He asked if she was ADHD and I said I didn't know, but I've actually begun to wonder about that myself. He said that could explain everything. He also said she has a personality disorder, which means that she doesn't respond to things as most people would.

After a lengthy period of mourning the loss of my daughter we came back together. I missed her, just not some of her behaviours. In the meantime, Teri-Ann had been diagnosed with borderline personality disorder (BPD), one of the most difficult disorders to treat. She gave me the book stop walking on eggshells: taking your life back when someone you care about has borderline personality disorder, a book that explained many things about my daughter that had caused me grief over the years. The last event was actually the last straw. To protect myself I had to distance myself. The book explained that BPD's have instability in specific neural pathways in the brain, and the problematic behaviours are not intentional or wilful. That was eye opening, because she seemed to have no idea of the effect she had on people, or why her anger was so frightening. My beautiful, bright daughter, who was fun-loving and helpful, also had a dark side. No wonder then that her relationships were difficult to sustain and that she chose boyfriends with addictions. She had self-medicated with pot and other substances since she was thirteen years old. Reading the book was illuminating, but also heartbreaking. My poor daughter.

Family and Food

Journal:

Wednesday, July 1, 2009.

Breeze in the butterfly woods. Blue sky. Drifting cotton from the cottonwood trees. Angie sitting beside a patch of daisies growing in the lawn, as patterns of shade and sunlight flicker about her. Black and white against the green.

Mom liked being in her room best, except to watch TV in the evening with me, although at that time she was still able to join me on the back porch for lunch or afternoon tea. We loved sitting there watching the yellow butterflies floating through the trees, listening to the happy sounds as chickadees flitted among the branches; we enjoyed the feel of the breeze on our faces and arms, as we ate our avocado, cheese, and tomato sandwiches, and sipped our tea. The temperature was so lovely there in the afternoon. Bridgey, Angie and Katie always joined us on the back porch.

Mom wasn't much for conversation in those days, but there were a few phrases she repeated often, sometimes several times a day.

Angie sure loves you," she'd say, smiling. "She follows you everywhere." That made me smile every time she said it. It was true that Angie followed me everywhere and watched everything I did with keen interest. She had imprinted on me, because I'd saved her when she was so young. If I was Mom to Angie, my mother was grandmother, another special relationship.

At other times, Mom sat in her easy chair in the living room, starring at the vivid painting of the raven that Lee Rawn had done for me.

"I love that painting of the raven," she'd say. I always agreed. That made me smile, too.

Mom looked forward to her daughter, Karen, who had lived and worked in Kamloops for some time by then, visiting on weekends.

She'd often ask, "Is Karen coming this weekend?" Ever hopeful. Her youngest child had our father's bright blue eyes and round face. Karen had been blonde as a child, just like our mother.

One weekend I bought corn on the cob. Mom clapped her hands together, "Oh, goodie," she said, with all the gleeful enthusiasm of a child. That is still one of sister Karen's favourite memories. Mom and I both looked forward to Karen's monthly visits, because she helped with the cooking, often cooking an entire meal herself, giving me a break. As a special treat on Sunday mornings, she made wonderful omelets for us.

Mom also loved Chinese food. When we lived in town, and she was still mobile, we would go out to a Chinese restaurant for a treat once a month or so. When we lived in the mobile and she didn't want to go out, my friend Dave would bring us a Chinese food feast. I'd set out the Chinese dishes that my father bought in China town in Vancouver, put on a pot of fragrant basmati rice, and steep Jasmine green tea in the tall burgundy tea pot designed with flowers, Chinese symbols, and bamboo handles. Mom still had an appetite then, and it was a pleasure to see her enjoy the meal.

Christmas, Easter, and birthdays were celebrated with family dinners, although as I became more and more exhausted, I swore that I'd never cook another Christmas dinner.

Mom enjoyed all of her children, grandchildren, great and great great grandchildren. John, Marilyn and Chantelle would join us for meals on occasion. Marilyn's son Eric visited when he was in town, and her daughter Marlena, Clint, and their children visited, too. Mike and Gloria would come from Calgary with their children twice a year and camp in the yard. Jim,

Kristy and Nick visited on a regular basis, too. Teri-Ann and Shasta would bring the grandkids, Ty, Robbie and Savanna much to our delight.

After our mother took the child psychology courses necessary to get her day care certificate, she confided to me that she cried on more than one occasion, thinking back to all the things she'd done wrong raising her kids.

She was a different person now that the stress of raising her five children, while living with my difficult father, was far behind her. I doubt if there's a parent alive who doesn't regret some aspects of their parenting. I was young when I became a mother, and yeah, I have regrets, but at some point we have to let that go and pray that our kids work through whatever legacy they have from childhood and grow up to be good people. Amen to that.

Saying Goodbye

It was September 10, 2009. "Marilyn, can you come over? Somethings wrong with Mom."

"I'll be right over," she said. She could hear the fear in my voice. Marilyn didn't think twice about the hour or that she had a new student arriving at her place early the next morning; it was nearly one thirty in the morning. She lived about a ten-minute drive away.

Mom's breathing sounded strange and she was in distress. I thought she was dying.

"Mom we're going to have to take you to the hospital," we said, and for once she didn't fight the idea, only nodded. We bundled her up and got her into the car. I glanced up at the thousands of bright stars before jumping behind the wheel. It always amazed me how stunning the stars were in the night sky so close to town, but it all seemed a little surreal under the circumstances. Mom had been taking antibiotics for fluid on her lungs *and I'd taken her back to the doctor a couple of days earlier when it didn't look as if the medication was doing much good. She was still coughing and her lungs were rattling.*

We reached the hospital in record time, much faster than if we'd called the ambulance. Marilyn helped Mom into the Emergency entrance—a beacon of fluorescent light in the black nigh—while II parked the car. They admitted Mom right away. Oddly, there was no one else in ER that night, which added to the surreal feeling we probably all felt.

Mom had a collapsed lung and congestive heart failure. It wasn't looking good. An ordeal followed for our mother, who could hardly muster the strength to fight one more thing. She hardly ate anything that was brought to her in the hospital.

After talking to one of the nurses, who said her recovery didn't look hopeful, I called the family. People arrived from as far away as Vancouver and Calgary; we visited the hospital in shifts: her grandchildren and children, her sister, an ex-daughter-in-law. I would have brought the cats in to say goodbye if I could have.

When Mom returned from Vernon, where they transferred her in an ambulance for a procedure, a nurse told me they found an aneurysm in her stomach, a shocking thing to hear. They decided they couldn't do the risky procedure that she'd been sent there for and that she wouldn't survive an operation on the aneurysm.

Blue Flower

It was September 11, 2009, the day before the launch of Deanna's novel Stalking the Wild Heart. *I was supposed to read an excerpt from my Raven memoir, had ordered flowers for the event. With my mother's life hanging in the balance, I knew I couldn't go. I phoned Sarah, my friend from Gardom Lake to ask if she could stand in for me. We had planned to drive to the North Shore Community Hall in Celista together that evening. She dropped by to pick up the gorgeous bouquet of blue flowers I'd ordered to go with the book cover that Natalia had painted. They may have been delphiniums, blue bells, blue moon phlox, bellflower, and maybe blue iris, but I didn't know the names for sure. Much later, I discovered that a blue flower is a central symbol of inspiration.*

A blue flower also symbolizes the beauty of things. Blue flowers are the colour of intellect and spirituality.

Ever since seeing a photo, the exquisite beauty of the Himalayan blue poppy thrilled me. They are rarely seen and thought to be impossible to grow, although the sheer beauty, perfect poise, and the clarity of the blue had the same effect on me as the blue stone had. Astonishment, awe, and the awareness that there is more to life than most of us realize. Both are dazzling gifts from nature.

Revealing Photos

Sept. 20, 2009

Mom makes a miraculous recovery that no one expected, although her doctor told us our mother was in slow decline. All the serious problems were non-operable due to her age and frailty. She was sent to Bastion Place for two or three weeks for physiotherapy to build her strength up enough to come home. She wasn't in any pain thankfully, and once she got through the worst of it, her spirits lifted.

Mom's doctor talked to Mom and me about a "Do Not Resuscitate" order. Mom said she understood, and agreed. She didn't register any emotion, whereas it hit me hard. Oh my God, why is this aging process so difficult. The doctor explained it meant that if my mother was in cardiac arrest for example, they wouldn't pound on her chest to bring her back. If they did, it would break all her ribs. That sounded logical, but didn't help me emotionally. How could I accept that if my mother was dying there were things they wouldn't do to save her?

    Marge and I maneuvered Mom's wheelchair up to a table on the outdoor patio at Bastion Place. Auntie Marge pulled the first album from her bag and laid it out on the table in front of Mom and me. The temperature wasn't quite as hot as the day before but the sun was shinning in our corner of the courtyard. We wrapped a blanket around Mom.

    Black and white photos. Marge pointing out various boys that Mom had dated. Mom quiet, nodding now and then, even that an obvious effort. One photo stood out because it was so un-Mom like.

    Marge pointed out Mom with her boyfriend. They were standing on a bridge and Mom leaned back against the railing in a provocative pose, a model's pouty expression on her face, her boyfriend, a grinning teenager, standing beside her. I stared at the photo, trying to fit this image with the mother I knew. How very interesting, I thought, never having seen the sexy side of my mother before.

    Mom's only sister, Marge, told me about ski trips, hikes, dances, the boys, all the fun—innocent fun—they had in the group of kids they hung out with.

    I wheeled my mother back to her room, where I'd removed the dark photos of foxes looking at her from the walls. "I don't like them looking at me," she said, so I replaced them with her favourite painting of the yellow glads in the turquoise vase.

    I visited her every day and made us both a cup of tea, the tea time ritual carried over from home. She didn't want a TV or radio, for even that was too much effort for her to watch or listen to; it was obvious to me that she was conserving her energy and biding her time until she could come home.

The Incredible Shrinking Mother

I watched my mother disappear, little by little. She lost several inches in height over the years; the woman who had always been taller than my five feet 8 1/2 inches was much shorter than me now—the brutal reality of osteoporosis and bone loss. When I helped her undress for a shower the first time, I tried not to cry. My mother's body had become almost unrecognizable, from the robust, big-boned woman she had been, to a tiny skeleton hung with crepe-like skin that looked as white as death. Illness and age had transformed her.

When we moved into the mobile home, I found a handy man in the park, who charged reasonable prices. Mom couldn't step over the height of the bathtub, and had long since given up bathing anyway, but for her to have a shower I needed a solution. Roger had the perfect plan, having just done this for another elderly person. He took the bathtub out and built waist high walls with a wide opening for Mom to step through. It worked perfectly.

My mother was a modest woman. The indignities of being washed by others, having what amounted to her diapers changed, and not being able to do most of the little things that she was used to doing herself, must have been difficult. But other than saying "I'm so sorry you have to do all this," she was resigned and uncomplaining.

She really was a lovely woman. Everyone who met her knew that. I don't know why I'd been ambivalent about her growing up. She wasn't grumpy or demanding like some elderly people I'd heard about. The only time she was difficult was once when it was time for her shower. We'd been doing fine, but that time for some unknown reason she refused.

"No," she said emphatically.

"Mom, you have to have a shower."

"No!" she said again, reminding me of a toddler digging her heels in.

Her defiant stance so surprised me that we skipped the shower that day.

One part of my mother that didn't change was her elegant, piano-playing fingers. She was proud of those long fingers and tapered nails. Karen was good at taking care of her fingernails and I took our mother to regular appointments at the foot nurse for a foot massage and the clipping of the toe nails.

The one thing my dear mother wouldn't abide, however, was if she thought her hair didn't look good. I arranged for a neighbour Mom liked to come over and cut her hair and give her a perm. That made her happy. Mom had always gone to a hair salon to have her hair—a beautiful full head of white hair—washed and set, but eventually it was too difficult for her to go to a salon.

John's Fall

Nov. 4, 2010.

The phone rang. It was Marilyn calling from a car speeding toward the Kamloops Hospital. "It's John," she said. "He's had an accident. It's bad." I heard a tremor of emotion in my sister's voice, a woman who was normally calm in a crisis.

"He fell down the stairs at the shop around 5:15 am. He's in a coma, Kay."

She told me Marlena, her daughter, was driving. When my niece Marlena showed up for work at the hospital, her mother was there. That's when she learned what had happened to John, her stepfather. They picked up Marilyn's youngest daughter, Chantelle and Chantelle's boyfriend, and headed for Kamloops where John had been transferred from the Salmon Arm Hospital.

John's head had cracked open.

I felt sick and numb. I told Mom that John had an accident and that I had to go to Kamloops. I called the woman next door to stay with Mom. Distracted as she was by the neighbour my mother didn't register what had happened.

Preparations for leaving didn't go well. It felt like an endless labourious task that I couldn't quite come to the end of. I couldn't think. The air was too heavy to move through. I've got to get out of here! Why can't I get going? The neighbour told me to take a couple of Tylenol to calm down. I knew I had to pull myself together for Marilyn's sake.

Karen called from the hospital badly shaken. She had left work immediately. "It doesn't look good." She could barely say the words. "How soon are you leaving?"

It seemed to take hours to get to the Kamloops Hospital, find a parking spot in the maze of parking levels, and finally to find I had to put money in a machine for a ticket to park. I couldn't figure out how to do it and a line had formed behind me. Fortunately, a kind man took pity on me and helped. My mind wouldn't work.

Marilyn hugged me long and hard when I arrived. Karen looked like she was in shock. Chantelle had collapsed into her boyfriend's arms, her face puffy from crying. Other family and friends were there, too. They had already heard that John's brain damage was so severe that the only brain activity left was partial breathing.

Holding onto each other, Marilyn and I entered the room where John lay so I could say my goodbyes to my brother-in-law. "We love you, John." I said over and over. "I wish you peace." I felt like my sister was holding me together, instead of the other way around.

Poor John. He had tried so hard, but when he fell, he fell hard; he fell off his program after years of sobriety. He fell off that as hard as he fell down the stairs. He was a goner the moment he took that first sip of alcohol. He was pronounced dead at 10:10 that evening.

Why is it that some people have so much to overcome? To society it looks like failure and weakness, but did John have a choice really, based on his background, and his genetics? When temptation flaunted its alluring face, the face of blessed oblivion when John was at his lowest point, he reverted to the life he was familiar with before he met my sister. He faced giving up the business he'd worked so hard to build, that he had pinned all his hopes and dreams on.

He was in his forties, which was too young to die. But he'd already said goodbye to several family members, including his mother, and a week before the death of his sister Gloria, who succumbed to cancer. John's Indigenous blood and upbringing left him susceptible. Blood, or genes if you will, and upbringing, make many of us susceptible to addictions and other disabilities. Alcoholism, also known as alcohol use disorder, is fifty percent an inherited disease.

Resilience isn't built into all of us. The ability to come back from disappointments, hardship, and loss, depends on our attitude to life's harsh lessons; cultivating a realistic positive attitude helps, and a good support system is crucial when overcoming stressful situations—and even then there are no guarantees.

Even Marilyn's love, John's Christian faith, and the church community hadn't been enough to save him.

Broken

The three things he loved most
were making people laugh,
family gatherings with his fun-loving Metis family,
and with our family, the educated white people
And my sister, who corrected his grammar
he loved her above all else.

The thing that pulled our beloved John
away from us
was something even more seductive
than his love of family, friends, and laughter

for when he fell into the cycle of addiction
he had left behind so long ago
it snared him—vulnerable and unsuspecting—like a trap
hidden in tall grass
the drugs, the alcohol
filled his brain, his veins
with longing
It broke him.
It broke us too.

Marilyn

Playing my Joni Mitchell CD, the song, River that I love .... identifying with the feeling, the longing, to have a river to skate away on.

Another Christmas. We got through it. Did turkey and all the trimmings. Sister Karen came. Teri-Ann and her current boyfriend and Ty were there. After a lengthy hiatus, my daughter and I had made peace with each other. Marilyn was there, although in body only.

Her grief was intense for the next year, but she did everything she could to cope: grief counseling, groups, a widow's retreat, church and prayer, but the experience changed her. Grief changes people. Trauma changes people.

What I didn't know then, and that I know now after reading Joan Didion's The Year of Magical Thinking, is that the person who appears strong after a shocking death, as Marilyn did in the beginning, may in fact be experiencing the common symptoms of shock, numbness, and the sense of disbelief. In Didion's situation the ER staff called her a "pretty cool customer." Some survivors experience the feeling of being inside a cocoon, or wrapped in a blanket.

Once the shock wore off, Marilyn experienced what is referred to as "complicated grief," the terrible kind of grief that occurs when the deceased and the survivor were very close and depended on each other. John and Marilyn did everything together and she worked in his business with him. Sadly, John wanted to throw away everything he held near and dear not long before his death, which further complicated my sister's grief. At some level he had given up. Would my sister give up, too, or would she find the strength to go on? It looked iffy.

I could have said to Marilyn mourn the person you were because she's not there anymore. I could have added, you've lost your innocence, but on the up-side you will become a deeper, more understanding person.

But I didn't know anything about that then. There has to be some benefit to standing at the edge of the abyss. Every experience contains a gift, say the spiritual teachings, although that's a tough idea to accept when life throws swift, disorienting blows our way. I leaned from Didion's book that of the two levels of grief, one is like having a serious mental illness; it's a milder form of manic depression. Grief is a form of madness, but no one tells you that.

About a year after John's death, Marilyn was diagnosed with stage three breast cancer just as her life was looking up. She had made new friends, was getting out again. She was smiling again.

Marilyn's diagnosis threw all of us into shock. Mom was in the hospital again; everything was up in the air and uncertain. Marilyn advised us not to tell our mother about her cancer. Marilyn, Teri-Ann, her boyfriend, and I took turns helping with Mom's meals.

By the time Mom was in the hospital that time I had high blood pressure, a thyroid imbalance, anxiety and depression, irritable bowel syndrome, which had become quite severe, back and neck pain, and constant headaches. I was on medication for most of it. I was falling apart, and didn't see a way to put an end to all the pain. Pain medication didn't help much.

Yet Another Diagnosis

During that time period I took on the task of organizing a book tour throughout BC for Caroline Woodward's latest novel Penny Loves Wade, Wade Loves Penny, a wonderful Canadian Odyssey story for adults published by Oolichan Books. It was a tonne of work lining everything up, but I was proud of the success of the tour.

Meantime, the eye surgeon gave us the bad news. Mom had age-related wet macular degeneration, the most serious kind. It leads to vision loss. Appointments were scheduled with a specialist in Kamloops. He was the only doctor doing the treatments, which meant people from all over the province sat together for hour upon hour in the small, stuffy waiting room. Hours of waiting, then a test, then more waiting to see the doctor, who had no time for niceties or pleasant conversation. He would stick a needle into both of my mother's eye balls! Mom, stoic and brave through it all. I couldn't have done it. I forget how long we went on like that, driving to Kamloops, sitting in the waiting room for most of the day, needles in the eyes!

Finally, the doctor told us that the treatments weren't working. Could anything be worse than going blind! But there seemed nothing else he could do for Mom.

I developed a habit of rocking, or kind of swaying. Marilyn said something about it. I guess I was comforting myself, as every day there seemed to be more bad news coming at Mom and I, and the movement seemed to help my back pain in some small way. I had to buy a nebulizer and give her medications for her lungs at regular intervals during the day. At one point she needed oxygen and that was another ordeal.

Marilyn was tactful and lighthearted when she mentioned the rocking thing, but one day I was sitting in the mall with her, having coffee, and I may have started swaying. She smiled and said it's okay to do that if there's music playing and just then a live band started up near us, which I thought was terribly funny, and we both broke up laughing.

Little Brown Bird

Waiting out winter at the bird feeder, my little brown bird. Solitary, silent, a symbol of resilience. She appeared one day after the chickadees had left. A small, nondescript brown bird sitting on the green lip of the bird feeder piled high with fresh snow. I wondered about her, but as the days went on I looked forward to seeing her. I would peer out the kitchen sink window and there she'd be—a spark of life in the silent white world, not forlorn, just biding her time, perhaps she even enjoyed the curtain of snow falling all around her. The overhang of the feeder gave some protection. The sight of her comforted me, gladdened my heart. She became my beacon of hope. If she could make it through the cold winter, then so could we.

Nightly Intrusions

The doorbell rang. Here we go again. It was time for the nightly arrival of the care aid. I'd reluctantly agreed to have someone come in the morning to prepare Mom for the day, and in the evening to prepare her for bed.

Mom was not in good shape and growing worse daily. She'd come out of Bastion Place the last time with a pressure sore, a nasty sore that's difficult to deal with once it gets started. I'd called the nurse in to look at it. Three women arrived, hovered over my mother, discussing her condition and photographing the sore. When they eventually left, Mom told me how uncomfortable she had felt with all that poking, prodding, and peering at her. Watching them do that to my mother, made me angry. I had to leave the room, even though on a rational level I knew they were trying to help, but on an emotional level it felt like a violation. But true to both our natures, we bore the unpleasant intrusion with dignified calm.

But the time had come. I knew that I couldn't continue much longer, as I had almost reached my breaking point. Actually, I probably had many times over but somehow managed to keep going. The agonizing decision had not been easy, but I was not in any shape to be caring for Mom anymore.

I had to have the dreaded talk with my mother about going into extended long-term care, but Mom, ever full of surprises, agreed with me. No tears, no argument, no apparent sadness. Just agreement. That did it. I burst out crying and couldn't stop. I phoned Marilyn, blubbering uncontrollably, and she came right over.

The head nurse said I would have to exhaust all the options before they could admit Mom to a care facility. What that meant was I had to accept a revolving door of care aids coming into our space two times a day. Mom and I tolerated these intrusions, not that all the women weren't nice, but it took us out of our own routine and we are both private people. It meant that with every new woman they sent, I had to show them the shower set up, and where everything was kept. Mom was compliant and didn't allow herself to show the uneasiness she experienced every time a new person had to give her a shower or get her ready for bed.

I opened the door to the care aid standing in the porch light. She was short, with a round, ruddy face and blue eyes. She was wearing a hijab, the veil that Muslim women wear that covers the head and chest as a symbol of modesty. Her body was covered from her chin to her feet in a loose robe that covered her arms as well. She was the only Muslim in Salmon Arm, and a Caucasian one at that.

We introduced ourselves and I led her into the living room where Mom sat in her easy chair with her feet up. We were watching TV after supper, as was our habit. A little TV before bed.

The care aid, Rosy I'll call her, sat down on the couch directly across from Mom. Mom looked at her, scowled, she actually scowled, something I'd never seen my mother do before, and said, "You've got to be kidding." My mouth fell open and I ventured a quick glance at Rosy. I noticed a deepening red in her already florid cheeks.

I blurted out, "Mom, this is Rosy and she's come to get you ready for bed." Mom scowled some more.

"I'll get you into your nightie Mrs. McCracken and then you can come back out to watch TV." Rosy did her best to maintain a calm, friendly tone. I, on the other hand, was agog at my mother's hostility. I wasn't even sure where it was coming from. I'd never seen any racist tendencies in my mother, but at that moment I really didn't know what to think.

Rosy didn't stay long, but none of the women ever did. In and out. I watched as she bustled out to her car. I felt for the woman who was only doing here job, but I felt even more for my mother. I guessed that she had finally snapped what with all the unnecessary nightly intrusions. Who could blame her? I was barely keeping it together myself.

The never-ending saga of my dear mother's declining health and assault on her dignity was a sobering look at what old age is like.

Lost

As I looked at Mom sitting at the table after breakfast, staring out the window, my heart ached at how small and frail she'd become. She would sometimes apologize when I had to clean up an accident or wash her. "It's okay, Mom," I would say. "I don't mind." And I didn't. Some elderly people become cranky and miserable, and who could blame them, but not my mother. I felt blessed that she was so easy going.

All I could do was try to make her comfortable and bring her favourite treats every day: a Cadbury Caramilk chocolate bar and the coffee she loved to get served in bed before coming out to breakfast—anything to make her last days a little happier.

Considering how close I felt to Mom, I still wondered what my ambivalence about her had been about, and when and why did that start? I felt there was something more.

Searching my memories one stands out. I walked to kindergarten by myself every day. Over the tracks, past the old men sitting on their porches watching me with dark eyes that frightened me. I walked and walked ... such a long way ... where am I? Am I lost?

Somehow, I always made it from lower town Revelstoke, though the Italian part of town and on through another section of town, until I eventually reached the main street where I found the church.

Why did my mother make me walk all that way alone? Even now if I'm under a lot of stress, for a split second or so nothing looks familiar, even on a street I travel on all the time. Where am I? Did I get traumatized somehow on that long walk?

What's surprising is that it took me so long to find a sense of belonging, to feel at home in the company of my mother, and to start writing seriously. The desire to write had always been there, but I didn't know who I was for most of my life. I hadn't yet learned that writing opens so many doors, including what lay beyond the blue door. Not only was my mother much more than I ever realized, but so was I.

Admitting Defeat

I wish I had a river I could skate away on.

Mom was in the hospital again, where once a day she was helped out of bed and into a wheelchair to have lunch. She needed help to eat, but even with me, Marilyn, Teri-Ann, or her sister Marge spoon feeding her she wouldn't eat much; maybe some soup, a spoonful of pudding.

One day I was there feeding Mom when her sister Marge and her daughter Noelle arrived with a special gift for Mom. Marge had knit a purple shawl for her sister to wrap around her shoulders in the hospital and had taken it to Juanita Austin, minister at the United Church, to be blessed. Mom was pleased and I was touched by the love in that gesture.

Even with all the care I could see that my mother was not getting better. She had descended to a place I didn't know how to bring her back from. Bringing her home if they released her from the hospital would not be an option. The time had come, but it was an ordeal getting my mother accepted into long term care. I had to stand up and fight the system, for both myself, and for my mother. A pressure sore had to be managed in the hospital by giving her a special mattress. She could no longer get to a bathroom. Mom handled all the indignities calmly, never complaining. Her stubbornness was still intact, however. If she didn't want to get out of bed to eat sitting in the wheelchair, there was no budging her. I'd seen a nurse and a physiotherapist, who tried to get her up walking, give up in frustration.

During evening visiting hours I brought Craig's novel Wakaw: A Prairie Lake Town, 1900 – 2011 to read to Mom. Wakaw is the Saskatchewan town where Craig grew up. He'd written an historical novel to coincide with the centennial celebrations in his home town in the summer of 2011. Three families through five generations are fictionalized in the fact-based history of a small prairie lake town. "Amidst a panorama of dreams, hardship, tragedy, corruption, murder and sex, the journey of Ukrainian, Hungarian and German immigrants are tracked from the oppression of the old country to the bitter hardships of their prairie farms, from the disillusionment of many to the empire-building triumph of others, from a lakeside Eden to a 21st century town with an uncertain future."

Mom loved my nightly readings and listened with rapt attention, her eyes shinning bright in the shadowy light, her bed separated from the one beside her and across from her by a thin curtain. I soon discovered that the other patients in the room were also listening, as were their visitors. They asked me the name of the book and told me how much they were enjoying it. By that time in the evolution of Gracesprings Collective, Carolyn

Woodward had gone her own way and I suggested we take my ex-husband, Craig Brunanski, on as a member of our collective with his recently independently published book.

Craig had grown up in a newspaper family that gave him an appreciation for the written word and for the power of story. He taught English in Edmonton for seventeen years before his marriage broke up and he moved to Vancouver with two of his three daughters. Eventually we met and married, although this second marriage didn't have a happily-ever-after ending either. I can't blame the failure of that union on being a pregnant teenager, as I was in my mid-forties by the time I married Craig.

During our courting period, Craig continued to follow his passion to write; he wrote, produced and performed in his 'great Canadian hockey play' Home Ice. Several other plays of his were well received. I recall Single Life with Condom produced for the Fringe Festival that played to sold out crowds every night due to the great publicity the play got. He wrote feature articles for a political magazine and plunged into acting, winning small parts in television and film, appearing in such shows as the Beach Combers, the X-Files and Scary Movie. Craig and I had remained friends after splitting up because I admired many things about the man. He was still family despite the piece of paper declaring us divorced.

On January 13, 2012, I wrote a letter to my doctor requesting that he send a letter to Community Care stating that I was no longer able to look after my mother. I asked Jim to help me figure out how I was going to deal with the current crisis. My own doctor had been asking me to get Mom into extended care, for the sake of my health, for years.

The day Mom was transferred from the hospital to long term care was the saddest day of my life, and that doesn't even begin to explain how I *felt. When I went to pick her up from the hospital, the staff already had her washed, dressed and sitting in a wheelchair. He hair was wet and plastered to her head, which made her look even smaller. Her expression told me how uncomfortable she was, possibly even in pain, but she didn't say a word.*

At Bastion Place the nurse said we had to cut all Mom's beautiful clothes up the back, because they needed to lift her onto the commode and the toilet, and that made it easier than taking her clothes off. The ritual of cutting her clothes felt like a violation, a final indignity for a woman who had always taken such pride in her appearance. She didn't, thankfully, register what was happening. I was asked to label all her clothes; my mother had probably done that for me when I went to summer camp, so once again, the strange reversal of roles.

Two of the women in the room with my mother were beyond conversing and the other woman turned out to be the neighbour that had lived across the street from Mom and Dad in Sorrento Place. She kept saying, "that doesn't look like Marion", which upset me even more. I wanted to yell at her, Shut Up! You'll upset my mother, but Mom wouldn't look at her or even acknowledge the woman. My mother had retreated into a place where I no longer knew how to reach her.

Leaving my frail mother lying in a bed in a room with three other women felt like I had abandoned her, a woman who had always been there for me to the best of her ability.

Love You Forever

Marilyn had her mastectomy on March 21st, which she bore with amazing calm and courage. My niece Marlena and I were in the doctor's office with Marilyn when her doctor delivered the news that she had stage three breast cancer. He told Marilyn later that Marlena and I looked like we might collapse, while Marilyn remained composed and continued to ask questions.

Mom was rushed back to the hospital from Bastion Place with an acute case of not being able to breathe. She lingered there for weeks until one day while I was visiting, her doctor noticed that Mom had turned a corner. The doctor took me out to the hall to tell me that it was time. She would arrange to have her admitted to palliative care at Bastion. I choked back my tears, as I thanked her for her care and compassion. Outside in the parking lot, my tears ran freely.

I sensed something had shifted, but it was my friend Dave's birthday and I'd invited him out for dinner. Reluctantly, I left Mom in the palliative care room where she'd been for going on two weeks.

"Dave, I have an uneasy feeling. I have to get back to Mom. Sorry that I can't stay for dessert." He understood, as he'd been through the same ordeal with his mother.

A woman that Mom and I knew from the pharmacy stayed with her while I was at dinner; she told me she had always thought that Mom was special somehow. She was still there when I returned. Nothing much had changed. Just a feeling I had. I asked the nurse what she thought, but she couldn't say. Eventually, I left Mom sleeping and went home to rest.

April 19th.

After coffee the next morning, I got ready to go back when a nurse called from Bastion Place. "You'd better come now. I think it's her time." The urgency in her voice told me more than her words. I made a quick phone call to Teri-Ann and Shasta, jumped in the car and raced to Bastion. Running in the main entrance, a nurse intercepted me, and the look on her face told me I was too late to say goodbye. It was my mother's birthday! Her 91st birthday! I wasn't there!

I sat down beside the bed, stared at my mother's ghastly pale, thin little body. The nurse wouldn't stop talking, asking pointless questions about siblings, trying to fill the sad space with words that had no meaning to me.

"Can you leave me alone with my mother please."

I was thankful when she left the room. I was also thankful that I hadn't shouted at her. I hoped that Mom's spirit might still be hovering, so I talked to her. I didn't want to cry then. I'd heard that you can hold people back if you show too much grief.

"I love you, Mom. I'm sure you're at peace. Thanks for being my mother and for everything you were to all of us, and always will be." I reached for her hand, which was still warm. I could have sworn I saw her stomach vibrating, almost imperceptibly. Is she still breathing? Maybe I'm hallucinating. Her mouth hung open in a fixed position, and her eyes were closed. There were no other signs of life.

I mentioned my concern at the nurse's station and a couple of people went in to check on Mom, stethoscope in hand while I sat near the entrance waiting for the arrival of Teri-Ann and Shasta, wanting to prepare them.

My face was wet with tears, as I waited. The tears were for my mother and for all she had been through and how she had borne it all with amazing grace. Although I felt terrible that I hadn't been with her at the end. Why hadn't I stayed that night?

When they arrived, Teri-Ann, Shasta, baby Riley and I went back into the room so they could say their goodbyes. Mom had missed meeting her latest great great grandchild by hours. The had arrived back from Alberta the day before and had intended to visit Mom that morning.

Shasta and baby came to stay with me that night and I was grateful for their company. They slept in Mom's bed. About four a.m. I heard my name called. Just once. Very clear. Not a voice I recognized; it didn't sound male or female. I wandered into Mom's room where Riley was just beginning to fuss a little.

"Shasta, did you call me?" No, she hadn't. Curious. I stayed with them awhile before going back to bed.

Everything after that was about dealing with the practicalities: calling family, arranging details with the funeral home, designing the head stone with Marilyn, getting an obituary written and into the papers, arranging a time and place and date for a memorial. As the executor of her will there were lots of details to look after, bills to pay.

A children's book that Mom loved, that made her tearful every time she read it, was "Love You Forever" by Canadian children's author, Robert Munsch. I had that engraved on her head stone. She would have liked that.

God, the Great Trickster

The day the funeral director gave me my mother's wedding rings because they were cremating her body, I fell into a morbid state. It hit me hard, the thought of her dear lovely body being burned to ashes. I was being consumed by grief, as Mom was being consumed by fire.

If I'd bought into the idea that it was just her body, that her soul or spirit had gone to be with God, or whatever divine spirit there might be, I suppose that would have comforted me. But I didn't believe in anything anymore, as I once had. It's all a pack of lies and fairy tales, I told myself. There is nothing else. She lived this long life, some of it difficult to bear, and now she's gone. What a weird concept. Where was she? How could she be gone? Anger. Sadness. Grief.

Death, the big black hole that eventually swallows us up. Nothingness. Damn!

I was no longer convinced there was an afterlife, or any rhyme or reason to life and death, period. On the way to pay my respects to my dying brother-in-law in the Kamloops hospital I shook my fist at the heavens.

"Why? What kind of God lets things like this happen?" I shouted. And this is just our family's personal tragedy. What about all the other atrocities that happen every day in every part of the world? Unthinkable horrors. I'm pissed!

Marilyn's Christian friends were helping her through her grief with their faith that God has a plan. Some plan, I thought! Marilyn said for the first year after John died, everywhere she went she carried that great hole inside of her.

I'd believed in an afterlife once, but that was after my father had passed away unexpectedly in 1990. Dad had fallen in the garden, snapping his leg in several places. I told Mom I wanted to drive up from Vancouver to Sorrento on the weekend to see Dad. She said there was no need, as he'd be out of the hospital in a couple of days.

A few days later, when Craig picked me up from work, I said please take me to the beach. I'd been in an altered state at work all afternoon and didn't understand why. At Jericho Beach I sat with my back against a massive willow tree, staring at the ocean, although not really seeing it. I felt trapped in a grey cocoon of sadness, the depth of which I didn't understand.

When I got home, I got the call from Mom. Dad had died suddenly of a heart attack in the hospital. I lay on a bed sobbing, when a calm presence, of what I can only think of as my father, descended over me like a soft warm blanket and conveyed, without words, that he was okay.

Sometime later, reading On Death and Dying by Elizabeth Kubler-Ross, I was comforted to learn that we would see all our loved ones again one day and that death was not the end, but a passage into a better place. Kubler-Ross, Swiss-born psychiatrist, pioneer in Near-death studies said,

"Dying is nothing to fear. It can be the most wonderful experience of your life. It all depends on how you have lived." I knew that my father had lived many years clean and sober by the time he passed, and that he had made amends to those he had hurt, mainly my mother.

And now mother. No word from her, although maybe the raven on the fence had meant something. I'd written about the spirit world in my Raven memoir. I'd believed in such things then. My current belief that nothing of us exists after death did not feel like a happy place to be. I railed against God. "God, if you did create this universe, then maybe you really are a Trickster! Native people had it right all along then. God really is a Big Black Bird, a Trickster.

Raven on the Fence

A day or so after Mom's passing a big raven sat on the fence in full view of the kitchen-sink window.

My mouth fell open. Ravens had flown over many times but I'd never seen one sit on the fence, beak open, making that resonant throaty call that only a raven is capable of. He, or she, kept up an insistent clamor, a sight to hear and behold. I thought my uncanny connection to these intelligent trickster birds was behind me. Was this visitation nothing, or something more than I could process at the time?

The next day a raven showed up on the other side of the trailer. Insistent croaking. Raven had been my touchstone, my connection to a mystical world, or at least that's how I saw it, during my time managing my bookstore, and later at Gardom Lake.

Some First Nations believe that raven brings messages from the deceased ancestors. As moved as I was by the two raven visits, part of me wanted to believe, and the other part of me was numb and didn't know what to think.

Beacon

Raven on the fence

proclaiming

I'm here

I'm here

pay attention!

croaking insistence

that there is more to life and death

than meets the eye

bold against the April green

perched on the weathered wooden fence

where one

never before was seen

beak open

my beacon

Mom, I miss you

Did you send the black bird

to remind me

that the wonder of nature exists

and that you, your spirit,

exists amid all that wonder, too.

The Honouring

A celebrated Irish novelist, poet, playwright and short story writer, Dermot Healy, known as the Celtic Hemmingway, said that in Ireland men with black hair are called Blackbird. In an interview with Healy on CBC radio he said that a character in his novel Long Time No See is called The Blackbird. I heard this two years after publishing A Raven in My Heart: Reflections of a Bookseller. After moving to Salmon Arm, in a strangely metaphysical turn of events, my deceased father, he of the raven black hair, came to me as a blackbird.

If my father was a blackbird, then my mother was the deep-rooted, sheltering tree that he, and we—her children, grandchildren, great, and great great grandchildren—took comfort in from time to time. We sought the beauty of her presence, just as birds flock to their favourite trees, trees where they find respite.

She would not be blown down by the winds of fate, no matter how hard they tried.

I read a shorter version of the black bird/sheltering tree analogy at my mother's memorial.

Mom didn't want a big funeral, just a gathering of family, however Karen suggested having something at the United Church, as Mom was a life-long member. I met with the minister, Juanita, to discuss what we would do. She had read my book, and perhaps because of that, she suggested having the memorial in the room with the labyrinth painted on the floor and arranging people in circles around the middle of the room. I thought that was a lovely idea. No one person standing above the others, no hierarchy, just a circle where everyone is equal and where we would honour our mother.

A prayer labyrinth is used to facilitate prayer, meditation and spiritual transformation. Walking the labyrinth involves releasing, receiving, and when one reaches the centre, they are said to be returning. At its most basic level the labyrinth is a metaphor for the journey to the centre of your deepest self and back out into the world with a broader understanding of who you are.

In the middle of the labyrinth a round low table held a beautiful photo of Mom, a bouquet of white flowers with a bunch of red berries in the centre, and a white candle burning in a red glass candle stick holder. I didn't consciously choose those colours, but at some level did I pick white for her innocence and red for her bold, brave self, for she definitely embodied both those qualities. It also seemed significant that she was in the middle of the labyrinth, a place where she would be returning to her spiritual home, to the God of her understanding.

Marilyn was going into the hospital for another surgery the day after the memorial, but she and her son Eric greeted people, with my nephew handing out memorial cards and asking people to sign the guest book I'd bought.

My young niece, Kristy McCracken, began the program by playing her guitar and singing "Hallelujah," Leonard Cohen's iconic song. To hear my beautiful niece sing it at my mother's memorial moved me to tears. The song means different things to different people with its blend of the sensual and the spiritual. It speaks of the contradiction we feel about having faith when we're broken and grieving. But in the end, it's always Hallelujah, an affirmation.

Jim spoke about the time he invited Mom and Dad on a white-water rafting trip and our mother didn't hesitate for a second. She had an adventurous spirit and wasn't afraid to try anything new.

In my eulogy I mentioned her physical strength, the fact that she could take my father down in an arm wrestle. And her mental strength. She *was always right and she knew it. When I as the eldest daughter moved in to take charge of her and her failing health, I found myself with a formidable challenge: two head strong women, both used to doing things their own way, butting heads. That got a laugh.*

I could have said, but didn't, that we are both Aries the ram, with Mom on the cusp of Taurus, the bull, which is where the image of butting heads comes from.

Karen read something she wrote about her admiration and love for her mother, and talked about Mom's love of mystery shows on television, especially Murder She Wrote, staring Angela Lansbury. My sister also honoured me for taking such good care of our mother over the years.

Marilyn played a moving piece of music for our mother, which was appropriate, because our mother loved music. She sang in Church choirs and the Glee Club. To her chagrin, after she married our father, she discovered he couldn't carry a tune, and that he couldn't dance. She, who loved dancing and singing.

Craig had come to pay his respects. When he spoke into the circle, he mentioned that we had been married and then he recalled the time that he, Jim, and another friend had been building book shelves for my bookstore, as I worked on other details. We put in long days, while Mom looked after Kristie and Nick, her grandkids. He said the thing was she never complained about doing that and considered it couldn't have been easy as she was in her seventies.

I had to admit that Craig looked very handsome. Alex, Deanna, Eric and Deanna's mother, Lorna, sat in the circle, as did friends from the writing community. Marilyn's friends from her church were also present. Teri-Ann and her son Ty, Shasta and baby Riley, all the nephews and nieces, and many other relatives filled out the circle.

My eulogy paid tribute to the woman I loved deeply, quirks, flaws and all. I had begun working on the sequel memoir that year. Beyond the blue door—beyond depression, anxiety and hopelessness—was a place where my mother and I eventually connected in surprising ways.

In my usual habit of going overboard, I planned a chili party at the mobile for family after the memorial at the church. Two kinds of chili, no less: one less spicy for those who didn't like the heat. I invited Deanna, Eric, Deanna's mother and my friend Dave to join us for this family gathering. Dave designed the memorial card, which meant we searched through many boxes looking for photos for the card. I planted pots of flowers on the front and back porches, mowed the lawns, cleaned the house and wrote the eulogy. I had consulted with auntie Marge on several dates and details, regarding the eulogy and the memorial card. Marge offered to organize and pay for the luncheon at the church, and that took a load off me. I continued to send out death notices.

Back at the mobile home, a bunch of us were sitting on the front porch, wine in hand, while others spread out on the front lawn with a beer. Some people sat inside, chatting and catching up.

My brother Michael took me aside to tell me what happened when they pulled up to the mobile home after the memorial service.

"We saw a white-haired woman coming out the front door," he said, pointing to Deanna's mother sitting on the porch. "It was a shock because it looked like Mom had just appeared." He still looked a little shaken. Lorna has the same full head of beautiful white hair like our mother, was wearing an outfit that could have come right out of my mother's closet, a rich royal blue.

All things blue, including the gift of the turquoise stone that had disappeared, became meaningful for me. The colour blue served as a symbol for those sublime, unexpected moments that filled me with awe and appreciation, reminding me that there is beauty and mystery in the world, and indeed, also in our relationships. In the years of care giving, I discovered who I'd inherited my strength, stubbornness, quirkiness, and anxieties from. I was my mother's daughter after all, an unexpected gift.

What's Next?

The family, including Craig, showed up for coffee at various intervals the morning after the memorial and chili party. I hadn't brushed my hair, my teeth, or washed my face, unheard of for me, when I found myself making pot after pot of coffee.

After everyone left, I stood at the kitchen window, facing a sink full of pots soaking in cold water from the night before, and the counter covered with dirty coffee cups. I sighed and glanced out the kitchen window at the bird feeders. No birds this morning. I wonder if I'll have to leave this place?

It was a strange feeling, facing an uncertain future again, like sitting down before the blank page, knowing I want to create a new story, but not knowing where to start. Once again, I have to imagine a different life. I've been here before. I have the feeling that my life has been nothing but a series of starting overs.

Another Writers' Festival coming up in a month ... already the end of April ... still have to come up with my part of the presentation for the Collective ... but at least that'll give me something to focus on.

Not Bridgey, too

Bridgey, as calm and stoic as my mother right until the end. Choked with grief, I was inconsolable in the Veterinarian's office when I knew what I had to do. My eldest cat had been sick; she wasn't eating, and I'd tried everything. Mom's ashes had only recently been placed in the ground at the Revelstoke cemetery in the English family plot. She wanted to be with her family, not lying beside her husband in the Sorrento graveyard. Should I read anything into that?

When the veterinarian said go have a coffee and come back when I was ready, I drove around sobbing. Marilyn was in the hospital having her chemotherapy treatment, so I couldn't call on her. I felt completely lost, then took a chance and called Dorothy. She dropped what she was doing to come to my aid. I asked her to wait in the waiting room, while I sat murmuring reassurances to Bridgey, as two women administered the drug that put her to sleep. I wrapped Bridgey in a special blanket afterwards and we took her home to bury her in the back yard. After my mother's death, Bridgey's seemed too much to endure. Thank god I had a friend to help me.

Dorothy suggested we each write something for Bridgey. I felt shattered and couldn't think, so I appreciated her suggestions. She asked if I had photos, which I dug out, and she asked me to tell her about my Bridgey.

I shared an anecdote from the eulogy I had written for my mother. I wrote about how much Mom loved our three cats, and other cats through the years. Bridgey, our large, overweight cat, was special because she would cuddle up to Mom on her bed and comfort her, especially during the last years when Mom was not well and she spent more time in bed. Bridgey could be a bed hog, but Mom never complained. She'd pet Bridgey, look into her big expressive eyes, and talk lovingly to her. Big beautiful Bridgey, all twenty-five pounds of her. She would talk to Mom with her tail, that talking tail, and those mesmerizing eyes.

I lamented my lack of faith. Where had Bridgey gone? Where was my mother? Dorothy assured me that my mother's spirit was nearby, looking out for me, and that the spirit world existed just beyond the veil.

Hopefully, Bridgey was there, too. Aboriginal people believe that animals go to the spirit world when their body dies. And why wouldn't they? If that's where we go, then that's where they go.

As Dorothy talked, I felt a little better. I wanted to believe her. No wonder people gravitate to religion and spirituality. The existential angst felt like a bog I couldn't crawl out of, but after Dorothy's reassuring words I felt I had at least one foot back on solid ground.

I gathered paving stones from the front garden, while Dorothy dug a hole under the cottonwood trees at the back. I picked nasturtiums and some wild flowers and set them in my mother's tea mug to place on top of the stones where dear Bridgey was buried. We read what we'd written for her and said a prayer for her spirit. I wasn't doing great, but performing the ritual felt like the right thing to do, just as the memorial and graveside ritual with my siblings had been for mother, an honouring of their lives. It didn't feel like closure, whatever that is, but we had sent Bridgey on in a dignified and respectful way, her passing no less painful than saying goodbye to my mother. I will always remember how Bridgey protected and comforted my mother, and how much they loved each other.

I thought about the voice I heard at four am after Mom passed on; maybe that was my mother. She may have been calling to let me know that she was okay. When I think about it, a voice from the other side wouldn't necessarily sound like the person did in life, would it? I guess it's up to me to believe what I want, especially since there's no way to prove it either way.

In Julie Cameron's book Prayers from a Nonbeliever, one letter to God is particularly telling. The man writing the letters to God says he started writing because the other options—more therapy, antidepressants, substance abuse, or a fling—seemed like dead ends; he already knew the probable outcome of those choices. Yeah, didn't I know it.

Maybe there is a guiding principle that every religion and every culture in the world has a name for. Maybe prayer connects us to that universal energy. Maybe my mother and Bridgey are together again, maybe even looking out for me. So many maybes. I knew it all came down to a matter of faith, but I still felt like an angry rebellious child.

Part Six

Starting Over

A River to Skate Away On

I had to figure out what to do with the mobile home, and the rest of my life. Lakeland Mobile Home Park disintegrated day by day; it began to resemble a graveyard for dead and dying trailers. As falling leaves left trees naked and the weather turned cold, I felt more isolated and unsafe in the park. Many of my neighbours had left already.

The first snow made me think about the long winter ahead, and I was facing it without my mother, or the great neighbours that used to help shovel me out now and then. I thought about Bridgey's grave buried under a blanket of snow under the cottonwood trees, and my mother's grave in the Revelstoke cemetery, where snow falls deep and silent.

Angie, Katie and I stared out the window at the falling snow.

The melancholy of Joni Mitchell's river song moved me as snow piled up. I also wished for a river to skate away on, especially with another Christmas coming on.

That song came from her Blue album. How fitting.

Unexpected Love:

One thing was for certain. Nothing stays the same forever. In a serendipitous series of events, I found that an apartment in town was available in the very place I wanted to live. My aunt Marge, Mom's only remaining sibling, owned an apartment on the third floor.

The fact that a rental became available that I could afford felt like a door had opened. I had to try to shift my life into town to a safer environment. I also felt like I wanted to be closer to the cultural life of the town and within walking distance to everything. I knew that with my back problems shoveling snow from the long driveway would be risking serious injury.

Making the shift took an enormous amount of energy, but with the help of Teri-Ann and her friend. I was able to make the transition. I sent a registered letter to the owner of the park giving my notice for the end of December and asking for a payout.

I gave in reluctantly, having sworn that I would be the last person to leave the park and that I would chain myself to my mobile home when they came with the bulldozers. But I had to let go. I had to turn the page.

I put up photos of Mom everywhere in my new apartment, and created an altar to the ancestors on a dresser in my bedroom. Along with photos of my mother, I placed the small blue urn of her ashes, a bird flying upward the only design. I'd requested some of her ashes be saved for that purpose and also for a small urn for Teri-Ann, while the rest of her ashes lay in the ground next to her mother's grave.

Like the blue stone, a blue flower, or even a turquoise feathered bird, the gift of beauty, and of healing came to me in unexpected ways. The privilege of caring for my mother, as I began to think of the last twelve years, had led me to the very heart of the woman. To my surprise I discovered that we shared many things in common. Like the love that grew between us, the gift of that relationship will always be deeply profound for me.

I'll never forget the day when I told Mom something, which I now forget, and she blurted out three times, "I love you, I love you, I love you," with such feeling that I was startled. My mother had never been comfortable expressing emotions. She had never told me she loved me before. I felt like she freed herself in that moment, and probably me as well. I had been telling her I loved her for years, through every terrifying health crises, she heard. "I love you, Mom," not only from me, but from her other children, grandchildren, and great grandchildren.

Many shades of blue had appeared in my life, sometimes lifting me up, other times burying me deep. If I can stay grateful for the full range of these experiences, that would be my song of songs, my hymn to the complexities of the human journey.

And who knows, maybe a different colour, and a new song will present itself in the next phase of my life.

In my journey through the labyrinth, I released old hurts and thoughts about my mother, received her unexpected love, and returned to a more realistic, more loving understanding of who she was. My love for my mother evolved into something deep and profound.

Afterword

As I wrote "Raven" I pealed back the layers on my own life and with each revelation of who I was at my core, my voice became stronger. I became stronger. I am the sum total of all that I have experienced, all the grief, loss and illness didn't make me less. By writing my truth, I hoped that my experience might help someone else. After publishing A Raven in My Heart several women told me reading that book had helped them understand their own lives. Nothing was more gratifying than hearing that.

Gracesprings Collective is alive and well after all these years. Alex Forbes and Deanna Barnhardt Kawatski have many more books to their names, some with Gracesprings and several with other publishers. Craig has written a murder mystery and is currently looking for an agent.

Lakeland Mobile Home Park was bulldozed. Gone are the old mobiles and the park in the middle formerly ringed with beautiful mature trees full of chirping birds, gone the wall of purple-scented lilacs on one side of our mobile, bringing such exquisite joy in the spring, gone the burgundy peonies, the elegant Japanese maple tree in our front garden, Shasta daisy plants, red rose bush, and the frilly daffodils along the back fence, heralding a new season. I planted many other flowers, including colourful poppies, and had two raised gardens beds of vegetables in the back yard. All gone.

New manufactured homes are appearing in place of what was, although one family managed to hang on. They wouldn't be coaxed out of the place where they'd raised their children.

My great grandson Robert and I drove through the desert-like landscape when he visited. I wanted to find Bridgey's grave. Robert saw it first. The three flat paving stones where Dorothy and I ceremoniously buried my dear feline friend under the cottonwood trees. The only place remaining were the woods behind our place that separated our home from the highway. I gave a sigh of relief and gave thanks that Bridgey's bones hadn't been disturbed, and that the woods full of wild roses and the extraordinary abundance of Mountain Lady Slippers had been saved.

Angie became sick at the end of October, 2014. "She's dying," the vet said. "She's in really serious trouble and may not even survive the X-ray." There was nothing I could do but have her put down. The shock was terrible. It had happened so suddenly. I cradled my beautiful Angie, who buried her head in the crook of my arm, as I sobbed. I managed to pull myself together to tell Angie that she was going to heaven, which I hoped was true. I will scatter her ashes in the woods behind where our mobile home used to be, where Bridgey is buried. Angie loved to wander among the wild roses and Mountain Ladyslippers.

Richard Wagamese, an author whose work touched so many, passed away on March 10, 2017, at 61 years of age, leaving grieving friends and family, and fans of his award-winning books. He wanted to move beyond mental illness, beyond mere resilience, to a place of genuine healing. *Embers: One Ojibway`s Meditations,* published by Douglas & McIntyre 2016.

Wagamese's novels helped Canadians understand the pain of growing up Indigenous in our vast country. The novel *Indian Horse*, published in 2012, became a national bestseller, followed by his next bestselling novel *Medicine Walk* in 2014. By telling your story, Richard, you touched the hearts and souls of so many people. May you be resting in peace.

Moving beyond mental illness, her hurts and fears, my beautiful daughter has found light and healing in a church of her choice. Her grandfather, my own dear father, found his redemption in AA. I found my own version of salvation—from a shy, self-conscious woman riddled with doubt about her worth—by telling stories. We each find our own way of breaking through the pain of our pasts.

Just one more thing: Mom *was* always right, about everything. But I didn't figure that out until after she was gone.

Bibliography

Aron, Elaine N, Ph.D. *The Highly Sensitive Person: How to Thrive When The World Overwhelms You.* Broadway Books, a division of Random House, Inc., New York, NY, 1996.

Atwood, Margaret. *Negotiating with the Dead: A Writer on Writing.* Published in Canada by Anchor Canada, a division of Random House of Canada Limited, 2002.

Brett, Brian. *Trauma Farm: A Rebel History of Rural Life.* Vancouver, BC: Greystone Books, An imprint of D & M Publishers Inc., 2009.

Brett, Brian. *Tuco: The Parrot, the Others, and a Scattershot World.* Vancouver, BC: Greystone Books Ltd , 2015.

Cain, Susan. *Quiet: The Power of Introverts in a World That Can't Stop Talking.* Published in the United States by Broadway Books, an imprint of the Crown Publishing Group, a division of Random House, Inc., New York. 2012, 2013.

Cameron, Julia. *Prayers from a Nonbeliever: A Story of Faith.* New York, NY: Jeremy P. Tarcher/Putnam, a member of Penguin Putnam Inc., 2003.

Chodron, Pema. *When Things Fall Apart: Heart Advice for Difficult Times.* Boston, Massachusetts: Shambhala Publications, Inc., 1997.

Didion, Joan. *The Year of Magical Thinking.* New York, NY: Vintage International, A Division of Random House, Inc., 2007.

Eriksson, Ann. *High Clear Bell of Morning: a novel.* Madeira Park, British Columbia: Douglas & McIntyre, 2014.

Goldberg, Natalie. *Writing Down the Bones: Freeing the Writer Within.* Boston & London: Shambala, 1986.

_____ *Wild Mind: Living the Writer's Life.* New York, NY: A Bantam Book, a division of Random House, Inc., 1990.

_____ *Thunder and Lightening: Cracking Open the Writer's Craft.* A Bantam Book, a division of Random House, Inc., 2001.

_____ *Old Friend from Far Away: The Practise of Writing Memoir.* New York, NY: Free Press, a division of Simon & Shuster, Inc., 2007.

Gottfriedson, Garry. *Glass Tepee.* Saskatoon, Saskatchewan: Thistledown Press, 2002.

_____ *whiskey bullets: Cowboy and Indian Heritage Poems.* Vancouver, BC: Ronsdale Press, 2006.

Healy, Dermot. *Long Time No See*. London, England: Faber & Faber, Ltd., 2011.

Jamison, Kay Redfield. *Touched with Fire: Manic-Depressive Illness and the Artistic Temperament*. New York, NY: The Free Press, 1993.

Keirsey, David, and Bates, Marilyn. *Please Understand Me: Character and Temperament Types*. 3rd ed. Del Mar: Prometheus Nemesis, 1978.

King, Stephen. *On Writing: A Memoir of the Craft*. New York, NY: Pocket Books, a division of Simon & Shuster, Inc., 2000, 2002, 2010.

Koestler, Arthur. *The Act of Creation*. London, England: The Danube Edition, 1969.
1st published May 1964. Reprinted '64, '65, '66. (paperback 2nd Danube edition 1976, Hutchinson & Co. (Publishers) Ltd.).

Lamott, Anne. *Bird by Bird: Some Instructions on Writing and Life*. New York, NY: Anchor Books, a division of Random House, Inc., 1994, 1995.

LeGuin, Ursula K. *Steering the Craft: Exercises and Discussions on Story Writing for the Lone Navigator or the Mutinous Crew*. Portland, OR: Eighth Mountain Press, 1998.

Lewis, Naomi K. (Editor) Altrows, Rona (Editor). *Shy: An Anthology* (Robert Kroetsch Series). Edmonton, Alberta: University of Alberta Press, 2013.

Light, Alan. *The Holy or the Broken; Leonard Cohen, Jeff Buckley & the Unlikely Ascent of "Hallelujah"*. New York, NY: Atria Books, A Division of Simon & Schuster, Inc., 2012.

Mason, Paul T. & Kreger, Randi. *Stop walking on eggshells: taking your life back when someone you care about has borderline personality disorder.* Oakland, CA: New Harbinger Publications, Inc., Second Edition, 2010.

Musgrave, Susan. (BC Bookworld, Vol. 29, No. 1, Spring 2015, page 3)

Pearson, Patricia. *A Brief History of Anxiety, Yours & Mine.* Toronto, ON: Random House of Canada, and simultaneously in the United States by Boomsbury USA, 2008.

Pew, Jeff & Roxborough, Stephen, Editors. *radiant danse uv being, a poetic portrait of bill bissett.* Roberts Creek, BC: Nightwood Editions, 2006.

Pinkola Estés, Clarissa. *Women Who Run With the Wolves: Myths and Stories of the Wild Woman Archetype.* Toronto, ON: Random House of Canada Ltd. and in the United States by Ballantine Books, a division of Random House, Inc., New York, 1992.

Solomon, Andrew. *The Noonday Demon: An Atlas of Depression.* New York, NY: Simon & Schuster, 2001, First Touchstone Edition 2002.

Stossel, Scott. *My Age of Anxiety: Fear, hope, dread, and the search for peace of mind.* New York, NY: Alfred A. Knopf, a division of Random House LLC, Toronto, ON: Random House of Canada Limited, Penguin Random House Companies, 2014.

Twigg, Alan. *Intensive Care: A Memoir.* Vancouver, British Columbia. Anvil Press, 2002.

Ueland, Brenda. *If You Want To Write: A Book about Art, Independence and Spirit.* Saint Paul, Minnesota: Graywolf Press, 1938, 1987 by the Estate of Brenda Ueland. First published by G.P. Putnam's Sons.

Vogler, Christopher. *The Writer's Journey: Mythic Structure for Writers.* Studio City, CA: Published by Michael Wiese Productions, Based on mythologist Joseph Campbell's writings "The Hero with a Thousand Faces", 2nd Edition, 1998. 3rd Edition, 2007.

Wagamese, Richard. *Embers: One Ojibway's Meditations.* Madeira Part, BC: Douglas & McIntyre, 2016.

Wayman, Tom. *high speed through shoaling water.* Madeira Park, BC: Harbour Publishing Co. Ltd., 2007.

White, Howard. *Writing in the Rain: Stories, Essays & Poems.* Madeira Park, BC: Harbour Publishing Co. Ltd., 1990.

Woodward, Caroline. *Light Years: Memoir of a Modern Lighthouse Keeper.* Madeira Park, BC: Harbour Publishing Co. Ltd., 2015.

Author Biography

Kay McCracken is the author of her memoir, *A Raven in My Heart: Reflections of a Bookseller*, a transformative tale about leaving Vancouver to open a bookstore in a rural area of B.C. Her sequel, *Beyond the Blue Door: a writer's journey*, published in 2017, explores Kay's relationships in the searing light of hindsight.

A Spooktacular Halloween, an adventure story for children, was published in the fall of 2012.

In 2003, Kay co-founded Word on the Lake Writers' Festival, a festival for readers and writers. She continues to write a monthly literary column, and is a member of the Federation of BC Writers, having acted as a board member and regional rep for six years.

Kay loves living in the diverse and friendly community of Salmon Arm in south east British Columbia, a beautiful area of the province known as the Shuswap.

Kay in her accidental garden, Lakeland Mobile Home Park